SHATTERING THE
GRANDEST ILLUSIONS

Harun Rabbani

Shattering the Grandest Illusions

Published by House of Nu Rah Publishing

Chief Editor:	Nikola King
Editor:	Sara Ellis
Cover design and photography:	Carolin Engel

www.exposeillusions.com

Disclaimer and Terms of Use: The Author and Publisher has strived to be as accurate and complete as possible in the creation of this book, notwithstanding the fact that he does not warrant or represent at any time that the contents within are accurate due to the rapidly changing nature of the Internet. While all attempts have been made to verify information provided in this publication, the Author and Publisher assumes no responsibility for errors, omissions, or contrary interpretation of the subject matter herein. Any perceived slights of specific persons, peoples, or organizations are unintentional. In practical advice books, like anything else in life, there are no guarantees of income made. Readers are cautioned to reply on their own judgment about their individual circumstances to act accordingly. This book is not intended for use as a source of legal, business, accounting or financial advice. All readers are advised to seek services of competent professionals in legal, business, accounting, and finance field.

ISBN: 978-0-9570879-0-3

Printed by Lightning Source in the United Kingdom, United States of America and Australia.

I dedicate this book to my beautiful children and to someone else who is very special to me, my mentor and friend, Konstantin Pavlidis.

SHATTERING THE GRANDEST ILLUSIONS

Table of Contents

Acknowledgments

This book has been in the making for four years. In that time, I have wanted to write several books that may help contribute to creating a better world for my children and all children to live in. This is the first. Therefore, it is of immense pleasure to dedicate this book to my beautiful children and to every child on this glorious planet. You are my joy and my inspiration. Of course, how can children exist without those who gave birth to them? Therefore, I salute and honour all mothers as you are the divine feminine who gives rise to all that is manifest. Your true genius and power has been neglected and, for millennia, often suppressed. But know this. It is changing now.

The writing and the completion of this book could not have happened without the exceptional support, guidance and teachings of my dear friend and mentor, Konstantin Pavlidis. It is with your guidance that I am at a place to finally get my first book to print. Thank you. I would also like to acknowledge the phenomenal support of my other family, Lance, Aniko and Carolin. I love you all.

The compilation of the interviews given by myself and with those at the forefront of science as well as experts in healing, geopolitics and consciousness could only happen with the generous cooperation of my interview guests that include:

Dr David Hawkins, Dr David Hamilton, Larry Crane, Nassim Haramein, Dr Jude Currivan, Dr Manjir Samanta-Laughton, Konstantin Pavlidis, Mark Abadi, Dr Dawson Church, Dr Dean Radin, Lynne McTaggart, Andy Tomlinson, Dr Konstantin Korotkov, Dr Bruce Lipton, Dr Joe Dispenza, William Whitecloud, Hugh Gilbert, Lindsay Wagner, Dr Elisabet Sahtouris, Dr Carmen Boulter, Ian R. Crane, Jaz Rasool, Dr Judith Orloff, Deepak Lodhia, David Hyner, Rob Williams,

Mary Trenfield and Richard Wilkins. I am extremely grateful to every one of you. Equal gratitude goes to the listeners of *The Consciousness Revolution Show*. You guys have helped me make my passion a reality by being there week in week out. Thank you.

Given the nature of publishing and the many challenges it holds, I am grateful to so many people who have given me priceless advice and guidance, including my good friends, John Sealey and Jenny Perryman. I also count myself incredibly lucky to have such amazing editors as Nikola King and Sara Ellis and for being unconditional in their love and support.

I am asked from time to time, who is my role model and inspiration, to which I smile. I am 'fortunate' to have chosen to surround myself with inspirational people. However, there are two individuals whose lifelong support is second to none. They are my brothers, David and Imran. Guys, thanks for kicking my butt when it needed kicking the most! Finally, I thank my Creator. Ultimately, all praises are to you.

Love and gratitude,

Harun

A Few Words from Friends

"Harun has clearly put heart and soul into this master-piece, travelling 360 degrees around his subject. His writing takes you on a journey from the tangible and physical to the intangible and metaphysical, then perfectly back to Earth again. Harun beautifully weaves his own personal insights into deep, experiential research and delivers a brilliant book in a unique and powerful way."

Martin Dewhurst
Founder of New Dawn Rovers
www.newdawnrovers.org

"In *Shattering the Grandest Illusions*, Harun sounds a wonderfully clear and timely wake-up call for us all. As a consequence of his own lifelong search for truth, he shines a profoundly truthful light on the illusions that hold humanity in thrall to the dysfunctional behaviours that have literally brought us to the edge of global breakdown. And in doing so he offers a great and empowering gift in helping us transform that potential breakdown into a collective breakthrough to a higher state of consciousness."

Dr Jude Currivan
Cosmologist, healer and author of '*HOPE - Healing Our People & Earth*'
www.drjudecurrivan.com

"Harun Rabbani's *Shattering the Grandest the Grandest Illusions* is a compelling read. It is the only book of its type that I have read cover to cover as it provoked, challenged and inspired in equal measure. Has it changed my attitude and behaviour on things? Hell yeah!"

David Hyner
Researcher, international speaker and motivational trainer.
www.davidhyner.com

"If you only read one book this year, you have it in your hands....it is thought provoking and life changing."

Molly Harvey
Leading authority on Leadership/Culture change, best selling author of the 'Seconds Away From...' management development books.
www.corporatesoulltd.com

"A far-reaching dismantling of the false edifices that make up modern, mainstream society. Rabbani has gathered nuggets of wisdom from the world's greatest thinkers and synthesised them into this intelligent, but reader-friendly treatise whilst adding his own personable touch. If you are looking for a wake-up call with a wide scope from science to economics to spirituality and more, then this is the book for you."

Dr Manjir Samanta-Laughton MBBS
Film-maker, author of 'Punk Science' and 'The Genius Groove'
www.paradigmrevolution.com

"I found *Shattering the Grandest Illusions* by Harun Rabbani to be a well constructed, highly informative read. The author suggests going and finding out the facts for oneself. Although, I thought I had researched much of what was conveyed in the book already, there were many new 'insights' into the 'illusionists' that I found mesmerising.

Being an active proponent of 'conscious creating' and helping others to take back control and to create their reality, I was fully absorbed and revelled in the latter part of the book's clarity and detail on the conscious mind and personal evolution.

Harun Rabbani has taken a bold stance to bring such vital information to the public in one publication. I highly recommend this book to anybody who may still need a reason to take back control of their reality."

Edel O'Mahony
Founder, Path of the Peaceful Warrior
Professional speaker, author and mentor
www.edelomahony.com

"This is a well written book and it offers many different points of view. I recommend that the reader take it all in, be open and come to their own conclusions."

Larry Crane
www.releasetechnique.com

"The sole purpose and achievement of this book is the liberation of the human mind. I warn the reader not to read this book unless they are prepared to have their eyes opened fully. I commend Harun for his book. This book is a lit matchstick in a dark room that instantly dissolves any doubt or ambiguity in the mind of a reader. I can assure any reader that by the time you finish reading this book, not only will your mind be enthralled but your eyes will be opened in ways you never thought possible. His book comes at a time when great minds with life-changing ideas are really needed. I recommend this as one of the must read books of the age.

Harun's unique literary style is clear, cogent, well-articulated and delivering highly sophisticated ideas yet simple enough for even a child to understand. The work stands out as a guide striking a chord in a wide range of readers from both skeptical intellectuals to modest   seekers of knowledge. Never before has anyone attempted to bring together the collective wisdom of the leading minds in one single, easy to read book that addresses the key issues in our life.

Harun elegantly weaves together the tapestry of expert knowledge from many angles to throw light on little known truths of today. I thank Harun for his considerable effort, recognisable literary genius and even more impressively his sincerity and dedication to the freedom of the human mind."

Chad Manian
Interdisciplinary Researcher/Senior Lecturer

"An extremely insightful and comprehensive account of human society, behaviour and belief systems, all of which have led to the status quo of life on Earth in our time. I feel that the issues raised and the topics researched should incite deep introspection and questioning regarding the nature of our existence and the purpose of our being. If these questions and issues do not achieve this goal, then we are already dead and need not look any further. Bless you Harun for your excellent work and may it act as a catalyst to awaken the truth in all humans, now and in the future."

Konstantin Pavlidis
Research scientist, movement artist and spiritual master
www.orassy.com

Foreword

Project your Present to the Future

"Yesterday is history, tomorrow is a mystery, but today is a gift. That is why it is called the 'present'."
Chapter 15 of *Shattering the Grandest Illusions.*

We live in the twenty-first century, but we do not fully understand what it means. Most people are involved in their everyday activities and they do not feel the winds of change. Every day we hear the news of natural disasters all over the world: earthquakes in Japan and New Zealand, floods in the USA and Australia, an avalanche of gale-force blizzards over the East Coast of the USA and unusually hot summers in Russia, the hottest in 1,000 years of history.

At least 100,000 people have died from earthquakes, floods and heat phenomenon. In Pakistan, record monsoon rains destroyed infrastructure, left thousands dead and millions homeless. Wildfires have erupted across several countries. In Moscow, this resulted in heavily damaged wheat crops and forced the city to impose an export ban that raised global wheat prices. While diplomats and scientists pondered over an accord that could replace the Kyoto Protocol, 19 nations were experiencing unusually high temperatures, including 53.5 degrees Celsius in Pakistan, the hottest ever in Asia. The 2012 Mayan Prophesy is coming true – the world is coming to an end!!!

But, is it really so? Should people all over the world stop their activity, close their shops and offices and wrap up in white blankets preparing for the coming Armageddon? Of course not! I am writing these pages in view of the beautiful landscapes of the Costa del Sol, Marbella, Spain: the blue sea, blue sky, green olives, and thousands of people enjoying sun, water and air; restaurants are full, shopping malls filled with lazy shoppers, and children continue to create their sand castles as they have done for tens of thousands of years. Life is going on. Life is going on!

Together with the Sun, the Earth is furiously moving through space and time. In different parts of the Cosmos, we are passing through areas of huge energies and eternal Cosmic Rays. Our Earth climate is the reflection of Sun activity, which in turn responds to the cosmic environment. In our millennium, we are spinning pass through the same areas of Cosmos repeatedly. Considering our observations of the movement of planets and other celestial bodies, we may detect only short natural cycles (11 years, 55 years, 110 years), but it is clear that these cycles are of much longer range.

So we ARE in the cycle of transformation in which we have been living since the end of the twentieth century. Our Earth's climate and human civilization are experiencing this tremendous transformation. All attempts to make long-ranged forecasts of weather and future are doomed to failure. Who could have predicted the abrupt crash of powerful Soviet Empire – the *Empire of Evil*? Who would believe, by the end of the twentieth century, the USA would be led by an African-American?

We do not know what will be in the next decades, let alone try to predict the end of twenty-first century. Only one thing is clear. We are living in Times of Change. For Russian people this is a normal state of affairs. From the beginning of nineteenth century, they have experienced one transformation after another. For the rest of the world this is still implicit – but it is coming! We can name quite a few symptoms of upcoming changes...

Transformation from the Material to the Informational World

The price of everyday commodities are reducing and, in principle, even now it possible to use many disposable, single-use items, like underwear, clothing, tableware, etc. Naturally, we may feel attachment to our dresses and table plates. They create an important part of our cozy environment. However, in the Informational World, we easily upgrade software and buy new programmes – better than previous ones. More and more people all over the world spend time with their laptops and iPads, opening up a World Without Boundaries.

Transformation from linear thinking to a more complex one

Development of modern mathematics and physics has led to them surpassing the boundaries of the medieval vision of reality. Whilst in the social sciences of biology and medicine, we are still trapped within the old model. Application of non-linear, complex, quantum approaches to modern science and life is an essential goal. We are at the threshold of the great renovation of the Western Scientific Paradigm – the new Scientific Revolution.

Transformation from the Oil Age to the Sun Age.

In our civilization, we are totally dependent on oil and oil money governs the world. However, we now understand how damaging this is both for nature and for our health and our pockets. Nowadays, we have technologies that allow us to get energy from the sun and run cars on water, but development of these technologies is restricted by Big Money. The next step is to get an unlimited energy from the vacuum. Slowly, but surely, it is coming. So let's see what might be the reality by the end of twenty-first century.

Transformation of the interest in consciousness from sneering curiosity to scientific exploration

Fifteen years ago, the study of consciousness was considered as somewhere between psychiatry and metaphysics. Now it is a serious branch of science. Creation of new quantum instruments has allowed scientists to study the operations of the brain in real time and to gain a deeper understanding of mind-body interconnections. Understanding of consciousness, as a pivotal factor in world safety, civilization development and individual health, is growing in the society.

Transformation from pharmaceutical medicine to holistic, integrative and quantum medicine

Tremendous achievements in modern medicine have greatly increased longevity in developed countries; mass implementation of heart, liver and cochlear implants; In Vitro Fertilization (IVF) and a many other modern developments. At the same time, we have also seen illustrated the weak points of modern medicine. This has manifested itself in a high increase in cancer, heart and brain problems and the onset of the supposed disease of the aged, senility, affecting people at a much younger age.

These all suggest that we lack some important elements in supporting people's health and well-being. These elements would allow us to move from curing diseases to preventing them, from a Medicine of Illness to a Medicine of Health. Not treatment, but prevention; not medications, but healthy life-style.

In principle, for life we need:

Sun
Water, and
Air

However, we need a lot of Sun, good structured water and fresh air. We also need supervision by clever well-educated doctors, who would guide us in life, taking care of our problems, providing us with proper nutrition, consulting us in the ways of life, food and movement. Some of these tasks would be taken by intellectual machinery, operating in 'clouds', but the last word would be the doctor's.

Our records would kept in a database and we would be supervised from conception to maturity. As you see, we are facing a great times ahead. Humankind has entered a new phase of its development, and we may only guess what wonders we could see, even in our time-span. Nevertheless, a lot depends on our own attitude to our life and our future. We may choose to participate in creating a new step, or we may choose to spend time without having any understanding of what is going on around us.

Your future depends on you now!!!

With your conscious attitude you may recreate your own life and contribute to the development of Humankind. Be aware of the power of your mind, do not be afraid to use it in everyday activity, accept your life as a precious gift, as a present from God, as a unique adventure, and project your positive thoughts and visions to the future. Your Angels will bring you everything you want, but you need to formulate your wishes, and make them clear and precise.

This book is divided into two parts: the first discusses the negative trends in modern civilization and the way money and power rules the nations, and the second discusses the way of transformation from personal evolution to global transformation. This is our destiny as humans, and I believe that we are only entering into a Shining New World.

"When there is a consciousness revolution, there is also an exponential growth in people's awareness regarding their day-to-day thoughts, feelings, attitudes and behaviours. That is how you change the world."
Chapter 18 of *Shattering the Grandest Illusions.*

Professor Konstantin Korotkov, PhD,
01 August 2011
Marbella – St. Petersburg

Preface

Exploration comes naturally to a young child. In my own childhood, I remember that I always questioned everything I saw, everything that there had been and everything that ever would be. I also questioned the status quo. Surely our lives could be better managed than this? Do we as humans really need to destroy everything we lay our hands on? Like me, a few people have chosen to retain that childlike curiosity for most of their lives.

As I entered my formative years, the familial, religious and cultural conditioning began to set in and take hold of me. Nonetheless, I retained my inquisitive mind and continued to question everything, but dared not voice those questions in case I was ostracised by my family and elders. My concerns were justified. I grew up in an environment that enjoyed spates of peace but moreover endured fear, aggression and violence.

At the time of editing this book, major UK cities like London and Birmingham (where I grew up in) had experienced the gravest civil disturbance, rioting and looting carried out by young people on British soil. So, why speak up and risk humiliation from the people whose care I was supposedly in? I was brought up to believe that I had no personal power and that I was at the mercy of my genetic inheritance and that it was an external God who had power over my destiny.

If things were difficult for me, then tough luck! It was my destiny. I had no choice but to grin and bear it. Although it frequently felt like I was destined for mediocrity, in little micro-steps, the world of infinite possibilities began to unfold in front of my eyes. By my late teens, I had read numerous books on business, economics, religion and health that were contrary to conventional thinking. So, what was 'truth' and what were delusions, fantasies and illusions?

Life around me exposed the differences with crystal-clear clarity. I grew up in a close-knit Muslim community in Birmingham that maintained a strong link with the religions and cultures of the Indian Subcontinent. As Muslims, we were taught about the all-knowing, all-seeing, omniscient and omnipresent God who created everything. However, if we dared to break any of the many rules dictated by the mullahs, He (God) would be angry and punish us in this life.

Worse still, if we pushed the boundaries of Shariah Law, we would be eternally damned to the pits of hell. I had difficulty understanding why my Creator would carry out such things as torture and retribution. How could someone who loved me punish and condemn me to eternal suffering? To even question God would have led to lashings from the Ustad's[1] danda[2], coupled with beatings and serious admonition when I got home.

Not surprisingly, at home I chose to be nothing more than a good Muslim boy! When I moved out of my parent's home at eighteen, I finally had the space and freedom to ask questions of the Cosmos and life around me. I began to have experiences that contradicted what I had been led to believe regarding matters such as family, God, politics, money, health and society. For example, why were we only taught how to read the Koran in Arabic during Islamic studies? Why were we not taught about the true significance of the words when the teachers did bother to translate the Arabic to English?

Why was the main focus of our teachers on those things that were forbidden? Why were we given intimate details of the punishment associated with evil so frequently? Why were fear, shame and guilt the main motivational techniques used to keep us in line? Why were we taught so little about the benefits to people who were 'good', loving, generous, compassionate

---

[1] Ustaad - Urdu for teacher or master

[2] Danda - Urdu for stick or lever

and law-abiding? What happened to the God who loved us? Where had all the love gone? Where did He fit into this picture? In fact, why was God a 'He' and not a 'She'? Or, were these just the questions of a naive immature child?

Throughout my life, I have been at a loss regarding the different identity labels that have been placed on me by others. Who was I? Was I a son? Nephew? Uncle? Father? Friend? Foe? Entrepreneur? Speaker? Muslim? Christian? Buddhist? British? Bengali? All of this was very confusing. Then it dawned on me. I am all of these things, yet, to me, none of the labels felt real. They do not present the true essence of what I am. They are all facets of me, some of which are transitory whilst others are more enduring. They are all perceptions that other people have of me according to their ow projections. These labels merely RE-present what I really am.

When I met my mentor and friend, Konstantin Pavlidis, I began the process of beginning to understand **what** 'Harun Rabbani' was. The more I discovered what I was, the more I realised how little I knew about me. That being the case, I can attest that most of the people I have met in my life also know very little about who they are, let alone what they are.

In *Shattering the Grandest Illusions,* my aim is to remove the multiple veils and disguises that are most common. That way, the reader can begin to get to understand their own true essence. The reason people are so lost is simple. So many are in a mad rush to achieve their heart's desires, they do not pause for breath to even notice which direction they are heading in. Or, many are lost and end up just going round in circles. How does a person know where they are headed if they have no clue where they are starting from? Everything, starts with the self.

It would be like building a high rise office block without foundations. If one chooses to grow to great heights, they better be darn sure their foundations are deep and wide and in ground that can hold them in place. Otherwise, they risk falling from a great height and end up with further pain and suffering.

There are countless examples of people toppling from heady heights. Many have achieved great status in business or politics, yet end up being some of the most miserable souls on the planet.

The examples of such failings are present. This book will allow the reader to dig through pass the layers of dirt in order to ensure they not only achieve their heart's desire, but they also enjoy the journey in the process of living. Part of the digging will involve looking at some of the major, global issues that affect everybody on a minute-by-minute basis. It has become evident that there are some parties who wish people to be so confused that they ignore fundamental global issues. The majority of the public, quite unwittingly, have been complying with the wishes of these parties.

There are numerous activities that are going on in the world that one may not agree with, such as the degradation of the planet, human rights violations, international conflicts, terrorism, human trafficking, etc. Unfortunately, people continue to believe that they cannot make a difference to the world by themselves and so they do nothing instead. However, there are things that everybody can all do to make real lasting changes to the planet.

Before we get to this place of transformation, it is worth considering just what it is that we are planning to change. Truthful, lasting change is not an event. It is a perpetual series of experiences. This book helps to shed light on areas that many may have neglected that also have consequences for people now and in the future. As individuals, humans are infinitely more powerful than they have been led to believe.

From time to time, some demonstrate this truth through the way they choose to live their lives. However, the most have been and remain in a deep slumber. The intention of this book is to share with readers observations and experiences that question those very obstacles that dumb people down and keep them asleep. One note of caution. Please do not believe a word I say. Do what all the great teachers of the past have said. Do your own research and be a seeker of truth.

"Then you will know the truth, and the truth will set you free."
John 8:32

The information presented in this book is a result of numerous interviews and conversations with some of the world's leading scientists and experts in the field of consciousness since 2007. Most of the interviews took place on *The Consciousness Revolution Show*. In this book, I quote those experts extensively. However, in order to ensure better readability, I have refrained from making references to the interviews for every pertinent point. There are far too many important points made on the show that need to be heard. To listen to the full interviews with the different world experts, please check www.exposeillusions.com.

I have also added anecdotes from my own experiences that may help to facilitate the reader's own self discoveries. Nonetheless, due to the particular relevance of their interviews, I am most blessed by the contributions made during the interviews with Elisabet Sahtouris, Bruce Lipton, Judith Orloff, Carmen Boulter, David Hawkins, David Hamilton and Konstantin Pavlidis, all of whom are doing phe-nomenal work at a global level.

In *Shattering the Grandest Illusions*, we will embark on a journey of SELF discovery that will help on your own journey of personal evolution. For any quest to be fulfilling, the adventurer needs to be equipped with the most suitable mode of transportation for the terrain and the prevailing conditions ahead. The mode of transportation for life is YOU: your mind, emotions, body, intuition and your spirit. This book offers you some of the resources to help you along the way.

Ultimately, this book is a guide to help reveal your own magnificence by means of a real, authentic and grounded approach. The disclosure of the grandest illusions in this book will help you to live a life beyond mere hopes, dreams and fantasy. This book is the first step in finding your centre of vision. Henceforth, the a most amazing life will begin to unfold as you take the appropriate steps to realise your greatest vision.

Enjoy the ride!

Introduction

"These grand illusions are used to control, deceive and manipulate humans on a massive scale."

In the beginning, there was light. From the movement of light through space, came sound. From the highly ordered state of an embryonic universe came disorder followed by a new order. Everything was in perfect harmony. Whenever disorder and chaos arose, a new order ensued. Amongst the glorious manifestations in the Cosmos, there came our divine Mother Earth. She gave birth to the mountains and oceans from whence arose bacteria, plants, animals and birds.

From amongst these beautiful creatures arose a higher conscious species, the human. From living in and with Mother Nature, humans developed into a species that organised, planned and controlled. An infinitely small proportion of this species began to enslave and control the majority of natural resources needed by the masses to live on. A mere 1% of the wealthiest people on the planet controlled 40% of all the global wealth.

Humans ceased to 're-member' their delicate symbiotic relationship with Nature and collectively tortured, raped and poisoned Mother Earth. However, She was compassionate, forgiving, loving and kept on providing. Finally, a time came where Mother Earth could no longer bear Her children's destructive ways. Some of her children estimated that 150-200 plants, insects and animals were becoming extinct every single day, 365 days of the year[3].

Mother Earth had been patient for thousands of years, nourishing and nurturing her children, without asking for anything in return. Today, She is reacting to the disorder and disarray caused by her children. Humans have a propensity to

---

[3] www.guardian.co.uk/environment/2010/aug/16/nature-economic-security

put things into boxes so that they have points of reference for comparing and contrasting. Even though they evolve through gaining knowledge and experience, they rarely question the original assumptions on whether their experience is truthful or whether they are living in fantasy?

This can be seen in all belief systems, including religion, science, politics, medicine, etc. The greatest and most powerful beliefs that people hold as truth, often central to their identity, are based on questionable assumptions. When an idea or belief is false, then it is an '*illusion*'. Some illusions can be inert and have little or no negative consequence, e.g. the belief in Santa Claus or the tooth fairy.

Some illusions may even be beneficial, such as the belief that a sugar pill falsely labelled as medicine can lead to healing. This is known as the '*placebo effect*'. However, there are far too many wide-reaching beliefs that have seriously destructive effects on them and the environment. These grand illusions are used to deceive, control and manipulate humans on a massive scale.

Unfortunately, the majority of people are completely oblivious to these illusions. How can they be expected to make a difference or create change? They have become like automated robots doomed to repeat the same old programmes over and over again. The grandest illusions are beliefs that have been propagated by people in places of authority and their weapon of choice is the mass media. These illusions are accepted as truth by the public.

Humans are so busy trying to keep up with daily life that few spend little, if any, time questioning the 'official' versions of events. For example, despite the vast amount of evidence piling up against the official version of the attack on the World trade Centre on 9/11 (provided by the *9/11 Commission Report*[4]), most American citizens still willingly accept the US governments findings. The public have relin-

---

[4] www.911commission.gov/report/911Report.pdf

quished their own power to heads of government, corporations and religious institutions. In *Shattering the Grandest Illusions*, I will be deconstructing some of the illusions behind issues which, hitherto, have been held as 'the truth'.

This book will also unveil vital information that will help readers to reclaim the power that has been dormant within themselves. A word of caution though. For some people, the information about to be revealed is one step too far from their 'reality'. Like Morpheus said to Neo in '*Matrix*'[5]:

"You take the blue pill and the story ends. You wake up in your bed and you believe whatever you want to believe. You take the red pill and you stay in Wonderland and I show you how deep the rabbit hole goes."

As you are reading this book, it may be prudent for you to take the red pill to help digest the information presented to you. Then you are free to make up your own mind and take the appropriate decisions and action steps. Again, please do not believe a word written in this book. Once you have read part or all of this book, do your own research in any area that either resonates with you or unsettles you. There is neither the time nor space to give all available information on any given topic discussed here. Thus, undertaking research is even more important for the readers own peace of mind.

Finally, to truly awaken to the truth, you must take the necessary action steps to complete the process. Purely reading this book is just adding further information and clutter to your mind. Once you have had your fill and, should you find this book of value, then please do not hold on to it. Pay it forward by passing it on to someone significant to you whom you feel will benefit from reading its content.

---

[5] www.en.wikipedia.org/wiki/The_Matrix

Chapter 1: The Story of Illusions

"...the US is no longer a democracy but has become a fascist dictatorship controlled by corporate interests alone."

What is an Illusion?

The most fascinating thing about the history of humans is that, despite the many lessons received, people continue to behave as separate individuals. Separate from the rest of the species and even more disconnected from the rest of Nature and the Cosmos. This perception of separation and individuality is the perfect breeding ground for the creation of multiple illusions, which, ultimately add to personal suffering. By identifying and understanding the existing illusions that have misled humans collectively for years, one can begin to dig deep into how they have accelerated the downfall of the human species.

Thereafter, it is possible to begin to consciously make decisions and take actions that will lead to the salvation of humans, not only as individuals, but also as a species. Let us first set the parameters for what will be discussed in this book. The word 'Illusion' comes from the Latin *'illudere'* which means 'to mock'. Interestingly, enough *'ludere'* also means 'to play'. Thus, those who are susceptible to illusions are merely being mocked and played. But, by whom? That is the billion dollar question. An illusion is the result of a person not being able to stay in touch with reality. It is their projected desires, hopes, wishes and even dreams. When dreams do not come true, a person becomes disappointed and at times, bitterly so.

They are not in touch with this particular aspect of their lives and they have minimal understanding of cause to effect and its resulting action. So how does the mind create illusions? When a person has a thought, it transfers into an emotion, an emotion transfers into a sensation and in turn that becomes a physical action.

Thought -----> Emotion -----> Sensation -----> Action

The action creates a task, which leads to a series of tasks that become a desired effect or result.

Action -----> Task...Task...Task -----> Effect (Result)

Illusions are a common part of people's lives because they do not interact with **Life**. They are too busy living their own life, i.e. their limited version of life or someone else's life, such as that of their parents or their spouse. When one is not truly listening to what Life is reflecting back to them about themselves or their situation, there is a conflict of interest. Therefore, there are two different frequencies or two different programmes running concurrently. They are singing from two different song sheets and are way out of tune. That is an illusion.

Who are the Illusionists?

Without a shadow of a doubt, it is the individual who is the primary illusionist and the one who has the most influence on their own life. The secondary level of influence is from those who have an immediate affect on individuals, such as parents, guardians, carers, teachers and peers. With the best will in the world, they merely pass down the programmes that they run in their own lives. The tertiary level of illusionists are made up of what I term as the 'indoctrination organisations'. These include education establishments, governments and religious organisations.

The fourth level of illusionists are 'master illusionists.' They include leading members of official organisations who covertly influence society, politics and control the mass media. These are the individuals and organisations who consciously choose to lie, deceive and manipulate the public. The majority of people on the planet have relinquished their personal power to the secondary and tertiary level illusionists without question.

Precious few are aware of the master illusionists and, therefore, cannot even begin to grasp how they have such a stranglehold on the human race. By revealing the key illusions, recognising them for what they are, i.e. nothing but illusions, and then seeking out the truth, it is possible to shatter multiple layers of illusion in one go. As this happens, there will be a natural migration of power from those who seek to control to their rightful owners, i.e. individuals. Although peeling back the layers of lies can be a difficult task to start off with, there is one thing that is worth remembering: the truth shall set us free.

The Grand Master of Illusions

One of the greatest iconic figures of the twentieth century was the Austrian neurologist, Sigmund Freud (1856-1939), the founder of psychology. The impact of his work is still felt throughout the world today. A lesser known figure whose effect is probably even greater was Freud's nephew, Edward Bernays (1891-1995). Bernays used Freud's work on psychoanalysis to manipulate the masses using the subconscious programmes inherent in all humans.

At the turn of the twentieth century, Bernays was heavily involved in the World War I propaganda machine on behalf of President Woodrow Wilson. Uncomfortable with its negative association with war, Bernays stopped using the term 'propaganda' and coined the term 'public relations'. The idea was this: by manipulating people's innermost selfish desires, it was possible to make them happy, and therefore, docile and malleable. Interestingly, the term 'propaganda' is still used in some countries by those people specialising in marketing.

Freud was able to unearth powerful and dangerous sexual and aggressive effects, reviving traces of a more animalistic past, that lay within the human psyche. Bernays aimed to make money by exploiting people's irrational emotions. For example, his most effective experiment was at a time when cigarette-smoking by women was considered a social taboo. He persuaded women that smoking was a way of exhibiting their feminine power.

After receiving a huge fee, leading American psychoanalyst, Dr Abraham A. Brill, advised Bernays that the cigarette represented the penis and male sexual power. If Bernays could find a way to associate cigarette smoking in women with challenging male power, then women would symbolically have their own masculine power! During the 1929 Easter Parade in New York, Bernays was hired by the American Tobacco Company to increase their cigarette sales. Bernays recruited a group of young models during a Suffragettes march to do his bidding on behalf of the tobacco company.

He informed the press that a group of debutante marchers would light 'torches of freedom' to signal independence from male domination. At his signal, the models pulled out their cigarettes at the same time and lit their 'torches'. Thereafter, the sales of cigarettes skyrocketed. After World War I, American corporations were worried they may overproduce goods beyond what people needed. The rich were familiar with the buying of luxury goods, but the masses would only buy goods they needed. A leading banker from Lehman Brothers, Paul Mazer, announced:

"We must shift America from a needs to a desires culture. People must be trained to desire, to want new things, even before the old ones have been entirely consumed...Man's desires must overshadow his needs."

Consumerism was born. Bernays became the most influential person in changing America from a worker society to a consumer society. In the 1920s mass consumer persuasion was maximised through Bernays' marketing ingenuity. This was supported by the banking industry, which were responsible for funding numerous chain stores across the country. He paid psychologists to write 'independent studies' stating that people should buy certain products as they were good for them.

Bernays' public relations machine for evangelising consumerism was on full throttle until the Great Crash of October 1929. The ensuing 12-year economic world depression polarised the powers in the US between the corporations and the politicians. The depression led to numerous riots and attacks on corporations by angry mobs. To take economic control back into the public's hand, President Franklin Roosevelt (1933-1945) introduced the New Deal which was a programme that involved creating giant industrial projects.

To the shock of corporations, the President was convinced that free markets could not be trusted to run modern economies. Nonetheless, the New Deal won the admiration of the Nazis, particularly Dr Paul Joseph Goebbels (1897-1945). Goebbels, the Reich Minister of Propaganda, was one of Hitler's closest associates and was known for his oratory skills and zealous anti-Semitism. As an avid follower of Bernays' work, much of Bernays' strategies on propaganda were implemented by Goebbels.

Roosevelt's political manoeuvres antagonised the corporations who decided to use Bernays' creative genius to combat the policies of the US government. This time there was an army of PR agencies across America who had been paid millions to instil the virtues of corporations and their products to Americans. The campaigns insinuated that modern America had been created by businesses, such as General Motors, and not by politicians.

All forms of media were used including billboards, television and newspaper editorials. This led to a bitter feud between corporations and politicians. In the end, the corporations won through to such an extent that governments today are hand-picked, funded and controlled by corporations.

Today, that battle has been completed. The US is no longer a democracy but has become a fascist dictatorship controlled by corporate interests alone. Corporations have fully utilised the strategies applied by Edward Bernays. The father of the greatest modern illusion-making machine.

Although the mass media still have a serious stranglehold on the psyche of the public, shifts are beginning to take place. Thanks to technological advances in communications and the internet, the public have much better choice of the media channels they wish to read, watch or listen to. They are moving away from mainstream media to these alternative choices. This is clearly seen in the downward spiral in advertising revenues earned by owners of television, radio and newspapers. When these factors are combined with a vigilant and discerning public, the truth is less likely to be corrupted.

A Brief History about Truth-Providers

As humans evolved into civilisations, the all-important questions that have been asked are:

"How did we get here?"

"Why are we here?"

"How do we get the most out of our time being here?"

When an individual is affiliated to a particular organisation, asks for such guidance, it is easier for them to accept the answers they are given. For example, a Sikh would be more likely to accept the guidance of their temple's elders or a Muslim would be happy with the guidance of their Imam. When an entire population make their organisation's system, the official truth-provider, it shapes and moulds the future of that civilisation.

Thousands of years ago, the first truth-providers for humans came through 'animism'. They believed that human entities are spiritual beings and spirit pervades through all

36

matter. All matter on Earth and the Cosmos are interconnected. They believed that there was no separation between matter and non-matter. Animism is a concept that was not, in itself, a religion. Animism was and still is present in many religions and especially prevalent in the belief systems of the Inuits, African traditions, Shinto Shamans and Native Americans. They believe, for example that all plants and animals have a spirit. Therefore, any animal or plant sacrificed for eating was balanced out by appeasing the spirits.

James Cameron's movie, *Avatar*, eloquently depicted this animist way of living amongst the *Na'vi* tribe of Pandora. The tribe do not see themselves as separate from the skies, the water, the trees, the animals or any part of nature. They are all connected by the great spirit, *Eywa*. As part of the initiation of being accepted into the Na'vi, Sully (the hero) sacrifices an animal to eat. During the sacrifice, he utters these words:

"I see you, Brother, and thank you. Your spirit goes with Eywa. Your body stays behind to become part of the People."

Later on, the truth-providers switched from animism to polytheism, most notably seen in Hinduism and the belief systems of the ancient Roman and Greek gods. In Polytheism, the spirits that belonged to matter were separated out into a tree and the god of the tree, i.e. two distinct entities. The polytheists took the spirit and made it part of the new entities (gods) which they worshipped. Eventually these truth-providers were, in the most part, replaced by a powerful new structure called 'monotheism'. This time there was only one god who was removed one step further away from the planet to a place called 'Heaven'.

Monotheism was practiced particularly in Judaism, Christianity and Islam. However, when Charles Darwin provided his *Theory of Evolution*, there was another massive shift to a new, more widely accepted truth-provider, called 'Science'. He provided an answer to the age old question of how people got here. This was a much more rational explanation than the one provided by the Church, which declared that humans were created by Divine intervention after the heavens and Earth had been created.

According to the Church, humans are the chosen species and God's most favoured creation. A human's job is to make sure they are on their best behaviour and must constantly praise Him...if they wished to join God in heaven after they die. In the 1800s, when breeding plants was at its peak, Darwin offered a plausible theory that seemed to fit people's paradigm. Given the choice between an invisible force that is separate from material existence that religion offered and this new theory of evolution, it was not surprising that Darwin's theory was accepted without too many questions.

Over a period of twenty years (1850-1870), the foundations of the Darwinian Theory of Evolution and its core principles were developed using a set of key assumptions. These original assumptions, from which a large part of modern science is derived, have never been seriously questioned until very recently. Some of the assumptions underlying today's illusions will be examined in this book as well as the illusions created by Darwin's theories and the acrimonious divorce between science and the Church.

This will be followed by a brief foray into one of the grandest illusions of all time. The cause of more mass murder and individual torture and killings than all other illusions combined - organised religion. Clearly, addressing the subject of religion fully would require much more than a chapter. In fact, it may be true to say that if all religious-based illusions were fully revealed, it may take a lifetime of investigation. Thus, in *Shattering the Grandest Illusions,* I will merely touch the tip of the iceberg.

Chapter 2: Science and Church

"...the master teachers were followers of the religions that represent them today. Buddha was not a Buddhist nor was Jesus a Christian!"

The Divorce between the Material and Nonmaterial World

During the era of Descartes and Newton, the Catholic Church had great power. For example, Copernicus, Galileo, Bruno and others of that time were offering up new ideas about the physical world. The ideas and theories created a furore, insofar as they endangered their own lives. Galileo was put under house arrest for most of his life. Bruno, who refused to be quiet, was eventually burnt at the stake for his proposals on the reality of the universe. These early scientists and philosophers trying to explore the natural world did so in the end through a deal they made with the Church. Rene Descartes was instrumental to that deal. He and others proposed:

"If we keep away from the spiritual world with our scientific exploration, then perhaps the Church can stay away from the physical (material) world."

Like a divorce between a married couple, the Cosmos was split into two halves, that of science and religion. Science got the physical world, whilst religion got the spiritual world. Although the earlier scientists were religious and spiritual (e.g. Newton was an alchemist), a schism started to emerge between an understanding of the physical world and the understanding of spiritual existence. Over time, to be free to continue that exploration, science and spirit were increasingly separated. In today's world, much mainstream science has become the new religion.

Instead of being science, it has become a kind of fundamental 'scientism'. Many people operating within that environment are terrified that, if they open to understanding the consciousness and spirituality, it will be equated to researching the old religious ways. Consequently, they want nothing to do with it. This is a real case of throwing the baby out with the bathwater. Whichever way it is perceived, both science and religion hold onto extreme fundamentalist views.

On one hand, there are the materialists who are in denial of anything beyond what they can see, feel, hear, touch or smell. Their deity is science. On the other hand, there are those who use their interpretation of religious teachings to guide their lives and to 'encourage' others that their way is the only way. Now, there is the situation of mainstream scientism that does not recognise that **scientism is not science**, as **religion is not spirituality**. At the leading edge of science, there are many people going beyond that limitation and fear. Science and spirit are now reconciling into the wholeness that the ancients intuitively knew about. This shift is helping people to awaken to the true oneness that is called 'reality'.

Approximately 13.7 billion years ago, the universe began with low entropy, i.e. a very ordered universe. It has been moving in a space-time cycle from that order of simplicity to ever greater complexity. Even though the universe started off incredibly ordered, it had a minimum amount of information within it. This is the ideal setup for allowing the disclosure of ever greater levels of complexity. Thus, as new information and experience arise, they are embodied by the unfolding universe.

In a way, this is not a choice of randomness. The universe is incredibly purposeful and ordered. Rather than say it is an intelligent design, it is more like an exquisite design for intelligence with ever greater complexities evolving throughout the 13.7 billion years. For billions of years, all that existed were hydrogen, helium and the formation of the first galaxies and stars. About 4.5 billion years ago, all the pieces of the solar system were in place for the next level of complexity to explore itself. Over the last 3.8 billion years, as the Earth cooled down and all the elements were in place for biological life to begin, it has been in a process of ever increasing complexity.

For the last 3.8 billion years, despite the fact the sun's energetic output has changed by over one-third in that time, *Gaia* (the living Earth) has held within it an amazingly stable biosphere that has allowed biological life to continue to become ever more complex. Now that people understand a little more about genetics, fossil records and the geological record, evolution makes much more sense without the randomness. Evolution is not without purpose.

As Einstein recognised, the universe has an innate order, an innate emergence and an innate embodiment. It is cosmic mind consciousness exploring itself through ever greater levels of complexity. Keeping this in mind, the aim of this book is to bring together both science and spirituality to gain the greatest knowledge to secure humankind's place in the cosmos. There is little value in separation and throwing the baby out with the bathwater by being fanatical about either science or spirituality. Both have a critical space within human lives. Nonetheless, there still needs to discernment between illusions and reality in both cases[6].

Organised Religion and the Great Master Illusionists

Although many religions have the common message of spreading love, peace and harmony, most have been corrupted by a succession of followers have distorted the original teachings of the founder of the respective religions. The so-called great religions of Judaism, Christianity and Islam (also known as the 'Abrahamic traditions') are renowned for the level of intolerance, violence and aggression towards their followers as well as non-believers.

---

[6] See Doug Parks' full interview with Dr Bruce Lipton on www.spirit2000.com

41

Other religions have not been immune to these behaviours. However, the Abrahamic traditions have instigated this aggression on a massive scale. That is not to say that the original teachings were bereft of wisdom, love, peace and harmony. Far from it. However, controlling peoples' lives by manipulating religious teachings has been far too tempting for religious authorities to resist. Incidentally, none of the master teachers were followers of the religions that represent them today. Buddha was not a Buddhist nor was Jesus a Christian.

I am sure that nobody needs be reminded of the Israeli-Palestinian conflict that has taken thousands of lives since the late 1940s. How about the many other massacres that have taken place in the name of religion? Have the Abrahamic religions not mastered fear, shame and guilt as the preferred method of controlling their followers? Who can ignore the honour killings of young women, the recruitment of soldiers for holy wars (crusades, terrorism, etc), the lynching of African-Americans, ethnic cleansing and many other horrific acts carried out in the name of religion?

At a more local level, religion has been used to control children and to maintain male dominance over women. One of the most widely talked about forms of control in current times, is the belief by some quarters that the burkha[7] is used to control Muslim women. However, other religions have also played their own part in suppressing women and subjugating them to male dominance. For example, unless they were from wealthy families, it was believed that English women were better off not being educated at all.

In Hinduism, the predominant religion of India, there still exists a strong caste system that favours one small group of people, the 'Brahmans', over other groups. One group, the 'untouchables', are considered so low that they are relegated to

---

[7] *Burkha* - a long loose garment worn my some Muslim women designed to cover the entire face and body from the eyes of the public

lifelong poverty and are given a label to exacerbate that predicament. Organised religion has turned from spiritual teachings and codes of conduct for daily life to a propaganda machine full of false promises and exaggerated claims.

Religion has become the most successful organisation in controlling the masses bar none. It has even humanised God and reduced the Creator to a white-bearded old man sitting amongst the clouds somewhere in Heaven. Apparently, after creating the Universe during six days of labour followed by a day of rest, God's job description became more clear. He was to keep watch over every thing humans do, every minute of every day, throughout their entire lives.

He even set out a list of ten things He did not want humans to do. And, if by chance, someone did one of those things, then He would put them in a place where that person would suffer agonising pain and burn until the end of time. That place is Hell. As the late comedian, George Carlin, adds,

"...but He loves you."

Many religious institutions have continued their behaviours contrary to the teachings of their founder. For example, Jesus had love and compassion for the meek and the poor. Yet, the Vatican is the most wealthiest organisation in the world that is not personally owned by a one or more individuals or a corporation. It is run like an empire by an emperor, the Pope. So, where did all this land, material possessions and money come from?

The Catholic Church also has influence over one of the largest populations in the world (1.08bn or 16.68% of the world population). When the other sects of Christianity are taken into account, the Catholics still have the greatest number of followers. The Muslim world boasts a world population of 1.57bn followers or 23% of the world population. However, at this moment, the influence on the Muslim world has been diluted by the disharmony within that community.

Judgement Day

In a world where chaos and disorder overwhelms families and communities, it was deemed necessary to have some form of accountability and responsibility with the purpose of maintaining harmony and balance. In their desire to propagate their religious messages, followers of master teachers developed systems that would, amongst other things, hold people accountable for their deeds. Unfortunately, instead of becoming adherents to the original teachings, they inadvertently became illusionists themselves.

Could there be any illusion greater than the idea of heaven and hell from which to control the masses? People are led to believe that if they followed every word laid down by religion, never questioned it, avoided the material world, sacrificed themselves on this plane in the name of God, then they would be rewarded infinitely in a place called 'Heaven'...after they die! There are also pockets of extremists who go one step further. They believe that, by strapping themselves up with, throwing themselves amongst the 'enemy', killing the maximum number of people (including themselves), their god would let them enter Paradise without a single question.

Amongst the Abrahamic religions, I find it most fascinating how every 'sin' has an associated punishment with it. For example, a person would be stoned to death for having sex out of wedlock. Another violent law that has been enacted by religion is to chop off the hands of anyone caught stealing. Despite the intimate details given for breaking religious laws, there is scant mention about the benefits associated with performance of 'pious' deeds. Does this mean the carrot-and-stick method works? Yes, it does...if the receiver is a lower conscious, fear-driven person. However, with an increasingly more educated, aware and evolving human species, the stick approach is losing its effect.

The more awakened the people are, the less effect fear, shame, guilt and even physical pain has on them. The author of *Man's Search for Meaning*, Viktor Frankl, was one of the victims of the concentration camps during World War II. Despite the barbaric treatment and torture inflicted on him as well as the murder of his wife and mother, he concluded that even in such a fear-ridden environment, humans cannot be deprived of purpose in their lives.

The Abrahamic religions took heaven and hell to new heights (and depths) in their respective belief systems. According to some of today's spiritual teachers, including Dr David Hawkins and Konstantin Pavlidis, ultimately, there is no heaven or hell. Heaven and hell is that which lies within all humans. Judgement Day is every day and individuals are their own judge, jury and executioner. People are constantly creating their own reality. They do not go to hell when they die. If hell is where they feel they are heading or it is the place they are trying to avoid, then it becomes their everyday reality. This is something I have observed on numerous occasions with members of family, friends and acquaintances.

In my experience, those with the greatest attachment to religious dogma become experts in creating hell on Earth when they can as equally have created heaven. Both my parents are devotees of Islam and they pay strict attention to their daily rites and duties. The root meaning of the word 'Islam' is 'salaam', which means 'peace'. A 'Muslim' is someone who 'submits their will to God' and attains their peace and salvation by completely surrendering to the Divine. Unfortunately, the daily religious practice is primarily based on the fear of not being able to make the grade and, therefore, not being accepted into paradise. It is of no surprise so many religious devotees experience huge stress on a day-to-day basis. Consequently, they are continually praying for forgiveness. Forgiveness: for what exactly?

Could this be Science's Achilles Heel?[8]

As a student of biology, chemistry and physics, we were taught the concept of 'assumptions' so we could better understand scientific phenomena. Whenever an experiment is carried out to test a scientific theory, key assumptions must be made to help test and validate that theory. So, how do assumptions play a role in science today? Unfortunately most scientists jump straight into scientific research without ever taking a course in the philosophy of science. In other words, they do not take a course about science as a human endeavour. Had they done this, they would know that science can only exist with a set of cultural beliefs as assumptions. These are what form the foundation of all the theories they are testing.

Theories cannot be made about the universe without having a concept of it. Science starts off with fundamental assumptions called 'axioms', which are critical for validating theories. However, the challenge arises when axioms are taken to be 'truths'. For example, it is a scientific assumption that 'the universe is a nonliving universe'. One can just as easily pose the belief that 'the universe is a living universe'. The existence of a nonliving universe has never been proven. Yet, in classical science, it is something that underlies all the theories about the universe. Consequently, it skews the way that those theories are presented.

Another fundamental assumption is that 'the universe can be studied objectively'. This means that the observer does not interfere or influence the outcome. Nor does the observer connect with the universe. This is another cultural belief. Both of these beliefs are just two out of many others. These kinds of beliefs would never have existed, for example, in devising Vedic sciences or Taoist science or, for that matter, indigenous sciences where the universe was always alive and participatory. Therefore, it is very important to recognise these assumptions

[8] Much of this section is taken from *The Consciousness Revolution Show* interview with Dr Elisabet Sahtouris

when looking at the kinds of things that are said about the universe in relation to theory.

One of the main aspects of the scientific model and the foundation protocols which scientists are meant to use has a fundamental flaw. The degree of intention and expectation that any one so-called objective observer has over the formulation and implementation of any experiment does affect the experiment itself considerably. In the West, there is a problem with the assumption of remaining objective and not interfering with the subject matter being studied.

Quantum science shows to a high degree how results are affected through intentions over a situation either through thoughts or expectations. The second problem is when something exists outside of the limits of the observer's own field of experience and reference point. It is difficult if an experiment does reveal something which is not within the scientist's point of reference. Frequently, such phenomena that cannot be understood are put into the box labelled 'unknown'.

Historically, in the wisdom traditions that involve metaphysics or ancient knowledge, science and those particular traditions were not seen as separate. There was a very strong understanding and foundation sense of unity. There was a theory of unification, which is contrary to classical science. The post-Descartes period is one of separation and explanation of phenomena after they have been separated, analysed and put into their component parts. Hence, the terms 'mechanistic science' and 'mechanistic physics'. Today, through physics, science itself has invalidated a number of the Darwinian assumptions, including the assumption about the nonliving universe.

A consequence of the assumption of a nonliving universe is that life comes from non-life, intelligence comes from non-intelligence and consciousness comes out of non-consciousness. In other words, consciousness is seen as a late emergent product of this material universe after billions of years of evolution when nervous systems can squeeze consciousness out. The Eastern sciences such as the Taoist and Vedic traditions were completely unified with consciousness because they took the opposite view. Rather than be a late emergent product of material evolution, consciousness was primary and material evolution took place within consciousness as part of it.

Consciousness can gel itself into matter by stepping down a frequency. This is the polar opposite view to the assumptions made in classical science. Scientists need to consider taking the important steps that will enable a more powerful advancement of science by asking:

"What are my untrue assumptions about science?"

"Do I still believe in a nonliving universe that gives rise to consciousness late in the game?"

"Do I acknowledge the view that consciousness comes as primary?"

The good news is, that despite following outdated assumptions for entire careers, many scientists have adapted their views to the polar opposite view. These scientists have been able to reconsider the assumptions they had been taught and examine the new assumptions they are now making. This will perhaps clear the path for more scientists to step forward and question some of the grandest illusions, such as the one that propagates the survival of the fittest paradigm.

We are merely Living to Survive?

Thousands of years ago, when there were far fewer human beings on the planet and a proportionately higher number of wild animals, it was imperative that humans had an effective threat-management system to tackle any danger posed to their lives by wild beasts. The genetic programme for 'survival' became a key part of such a critical system for harmonious coexistence of humans with nature.

When a wild predator got up close and personal with a human, the survival programme was responsible for activating the hormones for 'fight or flight'. At such a time, the rational human mind is not interested in the possibility of indigestion occurring as a result from running at a pace on a full stomach. The role of the human is either to get the heck out of there or confront the animal head on. The entire animal kingdom from the oldest reptiles to the most evolved mammals, possess this survival mechanism.

The hormones for survival are first triggered from the most ancient part of the brain, i.e. the 'reptilian brain'. In the case of a herd of gazelles in the African savannah, for example, the fight or flight mechanism is triggered when they sense the impending danger inherent in an approaching lioness looking for food. When the threat of being the main course passes, the fight or flight mechanism is switched off and normal biological activities resume. The herd go back to doing what they do best - grazing, playing, courting, mating, dumping, etc.

Since the chances of being feasted on by sabre tooth tigers have diminished in recent years, humans have adapted the survival mechanism for use beyond escaping death and into something more suited to the 'civilised' environment. The human species have discovered how to put themselves into survival mode on a near-permanent basis by allowing themselves to be triggered by a whole range of subconscious and unconscious programming.

When these programmes are triggered, a range of emotions are experienced. These are usually fear-based emotions. The resulting impact on people are undesirable and usually related to a sense of unworthiness, insecurity and a having little control over their lives. To fill these voids, people unconsciously seek out ways to feel more worthy, safe, secure and gain control of their lives. Consequently, most people's attitudes and behaviours are directly correlated to filling these inner voids.

The level of emotional security and maturity is directly relationship to the level of an individual's awareness and to the degree they are affected by their survival mechanism. Once the collective begins to comprehend the true power of consciousness, then they will begin to discover that their ascension to greatness will be fast-tracked by side-stepping the survival mechanism.

What has Consciousness got to do with Anything?

How can something as abstract as 'consciousness' be defined, let alone quantified? Very few people that I have interviewed or met can give a clear cut definition of consciousness either from a scientific or a metaphysical view-point. However, one person who taking it beyond definition by devising a method for measuring consciousness is Dr David Hawkins, author of *Power versus Force*. Using 'Kinesiology' or 'muscle-testing', the clinical psychiatrist and spiritual teacher, has devised a logarithmic scale for measuring consciousness called the *Map of Consciousness*. This system also demonstrates how our different emotions consume or radiate different levels of energy.

Each level of consciousness on the Map represents a different frequency or vibration of energy. Higher consciousness radiates a healing effect on the world and can be verified with the human muscle response. The response is strong in the presence of love and truth but weak in the presence of negative energy fields and non-truth. The Map begins on a scale starting from zero (death) and finishing at 1,000. Below the level of 200, the emotions are fear-based.

These emotions are great consumers of personal energy and consequently leave the individual with an ever-decreasing level of energy for other functions. For example, when some-one is in a state of anger, 80% of their energy is consumed on sustaining that emotional state. They are then left with only 20% energy to continue with normal bodily functions. On the other hand, when someone is in a state of apathy, 95% of energy is occupied with that feeling leaving them with only 5% of energy to use for survival.

It is no wonder that during a state of apathy the person feels so tired even though they are doing nothing. The level of 200 on the Map of Consciousness is where love-based emotions are accessed and where integrity begins to be present in an individual's life. On the Map, fear and guilt calibrate very low on the scale. Shame, interestingly, is one of the lowest levels of consciousness and is barely higher than the state of comatose!

Let's face it: the more one gets sucked dry by 'negative' feelings, the less energy they are left with to perform any other tasks to any degree of satisfaction, let alone excellence. The human mind and body are too busy trying to sustain the fight or flight instinct just so that they can survive a total shutdown of the body (i.e. death). The part of the brain responsible for taking humans to higher levels of consciousness (the frontal lobe) is deactivated during fear-based emotional experiences.

Over millennia, people in places of authority believed that they need only to keep the masses locked in fear to maintain maximum control and in a docile state. In such a state, the ability to use higher brain functions of awareness or 'awakedness' would be severely hampered. Effectively, fear was used to keep them asleep. Of course, the ultimate form of fear was either death or damnation to hell in the afterlife. However, as the collective consciousness steadily increased over time, so the methods of control became more subtle.

To reach their highest goals, master illusionists knew the best way forward was to keep humans in survival and away from creativity. The negative emotions that I am referring to, come under the headings of fear, shame and guilt. The lesser of the illusionists have demonstrated the use of fear, shame and guilt to good effect. How often do politicians use the fear of their opponents getting into power as a way of winning votes for themselves?

By handing over their responsibility to misguided politicians, the people have allowed them to get away with ridiculous policies based on personal greed and a desire to stay in power. No wonder corruption is so rife in most democracies. By keeping the voting public in a state of survival, they are stripped of their capacity to trigger the most empowering programmes that humans possess: creativity. It is this creativity that is the ticket to liberation and the key to salvation from a life of misery and suffering.

It is not remotely in the interest of the master illusionists to allow people to access their real creativity. That would mean becoming inspired, self-empowerment and self-actualised beings. How is it possible to control someone who is in such a profound state of self-realisation? It is not possible. The master illusionists do not like this. They know that the most efficient and effective way to enslave people is through what all humans are predisposed to...the need for survival. By programming and conditioning humans from the time they are born until they are seven years old, they have a ready-made slave willing to submit to the beck and call of the illusionists. The Jesuits understood this and had a saying for it:

"Give me a child until he is seven years old, I will show you the man."

Illusionists have created systems and exploited people's vulnerabilities because of their need for survival by propagating one of the most misunderstood and misinterpreted theories in science. The Theory of Evolution is probably one of the most important illusions fundamental to the existence of most other grand illusions. By truly comprehending the severity of the nature of this core illusion, it is possible to dismantle other toxic deceptions, too. This clears the space for individuals to enter the realms of creativity. The Darwinian nightmare is still strongly upheld by the establishment, indoctrination organisations and their mouthpieces. It is about time this whole delusion was over-hauled.

Darwinian Theory: Truth or Lie?

Before I sat my school exams when I was sixteen years old, I had to make my choice of the A-Level (pre-university) subjects I would be studying in senior school. Like most parents of Bengali origin of their generation, mine wanted me to become a doctor, lawyer or accountant. The alternative was to be a restaurateur just like 95% of all the other Bengalis living in the UK! Without too much hesitation, I opted for the medical route and chose to study biology, chemistry and physics.

However, I was also keen to study mathematics, except for one thing that held me back. Every person I sought advice from told me how terribly difficult maths was at A-Level. Given none of my advisors had studied maths, with hindsight, I should have asked them how they were such experts! Several years later, when I did study maths during evening classes, I could not believe how easy I found it. If only I had followed my gut feeling and not listened to the words of others!

Today I find a similar situation with the number of people who shy away from science as if it was some kind of disease. Sure, not everybody had fun learning science at school, primarily due to the education process not being tailored to make science relevant and up-to-date. Nonetheless, every person is affected by science on a daily basis. This ranges from the clothes people wear to how they cook food to how they heat their homes to how they travel. Others criticise the more recent sciences such as quantum physics (which is over 100 years old) as being a 'psuedo-science'. Yet, much of modern technology is based on quantum physics, from cell phones to television sets to the computers people use every day. Psuedoscience? Really!

There is one particularly important area of science that has had plenty of attention, but still remains a mystery for most. That is the story of 'evolution', which is another great fable told to emasculate humans from their innate power. The problem is that many of those who do take a stand against evolution theory put forward such preposterous arguments that they become the laughing stock of millions. Consequently, it polarises the rest of the world who then run and embrace the theory of evolution with open arms. Some religious zealots even deny the existence of dinosaurs and believe that God placed the dinosaur bones deep in the ground to test their faith! So how about shedding some proper light on the theory of evolution? The two questions to keep in mind regarding evolution are:

(a) Did evolution occur?
(b) If evolution did take place, what is the mechanism by which it works?

A distinction must be made at this stage. The Darwinian story of evolution is not the only theory. Thus, not supporting Darwinian evolution does not exclude supporting evolution per se. It means that the mechanisms proposed by Darwinian Theory are not being supported. Before his death, Charles Darwin himself did not support Darwinian Theory! He changed his mind and became more of a Lamarckian evolutionist. Jean-Baptiste Lamarck (1744-1829) created the theory of evolution the year Darwin was born, which was fifty years before Darwin's Theory came out. Thus, Lamarck had a theory of evolution that was the first scientific theory of evolution.

Next, if evolution takes place, is it according to Darwinian Theory? The answer is 'no'. The mechanism of evolution is much closer to that of Lamarck who said evolution was driven by the interaction between an organism and its environment. In other words, as environments change, organisms adapt to the changes by adjusting their genes to the new environment. Therefore, the driving force of evolution is the environment.

Darwinian Theory takes people the other way around. It says that heredity drives evolution and genes randomly mutate and, as a result, change the traits of an organism. For example, if two dogs were mated, the puppies in the litter will have the traits of their parents. Occasionally, there may be an anomaly in the offspring, i.e. the runt of the litter. THAT was the mutation that Darwin was emphasising in his theory. Every now and then, a mutated organism appears. Darwin said if mutants were bred with other mutants, then the offspring would have even more mutations.

At some point, the mutants will become a different species. Back in 1859 before television, video, computer games and the internet were around to distract people, breeding plants and animals was a popular pastime. When Darwin proposed his theory, everybody thought it made perfect sense because they were creating different variations of plants and animals by purposely crossbreeding them. That is when Darwinian Theory spread around the world like wildfire.

Everybody accepted the Darwinian Theory because the previous theory of evolution, the 'Genesis Story', had come from the Church who were the official truth providers. Genesis did not hold water compared to people's direct experience with breeding plants and animals. Darwin's theory made more sense than the magic of Genesis and, thus, science became the truth provider for civilisation. Once Darwin's explanation of how humans got here was preferred by the people over Genesis, the Church lost most of its power. Darwinian Theory took over.

Darwinian Theory says that humans got here in two steps. The first step was the result of an accidental mutation, which was a random mutation that took place every now and then. It only happened when the runt of the litter showed up. The second step was when a different organism appears on the scene. Does the mutated gene enhance the ability of the organism to survive or does it compromise the organism's ability to survive? In other words, the gene that mutated gives an advantage to this organism and it will live longer and propagate the mutated gene.

Now, the evolution of that species begins to head off in a new direction. Essentially, Darwin said that the first step is random mutation (by accident) and the second step is called 'natural selection'. This means Nature will select the stronger of the offspring to survive and it will eliminate the weakest ones. The issue is: why are humans here? According to Darwinian Theory, it was just an accident and there was no purpose for humans to be here. It was just a coincidence that human genes ended up the way they did. This whole theory is incorrect.

It was not accidental mutation that drove evolution. These mutations are now called 'adaptive mutations'. What this means is that when the organism finds itself in a new environment, many of the organisms adjust their genetics through an interaction with the environment. The organisms adjust their genes purposely to fit their environment to be better suited to those conditions and last longer. Organisms that are here did not get here by accident. They got here because of their ability to adapt and conform to an ever-changing environment. They are here as part of a plan to create a harmonious cooperative called the 'Biosphere'.

Evolution is based on cooperation yet Darwinian Theory says that evolution is based on competition and a struggle for survival. The entire world, which bought into the beliefs propagated by Darwinian Theory, now competes with each other in a rat race to get to the top to survive. If an individual does not get out and actively struggle in the world, then they will be beaten by someone behind them. The competitor is going to struggle harder than the next person, and beat them. Then, in the end, the individual realises their life is over. What a perfect way to use fear as motivation! Most people live in the fear that the world does not support them.

They are on an eternal struggle for survival and an eternal battle of competition.

People can be forgiven for thinking Darwin was right about a struggle for survival. What is the truth beyond this illusion? The struggle to survive is based on a belief system. When enough people believe the same thing, they create a world that equals that belief system. When the world accepted Darwin, the world accepted that violence and competition was a natural means of life. Evidence shows this to be absolutely not the case.

It was Lamarckian theory that said life was conforming to the environment and that humans are directly connected to nature. Humans are part of the environment, part of the ecosystem and the biosphere AND that is where they came from. What does that mean in today's terms? For the better part of history, humankind has lived without knowing that it was part of the environment and humans were groomed by evolution to be a cooperative element of the environment.

Look at the consequences of what humans have become and what they have done to their environment. They have become the exterminators of the garden. People have undermined the environment. They have broken the web of life to such an extent that a global climate change has been created which is throwing havoc into producing food. Then humans act as if it all happened by accident. None of this was an accident.

Humans have undermined the life-giving environment because they have always felt they were separate from the environment and that they got here by accident. When Nature evolved humans, they were seen as powerful entities to keep harmony in the environment. Without that knowledge, humans have turned backwards and destroyed the environment. Now humans are facing a strong possibility of their own extinction.

In 1859, the original theory of evolution that is referred to as Darwinian Theory came from a commoner and scientist, Alfred Russell Wallace (1823-1913). He sent his theory of evolution to Charles Darwin. At this time, Darwin did not even have a theory of evolution written. Darwin was a protégé of one of the leading scientists in the world, Charles Lyell (1797-1875). Both these scientists were upper class, which was of particular importance to Victorian England.

The fact that Wallace was a commoner was unimaginable to the Victorians. How could something as profound as the theory of evolution come from a commoner? Between Darwin, Lyle and botanist, Joseph Hunter a 'delicate arrangement' was made. They put Darwin's name first on the Theory of Evolution so it was seen as *'The Theory of Evolution by Charles Darwin and Alfred Russell Wallace'*. That was how it came out in The Royal Society[9].

The ordering of the names is quite profound in scientific circles. Effectively it implies that Darwin discovered this theory with supporting actor, Wallace. In real terms, it means Darwin gets all the credit. Furthermore, this theory was proposed by a lower class man with an upper class gentleman of society during the Victorian era. The lower class were not even supposed to look into the face of the upper classes. They lived in two distinctly different worlds.

Wallace came out with a theory that asked what the driving force of evolution was. He said that it was based on the 'elimination of the weakest'. The weakest individuals would die off and their genes would not be propagated. Darwin turned it around and said it was the 'survival of the fittest'. Even though it sounds like it is the same thing, there is a huge difference. Look at it this way. Take a choice of two worlds that someone could live in - *World A* and *World B*. The former (*A*) is based on the survival of the fittest, whilst *World B* is based on the elimination of the weakest. Which is the preferred world scenario? Living in a world based on survival of the fittest, there is a constant struggle to survive to be the Top Dog.

---

9 www.royalsociety.org

Living in a world that is based on elimination of the weakest means there is less work to do and life can be enjoyed more fully. In *World B*, all that is needed is not ending up as the weakest. This is far easier than being the fittest one. When Darwin was talking about survival of the fittest, he was emphasising the upper class of Victorian England. They were the evolutionary leaders and the lower class were the bottom layer and irrelevant supporters of the upper class.

Darwinian Theory was a philosophy that was created to support the existing status of Victorian society. They believed the upper class were separate and distinct because they were more superior than the lower class. They eliminated Wallace from the equation. Today, most people today have no clue who is, yet Wallace was the actual founder of what is known as 'Darwinian Theory'.

The Darwinian Theory of Evolution remains just a **theory**. There is plenty of evidence in nature that competition exists. However, there is equally as much evidence for cooperation in nature. The Catholic West had a strong preference for the Darwinian theory as it suits their purpose to think of competition as the entire purpose of evolution. Few people realise that in the Soviet Union, they were studying Pyotr Kropotkin's (1842-1921) *Theory of Evolution*. In his book, '*Mutual Aid*', he argued that cooperation and mutual aid are as important in the evolution of the species as competition and mutual strife, if not more so.

To add to the confusion, science has been politicised to suit the objectives of different sects. The secular state was born after the European rule by Church and State gave way to rule by entrepreneurs and science. Now science got to tell the Creation Story rather than religion. Science presumably understands the world, not through revelations but through research. Nevertheless, the foundation story of science is really not a scientific story but a cultural story.

The Lamarckian concept of life is about understanding the commensurate, the collaborative and the consequences aspect of life. Humans are constantly adapting to shifts and changes causing evolution to take place and transforming them. These changes are about growth and adaptation through necessity. It is something that involves an expanding and encompassing process rather than separation on the basis of survival.

The likelihood is that such a perception did not suit the powers that be. Therefore, they pushed it aside and gave reasons for why survival of the fittest should be promoted. It comes as no surprise that the Darwinian Theory was seen as such a strong theory. It is also a profound reason why the entire Industrial Revolution and Capitalist Theory moved in the direction it did and gained the power that it wields today.

Why is the Darwinian Delusion so Dangerous?

One of the biggest influences on both Alfred Russell Wallace and Charles Darwin's lives was Reverend Thomas Robert Malthus (1766-1834), an Anglican cleric, British scholar and evolutionary economist. Malthus' viewed the notion that humans would improve their condition in time with skepticism and cynicism. He was a true pessimist. In his mind, a proportion of humans would always be condemned to poverty.

The enthusiasm people attached to their future prosperity came from a desire for them to increase their family size. By doing so, the population would outgrow the resources available to support them. In other words, as populations increase, there would be less food and resources for people to live on. Hence, there would always be those who were too poor and too weak. Malthus' work prejudiced the work of Darwin and Wallace, the fathers of modern evolution theory.

Malthus proposed two methods, a positive and a negative one, for controlling populations which were facing the limitations of available resources. The positive method was through hunger, disease and war. The negative method included birth control, abortion, prostitution, celibacy or delaying marriage. He was against advancing technology that would lead to better agriculture and was in favour of Francis Galton's notion of *Eugenics*[10].

Galton's methods of population control and his support of eugenics was primarily aimed at the working class and the poor. After all, if the poor were not able to support themselves, then why should the government or the wealthy class help them? It must be Nature's method of population control. Although his theories were repudiated by eminent men of the time, many more prominent men such as John Stuart Mill (1806–1873) and Jeremy Bentham (1748–1832), intellectual elitists employed by the *British East India Company*, wholly supported the Malthusian views. Some of these men also later influenced British Prime Minister, William Pitt the Younger, in his extension of the 'Poor Relief', i.e. he withdrew the Bill to support the poor!

In its social interpretation, Darwinian Theory has become the 'Darwinian Delusion'. It has proved to be dangerous as it justified many inhumane acts, such as forced child labour through to ethnic cleansing and the Holocaust of World War II. Scientists objecting to this interpretation often unwittingly fail to recognise the politicisation of science. The Victorian illusionists wanted a continuous hostile struggle for survival and a competitive struggle. This is why they found Darwinian Theory so appealing.

The Industrial Revolution was powerfully supported by the theory of evolution and survival of the fittest. It gave birth to a number of other incentives which first started after the American Civil War (1861-1865), i.e. the creation of the 'corporation' and the ability to give responsibility to a body that did not represent people any more. The corporation was a composite existing company which could essentially dissolve into the ether when it came to pointing the finger and taking responsibility.

---

[10] www.en.wikipedia.org/wiki/Eugenics

61

Earth is a finite object that is a living, interactive being. The whole concept of the corporation involved assuming that humans can neglect their responsibilities by ignoring the consequences of their actions on Earth, Nature and other species. The individual is not held to account for their actions. They can disappear into obscurity and allow the corporation to take the slack even to the point where it is liquidated. This behaviour comes from the mindset of survival of the fittest.

The level of fitness is determined by the quantity of land, assets and resources acquired by each individual. What and how the acquired resources are used is nobody's business. It is mine, mine, mine! Consequently, the extraordinary ability to tap into universal creativity is neglected. The survival instinct is very powerful and supersedes everything in daily life, regarding one's inner creativity.

Competition does foster a certain level of creativity. However, when it is at the level of the individual, it tends to be driven by the necessity to gain, to show off and to prove. This is different to understanding the creativity which one engages in as a result of opening up. This creativity is when a person enters into the realm of Life, Nature, Earth and their own inner health. When these aspects interact with each other, it leads to wisdom. This creativity is a result of surrendering and being able to be guided by a power greater than one's own force. When an individual is driven by survival, they end up limiting themselves enormously by thinking and behaving within a very minute and self-destructive realm.

Eugenics: Eliminating 'Defective' Humans

In 1883, Sir Francis Galton used the work of his cousin, Charles Darwin, to develop a new field called 'Eugenics'. Galton's work was supported strongly by President Woodrow Wilson, President Theodore Roosevelt, George Bernard Shaw, John Maynard Keynes, John Harvey Kellogg, Charles Davenport and Nobel Prize winner, Linus Pauling. Galton's work was pioneered in the USA and expanded rapidly into many of the European countries such as Sweden, Germany and Belgium.

'Eugenics' is derived from the root words *'eu'* and *'genes'* which means 'well' and 'born'. Galton defined it as 'the study of all agencies under human control which can improve or impair racial equality of future generations'. Sound like fun? Eugenicists believe that, given certain (social) policies, the system of creating designer babies will improve the gene pool of the human race. That way, hereditary diseases such as haemophilia and Huntingdon's disease can be eradicated.

During the twentieth century, many governments allowed eugenics programmes to take place in their countries. This included marital restrictions, preventing birth of children 'prone to homosexuality', controlling birth rates, racial segregation and segregation of the mentally ill from the general population and genocide. Eugenics was, most infamously, engendered by the leader of the Nazi Party, Adolf Hitler, in his book, *Mein Kampf*, and then enacted through the mass murder of numerous ethnic groups, including Jews.

Today, eugenics has taken a different and more palatable guise and is called the 'Planned Parenthood Federation of America' (PPFA) or 'Planned Parenthood'. It is now an international movement[11] persuading many countries of the world to fulfill its mission. Again, the concept of survival of the fittest has been used more than once in eradicating and ethnically cleansing communities of millions of men, women and children. Despite the advancement of science or the good intentions of most scientists, there is always a real and present danger of good science being manipulated to eradicate not disease, but people.

The solution will not come from policing science or prosecution, but from individually and collectively raising human consciousness. This means learning how to prevent illusionists from taking hold of power in the first place. The

---

[11] www.ippf.org

first step onto such a path involves reclaiming one's own power by emancipation from slavery.

Chapter 3: The Invisible Shackles of Slavery

"The greater the number of laws there are,
the less freedom and liberty are enjoyed."

Crying Freedom

Most people in developed countries believe they have freedom of choice. Really? Freedom stems from the Latin 'libertas', which is also the root word for 'liberty'. Liberty is the state of 'being free' within society. Free from oppressive restrictions imposed by authority on one's way of life, behaviours or political views. Do oppressive restrictions imposed by authority in any country exist? Hmmm...let me think. Thinking's over. YES!

I cannot think of a single nation which does not oppress one or many groups of people within its borders. History shows that ethnic minorities in most nations have been under attack by mainstream nationals at some point. Today, we are no more advanced than we were 2,000 years ago. Some of the onslaughts on minority communities have been so devastating, that entire communities have been 'cleansed' of them.

Simply recall the Holocaust of the (1930s and 1940s), the Israeli-Palestinian conflict (1948 and still ongoing), the Rwandan massacre (1994), the Bosnia War (1992-5), Sierra Leone's civil war (1991-2002) to mention just a few. Need reference be made to the massacres during the Russian Revolution which claimed up to nine million lives? Nor the countless numbers who perished during and subsequent to the civil war in China led by Mao Zedong?

What happened to their freedoms? What are the real costs of attaining freedom? How about the freedoms that

Britain and America attained through the enslavement of African men, women and children? America, said to be the flagship of democracy and liberty and the land of the free, has got one of the most terrible track records for violating civil liberties. The UK, as ever, hang onto the coattails of American government policies. Here's a quick barometer for checking how much freedom there is in any country: the greater the number of laws there are, the less freedom and liberty enjoyed by its people.

Some of the more cynical individuals may claim it is unfair to cite these examples. OK. How about entertaining that notion for a moment? How about the freedom to practice religion openly in a place where the majority of worshippers follow one main religion? How much freedom would be granted to worship any god one chooses in places such as Makkah (Saudi Arabia) or in the Vatican? How about the civil rights of individuals who were being locked up in prison for 28 days without charge? Or when alleged terrorists are incarcerated in Guantanamo Bay?

How about the freedom to have an intimate relationship with someone of the same sex without prejudice? How about a child's right to retain their innocence without being molested, abused or raped by a person in a place of authority or by a trusted relative? How about the right to reclaim one's own land that was forcefully taken by the indigenous people by legalised militia? Ask the Aborigines of Australia or the Native Americans or the descendants of the African slave trade living in former colonies or the many indigenous tribes of the Amazon or the Tutsis of Rwanda about freedom. Most of them will have a different story to tell than the ones that the masses have been brainwashed into believing.

Illusionists, in the guise of certain politicians, often accuse people in the developed world of taking their freedom for granted. Fair enough. It may have been the case that British citizens had much more liberty than Iraqis under the dictatorial regime of Saddam Hussein. However, the cost of forced 'democracy' has been one million Iraqi lives since the British-American invasion in March 2003. By the end of 2010, over 4,000 US soldiers had lost their lives of which more than 54% were under the age of 25 years of age[12].

The political system in the UK is another example of the farcical choices available to the public. It has effectively become a two party democracy, i.e. the Labour and Conservative parties. The Liberal Democrats, a third party, had not been in power since David Lloyd George left his premiership in 1922. In May 2010, they predictably forged an alliance with the Conservative Party to get a whiff of government[13]. In the US, the illusion of choice of government is even more nonsensical. The choice of political parties is limited to two, Democrats and Republicans. How can this be a true choice for the electorate if neither party has policies that resonate with the American electorate?

Furthermore, whoever becomes the US President, de facto, becomes the President of the world's economic system; a potentially dangerous proposition. Another area where massive limitations exist is in consumer choice. The public have very few options in what company they can buy their fuel from. The choices that are left include the five major oil companies - Exxon, Royal Dutch Shell, BP, Chevron and ConocoPhillips. These five companies are all in the top ten largest companies of the world.

The banking world is not much better. In order of magnitude, the largest banks in the world are BNP Paribas, Royal Bank of Scotland, Barclays, Deutsche Bank, HSBC, Credit Agricole, Bank of America, Mitsubishi UFJ Financial Group, J.P. Morgan Chase and UBS AG. How many of these banks are seen in the local neighbourhood or on the high street? In the UK, most of the previously traditional safe places

---

[12] www.usliberals.about.com/od/homelandsecuriti/a/IraqNumbers.htm

[13] The department responsible for the British Prime Minister and his/her ministers

to keep money, i.e. the building societies, have also converted into banks. Hence, choice has been eroded further.

There are few choices of supermarkets with just a handful dominating the field in both the US and UK. In the UK, Tesco has almost the double the market share (30.7%)[14] of its nearest rival Asda Walmart (17.3%). Sainsbury's (15.9%) and even Morrison's (11.7%) have a significant chunk of the market, albeit much smaller than Tesco. US consumers have greater choice but the entire market is dwarfed by two giants, Walmart and K-Mart. Unfortunately, many of the smaller businesses (the real competitors) have gone out of business or are close to extinction.

In the judicial system, the excess of laws that have been erected by governments in an attempt to 'protect' citizens have led to many more people being imprisoned. In 2009, the US prison population was 2,297,400 with an even higher number in some form of correctional order. 92.9% were male with African-Americans making 38.2% and Hispanics making up 20.7% of the population[15]. Both minorities are over-represented in prisons compared to the general population.

In the UK, it is estimated that 72% of male inmates and 70% of female inmates suffer from one or more mental health disorder. What about their freedom to have the opportunity to reform or their chance to recover from their psychological condition? There may be those who are incurable, but 70-72% with mental disorders? This is a joke. Whilst on the subject of imprisonment and freedom, what about the death penalty that is still a legally accepted punishment in some countries?

The ultimate line of attack to strip an individual of their freedom is to kill them and is euphemistically called 'capital punishment'. Numerous countries still administer the death penalty for drug trafficking and murder. In the USA,

---

[14]
www.en.wikipedia.org/wiki/List_of_supermarket_chains_in_the_United_Kingdom

[15] www.en.wikipedia.org/wiki/Incarceration_in_the_United_States

capital punishment is legal in a number of states. Way ahead of the league in the usage of the death penalty, which is signed by the state Governor, is the state of Texas.

From 1976 until 2009, 464 prisoners were executed with 336 more on death row[16]. The most famous Governor of Texas in recent times, George W. Bush (1995-2000), who was also the US President from 2001 to 2008. Suffice to say, freedom and freedom of choice is truly a grand illusion. The protectors of freedom were monarchs, emperors, warriors and, in recent times, democratically elected leaders. Whilst monarchs, emperors and feudal rulers were often dictatorial, the new democratic form of rule was created to empower the people. How does democracy fare in the illusion stakes?

A Free Democracy

The Cold War (1947-1991) began in earnest shortly after World War II. It hailed the beginning of a standoff between the USA and its western allies and the communist countries of the People's Republic of China, the Soviet Union and its satellite states. The West were vociferous and took an aggressive stance in the spreading of democracy across the globe. Any country who dared to question or take a stand against, especially the US and Britain, were totally cut off from trade with the democratic countries.

Since communism was perceived as a threat to peace, prosperity and democracy, western leaders saw it as their duty to instigate further conflict to prevent its spread. One of the most notorious conflicts was the Vietnam War that began in 1955[17]. Consequently, achieving and maintaining democracy has been a major platform for American foreign policy. But, what does democracy mean? Democracy is a political form of government in which the governing power is handed down from the people either by referendum or by elected

---

[16] www.en.wikipedia.org/wiki/Capital_Punishment_in_the_United_States

[17] www.en.wikipedia.org/wiki/Vietnam_War

representatives of the people. The root meaning of 'democracy' comes from the Greek word '*demos*', which means 'people' and '*kratos*' meaning 'power'. Therefore, democracy means 'people power' or 'rule by the people'.

The term 'democracy' first appeared in ancient Greek political and philosophical thought. Plato[18] distinguished the difference between '*democracy*', the system of 'rule by the governed', with '*monarchy*' (ruled by a king or queen), '*oligarchy*' (ruled by a small elite class) and '*timocracy*' (ruling class of property owners). Each system of governance had their strengths and weaknesses but democracy was seen as the most fair and just system for Greeks who had previously suffered years of tyrannical monarchic rule.

Today, a developed country may consider itself as democratic because it allows the public to vote and be protected by the laws of the land. This would have been a significant breakthrough for many countries, who until a few years ago did not even have these basic rights. For example, British women were not given the legal right to vote until 1928. Started in 1872, the Women's Suffrage[19] movement led to the *Representation of the People Act 1928* being passed. This gave women the right to cast votes on equal terms as men.

When the concept of democracy was created by the Greeks, there were two further principles that were far more important than the right to vote and being protected by the laws of the land. The second principle of democracy was about 'being responsible' as an individual and as a member of the city. Hence, the term 'citi-zen'. In many of the democratic countries, especially in the UK, USA and European countries, the public have handed over their responsibilities to politicians supposedly representing their interests in all matters of local, regional, national and international.

---

[18] www.en.wikipedia.org/wiki/Plato

[19] www.en.wikipedia.org/wiki/Women's_suffrage_in_the_United_Kingdom

With the lack of individual responsibility has came the near total loss of public power; and the public voice has been effectively silenced regarding government policies. Modern day democracy does nothing more than give the public the illusion that they have choice. They have no choice. During the lead up to the Second Gulf War (2003-present day), numerous public demonstrations were held throughout the world protesting against the impending invasion of Iraq. In the UK, one million people descended upon London, whilst the biggest mobilisation of protesters took place in Rome with an astounding three million people[20].

Nonetheless, the British-American alliance ignored the pleas of their people and invaded Iraq as a backlash from the 9/11 attacks on the World Trade Centre and on the pretext of the Iraqis having WMD ('Weapons of Mass Destruction'). In the end, no WMD were found in Iraq. However, the war, led by Prime Minister Tony Blair[21] and President George W. Bush, still raged on. The horrific attack on the Twin Towers on 9/11 left 2,995 people dead, yet the ensuing invasion and occupation of Iraq has left over one million Iraqi men, women and children and 4,000+ US soldiers dead.

Not only have individual members of the public lost their sense of responsibility, it is clear that their elected representatives feel no desire to listen to them. The third principle was to 'be accountable' for that responsibility. If anything went wrong, individuals were never expected to blame others for unacceptable conditions and events, such as their politician, or the Prime Minister or President or even the political party. The situation was in their hands and they allowed it to happen. If the public wanted to implement change, they were the ones who needed to change to ensure the situation never repeated itself.

---

[20] www.en.wikipedia.org/wiki/Protests_against_the_Iraq_War

[21] www.en.wikipedia.org/wiki/Tony_Blair

If such a situation were to happen again, the lesson needed to be repeated until the public learnt and took the appropriate action to ensure that it never happened again. Therefore, in the example of the Gulf War and the deaths of over a million citizens, it would be the voting public who would be accountable for allowing such atrocities to take place. This exercise in democracy is beyond just taking responsibility and having accountability.

It is also about the ability to see cause to effect, to take action for that effect, to not repeat the previous negative outcome and finally to transform it. Therefore, there is something to look forward to for future generations by not perpetuating the survival of the fittest mechanism and by not just living for the now. There is a difference between *being present* and *living for now*. The former means accepting the current moment and acting accordingly with consequences for each decision and action.

On the other hand, the living for now means living without responsibility and consuming resources in this moment with no consideration for the consequences of one's own actions and with no thought for the future. In the case of the international conflicts, what really drives war? Weapons of mass destruction? The imminent threat of a terrorist attack by a group with no coherent leadership? The reasons are far simpler than one would like to think. The purpose for modern day warfare will be revealed in Chapter 5.

Chapter 4: Chasing Illusions

"It is out of fear and their need for survival, that the illusionists desperately want to control the masses."

Money: the Root of All Evil?

This is the BIG one. The number of times that I have heard about the importance of money is countless. Sayings such as the following are commonplace across many cultures:

'Money doesn't grow on trees'

'Money makes the world round'

'Money is the root of all evil' (infamously quoted from the Bible usually out of context and should read: *'the love of money is the root of all evil'*)

'Time is money'

'Money doesn't buy happiness'

What is it about the great illusion of money that causes humans to perpetually chase it? When I was working in my family curry house during the recession years of 1982-83, we struggled to survive with barely a few customers and the occasional drunkard. Nonetheless, as the oldest child, I worked for my father serving customers during the evenings seven days a week. Being 12 years old, I used to easily get bored during work hours. My main pastime was watching television and reading newspapers. From time to time, certain adverts in the papers would catch my eye. I remember one that stood out for me in particular as it promoted a book that guaranteed readers of the secrets to getting rich real fast.

Within a few weeks or months of buying the book, individuals could earn anything from £25,000 to £100,000. Of course, the book cost £25, which was a lot of money for 1982. The strategy for making money in this get-rich-quick scheme was very simple. The readers had to publish their own book on how to get rich quickly and sell it to members of the public gullible enough to spend their money. Worked like a scam...I mean dream!

In 1999, Niall, a life coach and trainer, approached me about a 'business opportunity' that would earn a shed load of money in only a few weeks. Immediately, I smelt a rat. He told me that I would have to find a few other people who would be interested in this opportunity and get them to do the same. Before I could say "It is Christmas everybody!" I would have earned a six-figure sum. Guess what the product was? A teddy bear pin! After I did a quick calculation in my head, I concluded that I could get very rich - as long as I signed up my contacts and my contacts' contacts and my contacts' contacts' contacts. You get the picture.

In the end, I would have sixty-million people, i.e. the population of Britain, signed up. However, Niall was not going to let my cynicism stop him from investing £2,000 of his life savings into this pyramid scheme. A year later, I asked Niall how he was faring with his business opportunity. The poor man had lost all his money and the people who recruited him could no longer be located or contacted.

The good news is that Niall learnt his lesson. He went back to doing what he does best - coaching people and talking about how much he enjoys coaching people. Unfortunately, Ponzi schemes[22], such as pyramid selling, which prey on people's greed using fraudulent strategies for making money, are not restricted to individuals. Entire government sanctioned organisations have also been running Ponzi schemes, e.g. the Federal Reserve (FED) of America.

Fast-forwarding to 2010, I was invited to attend a three-day internet seminar in London that featured the work

---

[22] www.en.wikipedia.org/wiki/Ponzi_scheme

of some of the best internet marketers in the world. I wanted to learn how I could use internet marketing to promote my book. The theme of the seminar appeared to be: how one could make as much money as quickly with the least effort? Nothing wrong with that. To entice the audience further, all the presenters kept emphasising how much money they were making through their own schemes.

The speakers seemed to believe that the audience were only interested in making a quick buck. That may have been the case for some. Their personal passions or their personal interests never came into the play. The only thing the speaker had a passion for was making lots of money...yesterday. So why do I mention these experiences? Having spoken to many of the 'investors' in a range of industries - pyramid schemes, get-rich-quick schemes, multilevel marketing (MLM), property investing, books, internet marketing, share-dealing, life coaching, etc; it seems the only people making good money are the ones who teach people how to make money.

Precious few marketers create real value. Yeah...I said it. I do not devalue the work and dedication of these players. However, I do question the false perceptions created by their systems, which contribute in propagating false hopes, dreams and aspirations. Let's understand money for what it really is. It is an ILLUSION! Money 're-presents' the value of a good or service. For example, gold has an extremely long life and certainly outlives many generations of humans and lasts aeons without degradation. What is it about gold that makes it useful to people in their daily lives? Can it be eaten or ingested? Does it bring inner peace or happiness? Can it lead to a state of higher conscious awareness? If not, can it lead to freedom from suffering or even to enlightenment?

Given this backdrop, what can be done with pieces of paper or metal coins (money)? They can be offered in exchange for goods and services. However, the efficiency in the exchange of goods and services using coins and paper is only as good as the word kept by the issuer of the coins and paper.

At any time, they can decide to ask for more coins and paper for the same amount of goods. And, they do.

In other words, working for something that promises to give something is no different to working for a meal that has been promised. The true value has not been given, it is just a promise. Money is like a meal that does not give nutrition or substance and does not give full value for what has been just eaten. It would be like eating a MacDonald's filet-o-fish. Shortly after eating it, the consumer is left confused whether they had any food earlier on or not!

Working for money alone is like working for an ideal. Working for a principle or a concept, on the other hand, is about receiving something with added value. In reality, money is the greatest example of an illusion that has been invented in the history of humankind. In the past, bartering would take place for the exchange of goods of value. For example, cave dwellers used sharpened flints, which were razor sharp and were excellent tools for either skinning or killing an animal. A few small animals would be exchanged for larger animals.

In later human history, the animals may have been exchanged for sacks of grain. All these tangible goods help to see what the normal human existence is based on and, as a result, how they are valued. Precious stones are only really precious if they offer something of value to the holder. In the past, these stones emitted a positive effect on human bodies and on health. Therefore, for a long time, stones such as healing crystals and metals were used as a foundation for value exchange. When this was transferred to printed images on pieces of paper, the true value became simply representative. That was the beginning of 'cyber-value'.

Money from Nothing

To confuse the public, the process of money creation has been made to look over complicated. Yet, people have allowed this process to control their lives. Economists have developed highly confusing language and jargon around the idea of economics and money. Due to the complexity in which it is presented, most students detest economics as much as they hate maths. Now, imagine the prospect of trying to get to grips with money when being presented with complicated maths to explain the economics.

The financial moguls are undoubtedly the most unquestioned illusionists that exist. Few people understand how money is created, how it is manipulated and it effects communities across the globe. To shatter this illusion, it is important to understand the basics of money creation. For all the complexities of money creation, it is a far more simple process to understand.

Imagine a simple community where there is no bank. Goods are bought and sold through a barter system. Every member of the community is a farmer who produces one or two goods. One of the locals, Susan, exchanges her chickens for bread with another local, Peter. Somebody else exchanges wool for butter, etc. Over time, the locals begin to trade with people outside the community. This time they exchange the goods for precious metals like gold.

Given how some people are like magpies (they like shiny stuff), the locals realise it may not be so wise to stash their hard-earned gold under mattresses. One day, Mrs Goldsmith offers to look after any local person's precious stones and gold in her highly fortressed building, which is protected by savage dogs. Some people decide to 'bank' their gold at Mrs Goldsmith's fortress. Of course, they do not hand over all their gold without getting a guarantee that they can have their gold back.

So Mrs Goldsmith, the only person with access to a printing press, exchanges a piece of paper in exchange for the gold. On this legally accepted paper, Mrs Goldsmith declares in writing that she promises to pay back, on demand, the entire sum of gold when the paper is 're-presented' to her. This paper is known as a 'promissory note' and is very difficult to forge and, therefore, is accepted in exchange for the gold.

As trust in Mrs Goldsmith community bank grows, the entire community deposit their precious gold in exchange for her promissory notes. This has two important consequences. First, the townspeople realise that everybody in the community has promissory notes in a variety of denominations. Since they trust Mrs Goldsmith without question, why not exchange the promissory notes with each other instead of bartering? The promissory notes are far easier to carry around and it opens up more opportunities to trade and exchange. That was how money was born.

The second outcome goes like this. Mrs Goldsmith notices that, at any given day, up 10% of the gold is ever demanded by her customers, leaving 90% stashed away in the 'safe'-ty of her 'bank'. Furthermore, she has been approached by enterprising people with great ideas who believe they can add value to people's lives by making and selling their wares. However, the only reason they cannot move forward is that it takes too long to save enough gold to buy the equipment needed for their enterprise.

So why not lend them the gold they need? At any one time, 90% of the gold is sitting in the safe doing nothing. Mrs Goldsmith figures out that, so long as there is a minimal 10% of gold in the safes, then there would be no issue in lending out as much as she liked. That was the birth of 'credit'. The use of this kind of credit in the banking system is called 'Fractional Reserve Banking'[23].

---

[23] www.en.wikipedia.org/wiki/Fractional-reserve_banking

Mrs Goldsmith is no fool. If these business people are keen enough to borrow from her, they may be interested in paying a little extra for the added services she is offering. Therefore, for every ounce of gold she lends, she can charge a proportional rate of interest, e.g. 10%. Therefore, for every £100 an individual borrows, they must repay the £100 plus £10 for every year they owe the money. The word gets out about Mrs Goldsmith's money lending service and, now, even more business people turn to her for loans.

To ensure that she maintains a 'reserve' of 10%, she needs to attract more customers or, alternatively, she must stop lending. She offers interest payment for savers to encourage more of them to save with her instead of stashing it under their mattresses. Remember, for every £100 of gold invested, she only needs to hold onto £10, whilst she can quite happily lend out £90 of that money. This simple example is similar to how the modern banking system works.

Money Equals Debt

The biggest borrowers of money in any country are the governments of that country, whilst the biggest lenders are their central banks. When the US government needs to borrow $10 billion, let's say to invest in a road-building programme, it calls up the Federal Reserve ('Fed'), the US central bank, and applies for a $10 billion loan. To facilitate this, the Fed agrees to buy $10 billion US government bonds. A government bond is a loan document that is 100% guaranteed that it will be re-paid by the government, which they call 'Treasury Bonds'.

It then puts a value of $10 billion dollars and submits them to the Fed. In return, the Fed prints a bunch of paper, which they call 'bank notes' and which have a value of $10 billion. They trade these notes for the bonds. The government takes the notes and deposits them into their bank account, which now becomes legal 'tender' (money). Here begins the bit that needs a little patience to understand.

By definition, the treasury bonds are instruments of debt. Thus, the word 'debt' can be used to mean 'bonds'. When the government borrowed money from the Fed, it created it out of debt. The money issued by the bank was created from where? Thin air. Why is it out of thin air? Because there was not a single iota of value created in the process. No gold, no silver, quartz, salt, coffee beans, pretzels, chapattis or any other form of commodity was exchanged to create the money. Crazy, I know. However, it is important to remember this to get better clarity about money.

How on earth can money or any kind of value be created out of debt? It cannot. However, the Fed and other central banks like the Bank of England do just that. Back to the plot. $10 billion is sitting in a commercial bank account. The Fed decides the legally required reserves for commercial banks will be 10%. Thus, the commercial bank retains $1 billion in its vaults, whilst lending $9 billion.

The real life situation is slightly different to this basic example. First, the Fed does not print the money but carries out electronic jiggery-pokery and 'transfers' the $10 billion to the government's commercial bank account. Second, instead of lending out the $9 billion from the original $10 billion Fed loan, the commercial bank keeps this money and creates another $9 billion out of thin air. Now there is $19 billion in the US money supply. The Fed, entrusted to monitor and retain legal transactions, simply allows the creation of money by the commercial banks because there is a demand for it from their customers.

When another one of the bank's customer comes and borrows money, the creation process gets more complex. The new customer deposits their borrowed money into another bank, of which a further 90% of that money is lent out. This cycle of lending out 90% of every deposit from the original loan can technically go on forever. In reality, the average money created from the original $10 billion leads to a total creation of $90 billion. This is all out of thin air with no value being created.

So, where does the value for the new money come from? Surely, if it did not have any value, then the numbers in people's bank accounts would be worthless? Well, the value of the new money comes from the existing money. If Mrs Goldsmith was the owner of the only bank, the actual total gold is given the value of, say $1 billion, and $1 billion dollars of promissory notes are made. Every time money is created out of thin air, then the paper value of the same amount of gold increases.

Hypothetically speaking, Mrs Goldsmith prints another extra $1 billion dollars that goes into circulation. Now there are $2 billion representing the same amount of the original $1 billion of gold. How does this affect everyone? If the original deposit of gold was given $1 billion dollars in value, then due to the new money created, the $1 billion held in paper is now only going to buy back *half* the amount of gold that was originally deposited. Welcome to the world of inflation...and the public have been punked by the illusionists!!!

Inflation is a hidden tax by the government on the public. Is it a coincidence that governments always try to keep inflation between a certain range above zero and not at zero? As more money gets printed, the purchasing power of the currency possessed by the public falls. This continual erosion of purchasing power can be seen by comparing how much it costs for a packet of crisps in only thirty years ago and today. As a child in 1977, I remember buying my favourite cheese and onion flavoured crisps for only 6 pence. The same equivalent packet today costs me 65 pence at the very least, i.e. a tenfold increase in the price whilst the value has remained practically the same.

One of the biggest con tricks by the government and economists is to 'attempt' to reduce inflation by increasing the money supply, i.e. increasing the inflation. Huh?!! The biggest farce played out in 2008/9 was during President Barak

Obama's attempt at stimulating the economy to 'save' jobs. He did this by pumping three trillion dollars into a beleaguered US economy. The real effect is to massively erode the value of the money held in the hands of the public.

The Fractional Reserve System that initiates an increase in money supply without an increase in real goods and services only serve to erode the value of any currency. This system is purely inflationary by nature. A nation's money becomes worth less and less due to the current banking system. In the case of the US dollar, there has been a 96+% devaluation from its value in 1913, which coincides with the lifespan of the Federal Reserve.

As already mentioned, money is created out of debt and debt cannot exist without money. In other words, the more money there is, the more debt there is. If every debt was paid off by every individual and organisation, there would be no more money in circulation. There will be no need for money. In the current monetary system, it is the poor who do indeed get poorer. The rich also get poorer as their savings become worth less and less. It is only the ultra-rich and the ruling elite who get wealthier.

The single most important factor that makes this entire pyramid scheme work is the use of interest (also known as 'usury' for some reason). When the Fed charges the government interest on its original loan, where does the money to pay the interest come from? You guessed it, thin air. The government has to borrow more money from the Fed to pay off the interest as well as the original sum (principal) of money. This becomes just like buying goods using a credit card and only making just enough payments to cover the minimum requirement. As the borrower's repayment begins to exceed their income, the debt goes into free-fall. At this point, the borrower may seek to get support from a debt-management agency.

The options are quite different for national governments with money problems to individuals in financial trouble. In the case of the US, bankruptcy is inevitable. No matter how many rescue packages are attempted, the system is designed to bankrupt the country. As the people who repay the debts are the public, it is they who are punished for the government's mismanagement of the money supply. More accurately, the debt created today has to be repaid by future generations who had nothing to do with the mounting debt. The repayment comes in the form of ever-increasing taxes.

Originally taxes were levied on the public to pay for wars. In the UK, the modern taxation system is based on William Pitt The Younger's proposal of 1798, to tax up to 10% to pay for weaponry during the Napoleonic wars. Successive governments have never looked back. Taxation on the public has increased consistently, peaking at 98% in the UK on the higher rate for high income earners in 1974 [24]. The advent of the *16th Amendment*[25] to the US Constitution modified the apportionment requirement in 1913, and since then the income tax has become one of the means of funding the Federal Government.

A Quick and Easy Way to Enslave the Masses

Banks are like any other corporation. They exist to make profit, much of which comes through lending money to individuals and organisations. The money that banks lend to customers, such as mortgages, is merely a digital transference of money to the borrower. However, if one is unable to keep up with repayments, even after honouring their debt for the majority of the term, the lending bank has the legal right to repossess their home.

---

[24] www.en.wikipedia.org/wiki/Taxation_in_the_United_Kingdom

[25]
www.en.wikipedia.org/wiki/Sixteenth_Amendment_to_the_United_States_Constitution

According to the 2010 figures of a recent study[26], a property was repossessed in the UK every fourteen minutes (103 properties every day), whilst someone was declared bankrupt every 3.78 minutes. Given the nonsensical monetary system that exists, it beggars belief that the fractional reserve system is allowed to continue, not just in the UK and the USA, but across most countries in the world. It is nothing less than a system of modern slavery.

As Peter Joseph points out in *Zeitgeist Addendum*[27], money is created out of debt. Therefore, to get liberation from debt, there must be an exchange of human labour for money. As money can only be created out of loans, how is it possible for society to be debt free? The point is it cannot. In order for people to 'survive' in modern economies, they must get into some form of debt. No matter how damaging it is, they queue up to become wage slaves and join the perpetual rat race with millions of others who are also caught up in the slavery.

During the infamous African Slave Trade, the victims knew they were slaves because they could see, feel and hear the chains and shackles around their ankles and wrists. Their slave masters were responsible for feeding and housing them. In today's 'corporate slavery', the slaves willingly house and feed themselves. As the 'corporate slave' cannot see the shackles and chains, they are totally oblivious to their own enslavement. Freedom is far from being a reality.

The people who benefit most from 'corporate slavery' are those who are at the top of the pyramid scheme - the money masters who own the banks (i.e. 'banksters'). Is money not created in a bank and does it not end up back in a bank? The other beneficiaries of corporate slavery include governments, certain institutions and corporations. There is an invisible war between the elite and the mass population.

---

[26] www.creditaction.org.uk/assets/PDF/statistics/2010/september-2010.pdf

[27] www.zeitgeistmovie.com

Debt is the elite's way of conquering entire societies and countries, whilst interest is their ammunition. The slave masters have created increasingly more elaborate mechanisms and schemes for their economic conquest of societies through organisations like the *World Bank*[28] and the *International Monetary Fund*[29] (IMF). The World Bank is responsible for lending money to nation states for capital restructuring programmes, whilst the IMF is responsible for helping to stabilise national economies. Bizarrely, even though it is one economic nation amongst many other countries of the world, the US holds 16.74% of the entire voting rights of the IMF. This effectively means that whatever the US says at the IMF goes. Thus, it comes as no surprise to see how IMF policies are so strongly correlated with US foreign policy.

The Unluckiest Baby in the World...

On 24th December 2007, the headlines of the Independent[30] newspaper in the UK read 'The Unluckiest Baby in the World'. It was about a teenage mother who had given birth to a baby in Freetown, Sierra Leone. In that country, one in four children do not make it to the age of 5, one in six mothers die during childbirth and the average life expectancy is 42 for a woman and 38 for a man. This situation had been exacerbated by the ten year civil war that ended in 2001.

After the war ended, the World Bank offered loans to rebuild the country. However, to qualify for the loan, the World Bank placed a stipulation on Sierra Leone. Their government were required to remove their railway infrastructure completely, meaning that future economic growth would be severely hindered. Why would the World

---

[28] www.en.wikipedia.org/wiki/World_Bank

[29] www.en.wikipedia.org/wiki/International_Monetary-Fund

[30]
www.independent.co.uk/news/world/africa/independent-appeal-the-unluckiest-baby-in-the-world-766732.html

Bank ask the poorest country in the world to remove one of its most important communication infrastructures? Who do the World Bank and the IMF really work for?

Why are they asking developing countries, their customers, to make massive sacrifices to qualify for loans that they have no hope in repaying? Me thinks something fishy is going on. When 1% of the world's population owns 40% of the planet's wealth, it is worth asking why and how this has come about? What roles do the IMF, the World Bank and the rest of the Banksters play in this charade?

Questions need to be asked why every day 29,000 children die in the Third World from preventable diseases. What is the World Health Organisation doing about this? What are the public doing about this? What has happened to the world's natural wealth when 50% of the world's population have to live on less than $2 a day? Why is there such a gaping disparity between the wealthy and the poor? What happened to compassion? When it is understood that the life blood of all institutions and corporations is money, then the real truth behind the smokescreens and the illusions will be unmasked.

What motivates the illusionists to use the Granddaddy of all illusions, money, in such a way? The simple answer is 'to control the masses'. The illusionists have a desire to acquire more and control more. That is the effect of their actions. The motivation, which will be discussed later in the book, is fear. It is out of fear and their need for survival, that the illusionists desperately want to control the masses. They see the masses as nothing more than possessions.

I believe, we are indeed living in a 'Matrix' where the slave masters are represented by Mr Smith, the 'Artificial Intelligence' programme, and you and I are one of the other characters who have taken the 'red pill' to awaken us to the reality of this universe. (Well, I'm hoping that you have taken the red pill by now!) When we see the Matrix for what it is, we intuitively know with certainty what the illusions are and how to move back to reality.

In the modern era, the enticement of quick money and instant gratification has been too much for most people to handle. The UK has led the field by having the greatest household debt in the world, including mortgages, at 164% of an individual's annual income in 2007[31]. This has not been helped by the energy cartels whom have inflated world oil prices and the public's insatiable desire to become a nation of landlords.

Although mortgages in the UK were previously offered on a basis of approximately three times that of the borrower's annual income, at the peak of the property boom, banks were lending up to five times the borrowers' incomes. How and why they expected this to be sustainable is beyond comprehension. Luckily for the banks, when it got too hot in the kitchen, they had their respective governments to bail them out of trouble with taxpayers' money.

On Becoming a Property-Owning Nation

For nearly a century, one of the favourite pastimes of the English has been the property game. This is a pastime that is loved very much by Americans, too. As land and property accumulation has a tangible asset value associated with it, the attraction to institutions who 'feel' the need for secure assets could not be greater. I am talking about the banks and other financial institutions. To turn the USA into a property-owning nation, the markets were rigged during President Roosevelt's administration.

The *Federal National Mortgage Association*, also known as 'Fannie Mae' was created in 1938 during the Great Depression as part of Franklin Roosevelt's 'New Deal'. Fannie Mae was established to provide local banks with federal money to finance home mortgages in an attempt to raise levels of home ownership and the availability of affordable housing.

---

[31]
www.independent.co.uk/news/business/news/personal-debt-hits-10year-high-45459 6.html

The US government effectively underwrote the loans and facilitated the interaction between borrowers and lenders.

However, not every US citizen enjoyed the opportunities afforded to the majority to become a homeowner. A real estate developer was ordered to build a wall in Detroit's 'Eight-Mile District' to qualify for loans from the Federal Housing Administration. These loans were to be given for construction of predominantly white neighbourhoods. On the other side of this wall were the predominantly black neighbourhood to whom loans were not granted as African-Americans were not considered creditworthy. This was known as '*Redlining*' - the practice of denying or increasing the cost of services such as banking, insurance, access to healthcare, access to jobs and even access to shopping areas for certain groups.

Even though banks would lend to low income earning whites, they refused to lend to blacks no matter what the financial circumstance. Segregation was a direct result of the Federal government policy. If loans were given to people who were on the 'wrong' side of the wall, they had to pay significantly higher interest rates than their equivalent counterparts living on the white side of the divide. Fifty years later, a loan for a person who was living on the white side of the divide became known as 'prime' and the black side was 'subprime'.

Money is an illusion and has only as much value as people put on it. Therefore, it means that it is up to the public to decide whether to accept being caught up in slavery or not. Slavery is not just enslavement of human labour. Worse still, it is the enslavement of the human mind and the shutting down of human consciousness. Shutting the human mind has been carried out to such an extreme that the masses have no idea to what extent they are being sacrificed for the sole purpose of the illusionists gaining further control by way of greater more profits.

Chapter 5: War - The Biggest Scam Ever

*"Without the mobilisation and use of the
conscious brain, are humans really that
different from the other less evolved animals?"*

War: What is it Good for?

Absolutely nothing. Actually, this may not be the case as far as the Military-Industrial Complex are concerned. They are corporations that are directly or indirectly linked to the business of war. Every year, at the 11th hour of the 11th day of the 11th month, millions across the world keep two minutes of silence in memory of those who died particularly during the First World War (1914-1918). This is known as *Armistice Day* or *Remembrance Day*. The First World War was supposedly the war that would end all wars.

Twenty-one years later, a far more devastating war raged across the globe. Given the atrocities such conflicts led to, logic would dictate that remembering the dead will, at least, slow down human conflict. World War I claimed sixteen million lives and left twenty-one million wounded[32]. It was never going to be the war that would end all wars. The contrary was true. The Second World War followed involved numerous countries across the planet. Straight after that calamity a new military standoff, the 'Cold War', was created between the USA and the Soviet Union, the repercussions of which are still felt to this day.

Since the creation of Israel, the Arab-Israeli Conflict has made headline news with little hints of peace in the Middle East. Not to mention, the Vietnam War, the Iran-Iraq War, the invasion and occupation of Afghanistan. Even though the level of consciousness on the planet has been gathering pace over

---

[32] www.en.wikipedia.org/wiki/World_War_I_casualties

the last century, mankind still finds itself at war 97% of the time.

The human condition has a predisposition to jump into 'survival' mode. When survival becomes the dominant modus operandi, people are controlled by fear-based emotions and excessive stress. Energetically, they contract themselves and see themselves as separate from other humans and separate from Nature. Under this kind of stress, human DNA strands get wound up like coiled springs. In such a state, they are seriously limited in their ability to access creativity and their level of conscious awareness stagnates or even falls.

It is this level of conscious awareness that shapes the forebrain and distinguishes people from primates and other animals. Without the mobilisation and use of the conscious brain, are humans really that different from the other evolved animals? When Charles Darwin put forward his theory of evolution, he did exactly that - he put forward a 'theory'. He should not be blamed for his theory. However, a key assumption of his theory was the concept of 'survival of the fittest'.

Darwin's theory has been a 'convenient truth' for many of the leaders and dictators who wanted a greater stranglehold on the public. The most infamous series of events influenced by survival of the fittest were during the Nazi propaganda that the Aryan race was superior over all other races. Therefore, Hitler's followers felt little remorse during the mass persecution and murder of non-Aryans.

Here are just some of the illusions associated with war.

1. *War is the means of last resort when defending a nation's security.* This may have been true several thousand years ago. Ever since the barbaric and brutal era of the romanticised Roman Empire and the Mongols, etc, the consciousness of humankind has evolved sufficiently enough to distinguish humans from animals. So, when it is said that war is used as a means of last resort to protect

one's own sovereignty, it means that logic, reasoning, discussions and debate, i.e. diplomacy has failed. Right? Wrong.

Other distortions of the word 'defence' have been in the use of pre-emptive strikes on a targeted enemy. In other words, attack and invade the enemy's country before they attack first. This strategy has been successfully put into practice by many dictatorships, as in the case of the Nazi invasion of Poland in 1939 and the Anglo-American invasion of Iraq in 2003.

2. *God is on the side of the God-fearing and pious.* Those who choose to raise arms against the God-fearing must be infidels. Not true. A disproportionate number of wars have been fought in the name of God. What was the real motivation for war when the Mujahedeen fought to the death with crusaders in the name of peace and in the name of their God? This has been the most farcical of justifications for war yet. Pound for pound, religion has been the single biggest lie to initiate violent conflict for millennia.

3. Ever since the tragedy of the 2,995 deaths during 9/11, the most quoted mantra was *'War on Terror'* against *Al Qaeda.* What is Al Qaeda? An invisible bogey man organisation that cannot be seen, felt, heard, smelt or touched. An enemy only made known to the public when the government propaganda machine decides the time is right? Who created Al Qaeda? An old man with a long beard operating from the highly technologically advanced headquarters of the Tora Bora caves in Afghanistan?

The word 'terror' comes from the Latin 'terrere' which means 'to frighten'. Even if Al Qaeda were a genuine threat, then who should people be afraid of more? Perhaps those that massacre hundreds of thousands, if not millions of innocent men, women and children, whilst causing destruction and mayhem through foreign invasion and the abuse of human rights? Perhaps those who blow themselves up and kill usually less than a hundred and maim hundreds more? Of course, neither should be exempt from judicial enquiry. However, the statistics bare out the facts that the vast majority of deaths during conflict have been inflicted by governments and coalitions, i.e. internationally recognised organisations. Governments have become more like organised crime syndicates like the Mafia. They are certainly being run by criminals who lie, deceive and manipulate the public...with a big fat Cheshire-Cat grin on their faces.

The wars that were instigated by the Roman Empire were little more than invasions and the systematic killing of men, women and children in order to acquire more land and economic power. The arts, philosophy and sciences associated with such cultures came much later. The Crusades, which were kick-started by the Catholic Church during the time of Pope Urban II in 1095 CE[33] (Christian Era), promised soldiers they would gain salvation from their sins. They would enter heaven regardless of how many men, women and children they killed. There was no sin killing an infidel, i.e. Muslims.

When Jesus, son of Mary, spoke of aggression, his followers were told to turn the other cheek. The contrary is true in reality. When Prophet Muhammad spoke of '*Jihad*', which means 'to struggle', he said that the greatest Jihad is the one that is against one's '*nafs*' (ego). Yet Christianity, Judaism and Islam are associated with some of the worst human conflict ever to darken the integrity of Humanity. All were carried out in the name of God. The Crusades were nothing more than the fight for the acquisition of land, relics and other wealth in the Middle East. There was nothing 'holy' about any of these wars.

---

[33] www.en.wikipedia.org/wiki/First_Crusade

As author and researcher, Jordan Maxwell puts it:

"The only thing holy about the Holy Wars is the stories about them. They are full of holes."

War is big business. It is the biggest business enterprise bar none. The single most fascinating observation over the past hundred years has been mankind's predisposition to war. Ever since the Battle of Waterloo (18th June 1815), war has become big business for a few globalists. This landmark battle between the Germans, Dutch and the British against the Napoleonic forces was financed by the 'Emperor of Waterloo', Nathan Rothschild.

To win the war against Napoleon, the British had to have enough money to sustain the conflict. Rothschild was a master of the bond (debt) market and was said to manipulate the markets to create a buying spree that left him £600m richer. The biggest reason for the success of the Rothschild dynasty was the sheer brilliance of the collaboration between the brothers across London, Paris, New York and Amsterdam.

The second major concern to benefit significantly from war is the 'Defence' industry. It is at times of war that they receive the greatest number of orders. Loans are taken out by governments from major banks like Rothschild's and the central banks of nation states, including the Bank of England and the Federal Reserve. World War I and World War II were nothing more than business transactions engineered by the ruling elite.

In the blockbuster internet movie, *Zeitgeist*[34], Peter Joseph gives a solid explanation of how, during World War I, American citizens refused to engage in a European war despite major bankers insisting on entering the conflict. It was only when the *Lucitania*, a cruise ship with 1,750 American passengers on board, was sunk by German submarines that the

---

[34] www.zeitgeistmovie.com

US public cried for revenge. This is precisely what the banking elite needed to motivate Americans to go into war. Before the sinking of the cruise liner, the German embassy in New York were vociferous about Americans not buying tickets for the Lucitania. Despite clear warnings in an advert in the New York Times, the cruise liner was fully booked. It entered waters where the conflict was taking place and was subsequently sunk by German U-boats.

Wars do not lead to winners. Wars create further separation between individuals and communities. This separation takes many generations to heal. However, there are individual families and organisations who gain enormously from war: the banking families, arms-maker, royal families and other members of the ruling elite, heads of multinational corporations, Big Pharma, agrochemicals and construction. The acceptance of a tainted freedom and democracy without questioning those behind the propaganda means that individual power is abdicated to the very people who are exploiting the masses.

War is a game that is played out by the ruling elite who are composed of. The mind boggles when one researches the incestuous relationships that have been forged between a small minority of illusionists through secretive organisations such as the *Bilderberg Group*[35]. Suffice to say, being conscious that war is not the absence of peace is a good starting point. Perhaps next time, the so-called democratic leaders cry out for war, the public can take a step back and ask: what is really going on and whose interests are being served? What will be the multiple consequences of this new war? How many generations will the war effect? Can government and media be trusted to tell the truth? What will be the real cost of war in terms of post-traumatic stress, environmental pollution, the lives of innocent men, women and children and the lives of

---

[35] www.en.wikipedia.org/wiki/Bilderberg_Group

young men and women engaged in a war that they have little reason to be part of?

What is the Role of the Media during War?

In the early part of the twentieth century, American media were owned by a wide range of people. Neither the media nor the public supported the war that was taking place in Europe. By 1916, Britain was on the brink of losing the First World War. The British economy had been ravaged and she was totally dependent on external support. There were less than three weeks of food supplies in the UK and the government was seriously considering initiating talks with the Germans to call a truce[36].

At this point, the International Zionists approached the British government and offered them an olive branch. They proposed to 'bring in the Americans' to help the government and, consequently, persuaded the British to not call a truce with the Germans. In return, they wanted the British government's help in establishing a Jewish homeland. The International Zionists went to the US and bought fifty of the regional newspapers. Until this time, the American media were showing a lot more sympathy towards the Germans than the British.

Having bought up the fifty American newspapers, the international Zionists turned the propaganda from being pro-German to pro-British. Through that campaign and the continued reference to the attack on the cruise ship Lucitania, which took place the previous year, they managed to bring about the American public's support to enable President Woodrow Wilson to take America into the war. Thereafter, the balance of power changed in the First World War and the Germans lost to the Anglo-American allies.

---

[36] This information was extracted from *The Consciousness Revolution Show* interview with Ian R. Crane.

This demonstrated the power of the media in presenting a particular propaganda and how they had sufficient influence to sway public opinion. The ability for the press to sway public opinion has been used ever since that time to the present day to manipulate the public. Today, the entire western media is in the hands of six people. The most prolific of these owners is Rupert Murdoch who owns Fox News, the New York Post, News Corporation, The Sun Newspaper, The News of the World, The Times, Sky Network in Europe, the Star Network in the Far East and India as well as the Australian network and much more. Between his son, James, and himself, they own a significant proportion of the world media.

The most influential political writer in the UK, Trevor Kavanagh, was employed by Murdoch through the Sun, a daily tabloid that is read by thirteen million people in the UK. Hence, what is written by the media has a profound effect on the British public. For example, the Sun was instrumental in supporting Tony Blair's New Labour government getting into power in 1997. The media are nothing more than the paid-up mouthpieces of the illusionists to propagate the business of war as well as the interests of the globalists.

Who Gains Most from Wars?

Leading up to and during a war, the government of a warring nation must sharply increase their expenditure on arms and ammunition. These are produced in vast quantities at high prices by so-called 'Defence' contractors. According to the *SIPRI Yearbook*[37], global expenditure on arms in 2009 was estimated at US$1531bn, which is 2.7% of global GDP (Gross Domestic Product). This represents an increase of 49% since 2000. The estimated military budget for 2011 is US$1.06-1.449 trillion![38]

---

[37] www.sipri.org/yearbook/2010/05

[38] www.en.wikipedia.org/wiki/Military_budget_of_the_United_States

The incredible sums of money needed to pay the contractors do not sit in the government's bank vaults. They have to borrow it. Who is the lender? The Central Bank of that country, e.g. the Bank of England (UK) and the Federal Reserve (USA). Whichever way a war ends, whoever the victor is, the biggest winners of war are the banks. The defence contractors and their suppliers are clearly major winners in the game of war, too. Major arms suppliers included companies such as British Aerospace, Boeing and Lockheed Martin [39], for example.

These are some of the biggest companies in the world. They did not achieve such magnitude of success through honesty, integrity and peaceful means. As seen from the two Gulf Wars in Iraq, there is a military strategy that is deployed by the aggressors that is commonplace during war. That strategy is to destroy major infrastructures of the invaded nation whose loss of such buildings and utilities will then cripple the nation.

The infrastructures include oil wells, power stations, communication and transportation networks, factories, schools and other buildings of important national interest. At this point, the second line of contractors, i.e. the builders, come in. After the second invasion of Iraq in 2003, the Anglo-American allies devastated the country's major infrastructure. The subsequent tenders to rebuild the country were mainly given to American companies with Halliburton as the greatest winner. Of course, there should be no surprise that the then current US Secretary of State, Dick Cheney, also happened to have been the Chairman and CEO of Halliburton since 1995 [40].

The business of war is clearly illustrated in other conflicts. During World War II, the Germans had developed a prototype engine that could fly faster than other planes. It could carry a 1,000 kilogram (2,200 pound) bomb that could

[39] www.en.wikipedia.org/wiki/List_of_modern_armament_manufacturers

[40] www.en.wikipedia.org/wiki/Dick_Cheney

be dropped on the enemy from 1,000 kilometres (600 miles) away. These would be too fast for the British Royal Air Force's interceptors. The Nazi's were desperate to mobilise these more advanced killing machines. However, there were two problems with their dastardly plans.

First, they did not have the money they needed to make the planes and nobody would lend them the money at this time. Second, it needed a new specialised derivative of the existing fuel to make it fly. They overcame their financial obstacle when they eventually convinced an American finance company, Brown Brothers Harriman to lend them the money. A key director of Harriman was the US Senator Prescott Bush[41], father of President George H.W. Bush and grandfather of President George W. Bush. The dilemma of acquiring the fuel was solved by another American company, Standard Oil, which is owned by Rockefellers and IG Farben, the German chemical company (world's largest chemical company at the time). IG Farben, as will be shown later, proved to be the biggest corporate supporters of the fascist Nazi regime. Curiouser and curiouser!

There are many reasons why wars take place but we cannot forget who fights these wars. It is the brave young men and women who take pride in their countries and choose to join the military to protect their families, their homes and their way of life. These are noble attributes. However, little do they realise that they are mere pawns in business dealings where the major winners play both sides of the game. The conditioning and the brainwashing that takes place to entice them to the military starts from the moment they are born. These strategies have been well thought out by the illusionists and perfected to an art form through centuries of practice.

[41] www.guardian.co.uk/world/2004/sep/25/usa.secondworldwar

One World Government: the Mantra of Fascist Dictatorships

Ever since the dawn of time when men discovered they could gain control of another person's property and possession by killing them, there was always going to be individuals who had ambitions far greater than one could imagine. They may not have had admirable qualities, nonetheless, they did have qualities that distinguished them from the crowd. These men include Alexander the Great, Julius Caesar, Genghis Khan, the crusading monarchs and aristocrats of Europe, Ivan the Terrible, Mussolini, Hitler, Stalin, Mao Zedong, etc.

They all wanted one thing - world domination. All of them succeeded in their own way. As time passed, many of them became romanticised by historians. It has to be said, Alexander (356-323 BC) was probably the greatest of the empire-builders. He managed to invade and rule over the largest part of the known world at the time. One thing to keep in mind is that history is written by the victors. Of course, it is going to be ostensibly one-sided. All empires that were created also fell, including the longest-standing one, the Roman Empire.

Some may argue that the Roman Empire never fell. It just got transferred into one of the most vicious of all the illusionists, the Vatican Church, which influences the lives of over two billion people on the planet. Today, the illusionists are implementing a far more pernicious strategy to gain world dominance. The men in power realised that empire-building could no longer be left in the hands of one individual or one dictator. So, they created an entity that would be far more subtle and would be much more longstanding. Its agenda can be carried out under the radar without the masses even batting an eyelid. This entity is the 'corporation'.

The corporation took on its own identity and was no longer under the control of one single individual. It was like a Frankenstein monster because it was given free reign according to the law of the USA. As a result, individuals who were part of the corporation were not responsible for the actions of it. 'Responsibility' was that of the corporation. An invisible entity was created, one that could not be held accountable, but would still have full power over the masses. It was almost like giving license for free reign to make the world its oyster without limits or constraints. This has led to many unscrupulous ventures being started under the guise of the corporation.

The number one business, war, turned out to be extremely lucrative. The US very intelligently packaged and marketed it better than any other country. The corporate entity was created as a direct result of the American Civil War between the Union and the Confederates (1861-1865). The war cost in the vicinity of 620,000 lives with, at least, another 100,000 permanently maimed.

The cessation of the Civil War led to new laws being created that gave rights to people. One of them was the creation of the corporation. As a result of this, they lifted away and expanded what they saw was the beginning of a new empire. The US went into countries like Cuba, Vietnam and the Philippines. When they went into the Philippines in the late 1800s, they went on the pretext of offering freedom to the Filipinos from their European colonialists.

Having assisted them, the nationals thanked them enormously and expected the Americans to leave. The Americans, on the other hand, had other plans and wanted to stay. This was the beginning of a new type of colonialism by coming in on the back of being liberators. Incidentally, 500,000 Filipinos were murdered in this process. The US packaged and marketed warfare like no other nation. In the movie, *The Last Samurai*, the US not only sold arms to the Japanese, but they also sold uniforms, strategies and military manouevres. They also taught a new way of controlling the people within the country. The business deal was not just a one-off transaction. It was on a contractual basis which included renewal of weaponry, ammunition and tactics. This went on through to the beginning of the First World War.

During the Great Depression, the US used very cheap labour to create a gigantic navy fleet and air force that was only matched by the German air force and fleet. They were waiting on the sidelines for the Japanese to attack Pearl Harbor in 1942. One of the strategies the US deployed was to supply ammunition and weaponry to the Chinese whilst they were at war with the Japanese. This was a flagrant breaking of international law by the Americans, which angered the Japanese.

The Japanese issued warnings to the Americans to stop supplying the Chinese. These were ignored. The Japanese then sent gun-ships and air-carriers towards the US. The American government knew of this three weeks before the attack on Pearl Harbor. The American public had no idea what their government were up to and had no interest in getting involved in what they saw as a European war. However, when the shock of Pearl Harbor sunk in, they did what lifelong programming and conditioning does to any American individual. Their patriotic hot buttons were pressed and they cried blue murder and wanted immediate retaliation.

This was the most intelligently orchestrated and executed business capital venture that has ever been planned and implemented in the history of humanity. A deal had been cut between President Roosevelt and Churchill to assist the British. The conditions were that every one of the British colonies would allow the Americans free reign to enter into and start doing business. That included oil and the distribution of US products throughout the world.

The US had learnt from their European ancestors whose main focus was on taking the land itself. They would attack or take over land belonging to people who were found more inferior in military tactics, skills or weaponry. They learnt that whoever wins the war actually loses it. The victors have to pay three to five times more to sustain the land of the people they have taken over. The Americans cleverly decided that using psychological warfare is more profitable, less obvious, less conspicuous and far more successful in the long term. This is because once people have been hooked and reeled in by consumerism they have been caught for life.

According to Jordan Maxwell's research, the United States of America is itself a corporation. US citizens are considered as possessions belonging to the corporation of America. The corporation has one agenda - global domination. How do they intend to pull it off? Through globalisation. One may say: *"what about British and foreign multinationals, such as BP or Royal Dutch Shell? They are not American companies."* That is precisely the point.

The globalists care not about nationalism and patriotism. However, they will play on people's patriotism to those gullible enough to fall for that kind of mass programming. Corporations own countries and the people living within them! Most people believe in the illusion that they, the public, decide who will be the next British Prime Minister or the next President of America. This is exactly what the globalist corporations want the public to believe.

Dangling the carrot of a free democracy through voting has been one of the finest con tricks played by the illusionists. There is a much more compelling argument and enough freely available research in the public domain that, for the open-minded, will begin to shift anybody's narrow, romanticised view of the matrix that humans live in. (See Resource page at the end of the book for more details.)

In summary, the globalists have a set of key objectives that they have clearly stated at numerous times, including:

1. To reduce and maintain a world human population of 500,000 people. (A work in progress.)
2. To create a one-world government through the unification of several economic unions, such as the European Union, ASEAN and the soon-to-be North American Union. This has been in motion since the formation of the United Nations. (A work in progress.)
3. To create a one-world military representing all nations, NATO or 'North Atlantic Treaty Organisation' (Done.)
4. To create a global central bank, the World Bank. (Done.)
5. To create a single global authority who is the key decision-maker in all things medical, the World Health Organisation. (Done.)

This is a basic list and highlights only a few key objectives. The important thing to remember is that the men and women behind the globalisation agenda are the master illusionists, whose timeframe to fulfill their agenda is completely different to normal people. Some people do not see beyond next month's pay cheque let alone one or two years ahead. Others live from week to week, whilst there are also those who live from day to day or one meal to the next. The agenda of the illusionists go as far as 50, 100, 500 and even 1,000 years.

However, there is hope that things will change. The illusionists are running scared. Later on in this book, there will be an examination into what changes are need at the individual level to have an impact at the global level. Remember this - the illusionists work off one principle - fear. If they can, and they have, created enough illusions to trigger people's survival mechanism on a consistent basis, they have them hooked.

Childhood programming and conditioning are such that it takes little effort to trigger a fear-based emotional response, such as pride, anger, lust, feeling scared, grief, apathy, shame and guilt. There are numerous other negative and draining emotions which all fall under these different categories. As long as one lives from a place of survival, the illusionists are happy because THEY are in control. Ultimately, globalisation is the quest by a very small group of people who believe themselves to be the rightful rulers of a planetary fiefdom. Their objective is to create a one-world government (i.e. their government), a one-world economy (managed by them) and a one-world religion, i.e. the one that they condition people to believe.

The broad objectives of this group are laid out in the *Georgia Guidestones* [42]. This is a massive henge that appeared on a hilltop in Georgia in the southern states in 1982. It was attributed to an anonymous person by the name of R.C. Christian. There has been much speculation about who R.C. Christian might or might not be. On the stones, in eight different languages [43], are inscribed the goals and objectives [44] of those who believe themselves to be the rightful rulers of this planet.

The first of the ten goals is to reduce the number of people on the planet to 500 million, which is a 93% reduction of the planetary population from its current 6.8 billion. Clearly, this is a very significant reduction. Globalisation is about implementing policies and philosophies which will bring about the goals and objectives as described by the Georgia Guidestones. During my time as an undergraduate student of economics, we were led to believe that the best economic policies were those that removed all barriers to trade, unified

---

[42] www.thegeorgiaguidestones.com

[43] English, Spanish, Swahili, Hindi, Hebrew, Arabic, Chinese and Russian.

[44] See Appendix for the goals and objectives on the Georgia Guidestones.

economic policies, and reduced currency fluctuations by using a single global currency, etc.

In the intervening years since my graduation, I realised that the education establishments were effectively being used to promote political philosophy. This is another objective of the globalists and the extreme capitalists. As far as the illusionists are concerned, human life does not matter. The only important thing is driving corporate goals and realising the personal greed of the owners of corporations. The puppeteers at the core of the agenda are not interested in monetary gain. They have more than they could ever spend. They are merely interested in unadulterated power.

From an economic standpoint, the wisdom of assuming the barrier-less planet as beneficial is highly questionable. The 2008 global financial meltdown bore witness to a classical symptom of a globalised economy. Establishing a barrier-less global economy means that there will be great inequity between nations. The poorer and less developed nations will be plundered for their natural wealth, whilst the corporations who set the agenda, will gain abnormal wealth and power over the rest of the planet.

The Empire Strikes...it Rich

Until a hundred years ago, civilisations seen as economically advanced, invaded other countries, killed thousands of people and subjugated their laws onto the indigenous people. They increased the size of their economic wealth by paying low wages to the local workers, if at all, and by depleting local natural resources. The biggest modus operandi for military or economic invasion in recent years has been to acquire and control one of the most important natural resources in history - oil.

A number of countries have realised that it is far cheaper to economically take over a country than to instigate violent conflict to acquire this oil. Empire-building transformed itself from being projects of mass violence to aggressive economic takeover by controlling those who control the money, i.e. the countries Presidents and governments. In *'Confessions of an Economic Hitman'*[45], John Perkins describes how, when presidents and governments refused to cooperate with the CIA/US government, they have been toppled by economic hit-men. The first of such hit-men was CIA-employed Kermit Roosevelt, grandson of President Theodore Roosevelt. He was charged with taking out Dr Mohammed Mossadegh, the democratically elected leader of Iran.

Mossadegh was vehemently opposed to the vast sums of money exported by the Anglo-Iranian Oil Company (AIOC) to Britain from Iranian oil reserves without leaving any for the people of Iran. The Iranian leader dared to ask for some of the oil money to be retained for his people to fight poverty, disease and to meet their government's national budget. The British Prime Minister, Winston Churchill, accused the Iranians of going down the communism route at a time when anti-communism sentiment was at a peak in the USA. The US government under the leadership of President Dwight Eisenhower and Churchill's government took a decision to overthrow Mossadegh.

With a mere few million dollars, Kermit Roosevelt managed to initiate a coup d'etat which left 300 Iranians dead but with no casualties on the British or American side. Under pressure from the US government, Mossadegh was arrested under the charge of high treason. His replacement, Fazlollah Zahedi, was appointed by the Shah. An agreement was reached with foreign oil companies from which the majority of revenues were reaped by the US and Britain.

As a return gesture, the US government financed the Shah's government until he was overthrown during the Iranian Revolution in 1979. The case of economically taking over the control of Iran's vast oil revenues by using economic hit-men

---

45 www.economichitman.com

has helped the US tremendously. Coupled with other policies, the largest economic empire in history has been able to fund its exponential growth within the shortest time.

The 122 countries under the US's economic grip and control equal more than the number of countries under the control of all the other empires (e.g. British, Belgian, etc) combined. The plot is simple. The Empire targets developing countries in desperate need of aid and support. They offer them financial aid at exorbitant interest rates that the borrower cannot possibly repay. Consequently, the desperate countries have interest payments that exceed the original debt. Sound familiar?

At this point, the Empire, through the IMF and the World Bank, offer to help the developing country in return for them selling their country's reserves/infrastructure to private multinational companies. If the leader of the country refuses to comply, then economic hit-men or 'jackals' are sent in to assassinate the president. Such was the case of Jacoba Arbenz Guzman (1951-54) of Guatemala, and Saddam Hussein (1979-2003) of Iraq.

Why Pay for FREE Energy?!!

The Industrial Revolution of the 1800s has been one of the greatest milestones in the history of slavery. Before the Industrial Revolution, Britain was known as a 'nation of shopkeepers'. Individuals and their families worked together and specialised in arts, crafts, baking, farming and so on. They sold the fruits of their labour at the local market. However, the attraction of making a lot more quick money was enough of an incentive for rural dwellers to pack up their belongings and move into towns and cities to work.

A huge proportion of the work was on assembly lines in large factories and cotton mills. During this era, empire building was at its peak with cheap raw materials being imported from colonised countries to be manufactured into finished goods by the colonialists. The empires never had it better. Whilst coal was the predominant source of energy for business and domestic use in the nineteenth century, oil took over in the twentieth and twenty-first century. The majority of the world's energy requirement has been met by oil.

In the last 150 years, this has given oil companies a stranglehold on the world economy. It is hard to imagine the extent to which oil price affects individuals enslaved to the system. In simple terms, when transportation modes are dependent on oil as fuel, then people and goods are affected by any price fluctuation of fuel. Bananas bought from a local supermarket in London get picked up from the plantation of a tropical country, which are sent to be packaged in factories and then loaded onto ships. Then, they are imported into England by ship, taken by road from the docks; and finally the bananas arrive on the supermarket shelves in London.

The bananas would have required a minimum of three to four transportation modes with each one consuming vast quantities of oil-based fuels. Does it come as a surprise that oil companies are some of the most powerful organisations in the world? According to Forbes, six of the ten biggest companies in the world, by revenue, are oil companies. They did not get there by accident or through sheer effort. Nor are they likely to give up their super-monopoly position in a quick hurry.

The sales turnover of these companies is greater than the entire gross domestic products (GDP) of some countries. For example, the annual turnover of the five biggest companies in the world[46] - Walmart (US$419b), ExxonMobil (US$370b), Royal Dutch Shell (US$368b), BP (US$297b) and Sinopec (US$289b) - exceeds the GDP (gross domestic product) of Bangladesh (US$259b)[47], the country my birth. Not only have humans been held to hostage by illegal oil cartels (they collude to determine oil prices in order to make more profit), but they

[46] www.en.wikipedia.org/wiki/list_of_companies_by_revenue

[47] www.indexmundi.com/bangladesh/gdp_(purchasing_power_parity).html

have also been a major catalyst in the degradation of the environment in many parts of the world.

This does not even begin to consider the destruction in and around sea-based oil rigs. Why are people so dependent on oil? The answer is: they are not. Given the abundance of clean, renewable energy sources such as solar, wind and tidal energies, why is it that economies are so heavily reliant on oil? For example, there is enough potential for free geothermal energy (ground-based heat energy) to keep the planet going for several millennia.

The problem is that many of the inventions that provide viable means of extracting alternative energy sources get swallowed up by big corporations, never to see the light of day. One such invention was created by one of the greatest minds of the twentieth century, Nikola Tesla. His wireless transmission of electricity to all parts of the earth was the main objective in the famous *Pike's Peak Experiment*. He discovered that tremendously destructive forces could be unleashed in the earth by means of uncontrolled electrical resonance electricity.

Funded by the banker JP Morgan, Tesla demonstrated the feasibility of transmitting electricity through the earth without the use of wires in 1899 in Pike's Peak, Colorado. He chose Pike's Peak because of its remote location, and the availability of electricity from a local power station. Tesla discovered that the earth was a very good conductor of electricity. He could set the earth in electrical oscillation just like the mechanical oscillation that almost caused an earth-quake in Manhattan.

Power was supplied to the primary coil by the local power station. The secondary coil was grounded to the earth, producing waves which travelled to the opposite side of the world. The returning waves were discharged through the atmosphere. When Tesla demonstrated the feasibility of his wireless power system, he rushed back to New York to begin construction on a transmitter located at Wardenclyffe, Long Island, New York.

Construction began immediately on Tesla's Wardenclyffe Tower (also known as the 'Tesla Tower'). It was never finished and the project literally bankrupted Tesla. On discovering that Tesla was proposing to provide energy to the world for *free*, J.P. Morgan stonewalled him and created a panic on Wall St. in 1907. Today, most people have never heard of Tesla as his name disappeared into obscurity. Yet, Edison's name is synonymous with electricity and the light bulb. Nevertheless, some of Tesla's legacy does live on as his name is given to the unit of magnetic flux density.

Consumerism: The Deadly Invisible Disease of Modern Day Slaves

To get a tighter grip on the masses, the illusionists use propaganda to scare the public into survival mode. In the last hundred years, there has been a disease that has been brought to the forefront of people's minds called 'cancer'. At the beginning of the twenty-first century, the numerous forms of cancer were responsible for one in every three adult deaths in the developed world.

AIDS crept in during the 1980s and people were running around like headless chickens worrying about their one or many sexual partners. The third disease that has been introduced into the equation, and the most successful of them all, is called *consumerism*. This is a disease which infects people in such a way that (a) they do not even realise it has happened and it creeps up far more cleverly and mysteriously than AIDS or cancer; (b) it leads to people doing things like buying goods that they do not need, but cannot help buying them. Ever heard of retail therapy?

Then, the accrued mountain of debt is so high that they end up strangling themselves with repayments. How are they able to repay their debts? Simply by exchanging their labour for money with a corporation. They use the money they earn to survive, repay their debt and then get into even greater debt. Such is the vicious nature of becoming a wage slave.

In the UK, total personal debt has been rising consistently so that by February 2011, total UK personal debt was £1.454bn (US$2.398bn). The average household debt, including mortgages, was £57,697 (US$95,161). However, when this is combined with the public sector net debt, it rises to a staggering £109,919 (US$181,284) per household[48]. According to the OECD[49] (*Organisation for Economic Cooperation and Development*), the household debt as a proportion of personal income for Britons was 159% compared to 135% for US citizens.

Australia, New Zealand and Netherlands have much higher personal debt than the UK and USA, with Denmark leading at 260%. Consumerism is a self-imposed slavery where a big fat carrot is dangled in front of people and they are given the opportunity to buy something with the money they have or even money they do not have. In the past, there were no such things as credit cards. If a person saw a little doggie in the window they wanted to take home, then they better have the money with them. They could have used a cheque, but only if the store owner personally knew them.

Otherwise, if they wanted to buy something, they would either save up money was left from their earnings or they just simply did without. The entire idea of credit is a one-way ticket to self-imposed slavery. Before the financial meltdown in 2007/8, people could get hold of cards that had credit limits far more than what their annual income could realistically allow. Even if they were able to pay it back, they were caged in until they were released from their bond by clearing their debts.

Of course, if they could not pay the debts back, they could go bankrupt for three to five years and then start all

[48] www.moneybasics.co.uk/en/resources/money_information.html

[49] www.oecg.org

over. This is an interesting idea that has been pioneered in America, the land of the free. This has developed a licentiousness and a lack of responsibility in the users. All that has happened here is a massive schism between those who lend and those who borrow. In the end, the result is that people end up further and further apart from their hopes, dreams and aspirations in achieving their goals. On the other hand those who have lent them the money, get closer and closer to their desires very rapidly.

Consumerism was started by a handful of very clever, narrow minded, short-termed, greedy individuals, including Edward Bernays and Paul Mazer of Lehman Brothers. It is a type of disorder and psychological dysfunctionality because it operates on the principle of survival of the fittest. It is very much driven by the survival instinct and is similar to a predator-reptilian relationship. Consequently, everybody else suffers with very few at the top doing extremely well.

In 2011, whilst a supposedly deep recession was taking place in the UK, the Sunday Times produced their annual 'Top 1000 Rich List'[50]. According to their figures, even though Britain was experiencing one of the most devastating depressions in its history, the top 1,000 people increased their wealth by an average of 18%. Yet, at the same time, unemployment in the UK had rocketed. So long as people choose to ignore what is happening right under their noses, then consumerism will not only eat them up; it will remain the engine that fuels the oil of the greatest illusionists.

Take again the example of energy. Currently, the majority of the world's engines are powered on oil-based energy, including all modes of transportation, factories, the electricity we use to power our homes and our domestic appliances. The majority of the supplies of oil-based technologies are provided by five super-sized multinational

---

[50]
www.thesundaytimes.co.uk/sto/public/richlist/?CMP=KNGvccp1-sunday+times+rich+list

corporations who have one motive - profits. Considering the owners of such companies are hugely (not wholly) responsible for the devastation of the environment, the destruction of the forests, the pollution of the oceans and freshwater, would it be worth examining this matter a little further?

These businesses enjoy annual profits that are greater than the GDP of many countries. They seem to be exempt from many laws that the public have to abide by. The same companies are responsible for propping up corrupt presidents and removing presidents who dare put the public above the interests of their companies. Presidents who have been 'taken out' include Jaime Roldós Aguilera (1940-1981), president of Ecuador, and Omar Torrijos (1929-1981), president of Panama. They were both victims of assassination plots carried out by illusionists who could not persuade them to submit to the wishes of the US government.

The presidents who are propped by these corporations have the interest of their paymasters in mind only. Many of them take into government other more powerful corporate voices. President George W. Bush, Dick Cheney and Donald Rumsfeld are all examples of governments being led by the interests of big corporations alone. When a nation organises itself according to perspective of the corporation, which includes its values, systems, processes and includes the political and economic systems, it is defined as a *fascist government.*

Does this not describe the government of the United States of America? Sadly, most American citizens are wholly unaware of the regime that they are controlled by. A fascist dictatorship gives lip service to democracy at best and has a strong contempt for democracy at worst. Forget what the newspapers and the media say. If the government that is voted in is being sponsored largely by corporations, then the following question has to be asked:

"To what extent is this government going to be influenced by the corporations rather than the people who voted them in power?"

I truly hope that the readers of this book do their own research. Critical thinking need not be a dead art. Perhaps it is time the public took personal responsibility for their own destiny and worked with their community to determine their collective destiny. This means looking at the degree to which each person and the public have been programmed by illusionists. It is easy to point to the media and accuse them of mass manipulation. That may be true. However, the story starts much earlier than that for most people. How about if I said the disease begins at Kindergarten?

Education: the Beginning of the Indoctrination Cycle[51]

By adulthood, most people would have been conditioned and programmed by the master illusionists through the media, establishments, religious institutions and cultural 'norms'. The indoctrination process begins as early as the age of five in many developed countries such as Britain. Children experience the trauma of separation when moving from their families to preschool. Then, they have the added trauma of moving from a place of creativity and self-expression to their first year in school where discipline, orderliness and conformity are the only accepted standards.

Standing out and being different is a no-no. The more naturally creative and physically self-expressive a child is, the deeper their level of trauma. I remember how upset my own children were particularly in their first year at school. They found it incredibly difficult to adapt from a self-expressive environment to one that required them becoming like sheep.

---

[51] This section is based on the author's interview with Dr Carmen Boulter on *The Consciousness Revolution Show*

The education system in the majority of developed countries is concerned with one thing only: to create worker bees of the future, i.e. to become tomorrow's labour force and wage slaves. Is it a surprise that governments focus so much on homogenising education through predetermined national curricula, taking away freedom of choice for children? Hey, what is the big deal? They will have to get used to their freedoms being eroded later on in life. So, why not start early?

In the UK, there is a great emphasis placed on the three R's - reading, writing and arithmetic. Go figure! I agree it is important that a child is able to read, write and perform basic calculations. They will need these skills for future tax returns! The entire process of school examinations is effectively testing whether a child is able to perform well under fight or flight conditions. Those that perform the best are fit enough to be considered as a viable candidate for their future participation in the Rat Race. As a student at secondary school, I could not understand nor conform to the level of attention placed on understanding every little detail about English grammar and language and, as a result, I failed my English exams at sixteen years of age ('O'-Levels)...twice!

Bizarrely, I did very well in chemistry, physics, maths, Latin and even in the more difficult subject of English Literature. However, research reveals that many people reading and learning styles are quite different to what is emphasised at school. Here is something I found on a placard on the wall of a parking lot in downtown San Francisco:

Subject: Rscheearch

Aoccdrnig to a rscheearch at Cmabrigde Uinervtisy, it deosn't mttaer in waht oredr the ltteers in a wrod are, the olny ipr-moetnt tihng is taht the frist and lsat ltteer be at the rghit pclae. The rset can be a total mses and you can sitll raed it wouthit a porbelm. Tihs is bcuseae the huamn mnid deos not raed ervey lteter by istlef, but the wrod as a wlohe. Enojy the wkeened. Amzanig, huh?

115

So, what does that say about conventional thinking regarding the education process? The motivation behind the schooling system is to educate young people so they can be economically productive citizens of the country. The question is: who are they producing for? In Britain, are there not enough houses, cars, televisions, kitchen units, clothes, energy, doctors to keep everybody going? Clearly not, according to the government, especially when economic activity 'slows' down during a recession. Britain is no just a consumer society. She is a producer society where economic activity and tax collection defy all logic and reason.

Why is the current education model so outdated and used for the purpose of control? Understanding the meaning of 'education' may shed some light on this. The Latin derivative of 'education' is 'educere' which means 'to draw from within'. The ancient Greek philosopher, Socrates, was the first recorded teacher who used a systematic approach to drawing knowledge from within the student through logic and reason. The student was responsible for the development of their own faculties.

Today's schooling primarily relies on the teacher passing down their knowledge to the student in parrot fashion. The student takes 'responsibility' to learn the information by rote and to recall that information whenever the need arose during tests and exams. Students are trained to become memory machines rather than someone studying to gain true knowledge and become capable of critical thinking. Knowledge is limited when it is primarily based on just one faculty - thoughts - and only the logical left brain variety, at that. The ancient Chinese sage, Confucius, said something to the contrary:

"To know and not to do is not yet to know"

How did the education system fall into demise? The modern education system is based on the eighteenth century

Austrian schooling system. During the Napoleonic wars between Prussia and France, the French leader could not understand how the Prussian soldiers were much more effective killing machines than his own soldiers. This was despite both factions having similar backgrounds, i.e. being farmers and peasants.

On further examination, the French discovered the Prussian peasants and farmers were being trained and indoctrinated from a very early age to be obedient to their superiors, follow orders without question and to never quit in battle. On the other hand, the French had a much more ill-disciplined and rebellious attitude towards war. Under Napoleon's order, a schooling system was created to educate the males to be obedient to the flag and to listen to orders without question. The rest of the world were incredibly quick to adopt this form of education system that created obedient workers who were all too ready to obey their masters' instructions without question.

The modern education system is undergoing a crisis in many developed countries. The continual intervention of governments into the education system has left too many teachers performing management duties instead of teaching. Many teachers are forced to spend excessive time dealing with behaviourally challenged students. Physical activity such as sports and skills-based activities like woodwork, have been all but eliminated from the curriculum. More and more students are getting better grades in academic subjects and fighting for fewer university places. But, at what expense? Has the education standard fallen to get more 'qualified' workers?

Britain is a creative nation. This means, as a nation, the UK has more creative and innovative people than any other personality type[52]. When an individual has strongly developed creative abilities, they tend to have more need for physical movement and practical learning. Some become artists, whilst

---

[52] Hamilton, R. *Your Life, Your Legacy*

others become sports people, dancers, artisans, mechanics, musicians, actors, etc. The education system in many developed countries, such as Britain, take little notice of these natural creative abilities. The consequences are very simple. Students develop emotional and behavioural problems from a lack of integration of their innate qualities with that of the education system that they are subjected to.

Over a number of years, I have had the pleasure of experiencing working with hundreds of 'difficult' school children. My interaction with many of these ostracised young people has been revealing. Many of the lowest performers were amazing geniuses even though they were not academically inclined. By not harnessing their innate abilities, the schooling system has neglected the children they have been charged to nurture and guide.

Many of these children end up becoming socially deprived (if they are not already). There are associated health, financial and relational issues that accompany such social exclusion. Left to fend for themselves, these worker bees have little chance of gaining employment. A few have the good fortune to get out of the system and go on to succeed in other areas of life such as business, sports and music.

The modern day education system is a patriarchal system that has one person leading and the masses (worker bees) who are supposed to follow. Today's education is like the banking system where the teachers deposit information into the children. It is then on the children's shoulders to give the information back by getting a test score. As the children progress through the system, the information gets increasingly harder and they get more of it. When there are better grades and more exams taken, the public celebrate that the education standard is getting better.

However, technology has advanced to a level where anything can be Googled to find a 'fact'. The idea of having to memorise a fact is absolutely and unequivocally obsolete. This is because facts are now at everybody's fingertips.

Furthermore, if all the facts in the world were memorised, they would be out of date within 15 minutes as information changes very rapidly. The illusionists have been trying to create worker bees since the Industrial Revolution, which is still about the few who own the majority of the wealth and the many who are slaves to the system.

In fact, the people who built the schooling system in America were also the same people who built the penitentiaries, i.e. not too many windows and little space for movement called 'classrooms' or 'cells'. In many of the schools in Canada, USA and even in the UK, there are police or security guards at schools to check the students for weapons and drugs. It is not permissible to leave the classroom until the bell rings even when the work has been done. Such an environment is just not conducive to creativity.

The students do not like such environments and, consequently, there is a lack of respect and increasing levels of conflict. The countries that apply such education systems are in serious trouble as they are neglecting the most empowering form of education - 'learner-centred learning'. As this is a big paradigm shift from teacher-centred teaching, there is still a huge amount of resistance from those who operate such a system. The old guard still cannot get themselves to move from being the 'sage on the stage' to the 'guide on the side'.

Corporations and governments remember the Industrial Revolution with pride. However, they neglect to talk about how the Industrial Revolution has led to the dumbing down of people to such a level that they were grateful to have a tiny subsistence wage. At least, they could eat and live till the next day. It is the big guys paying these wages that are doing little or no work but are getting all the money. This is a patriarchal way of being and thinking where it is 'power over' people instead of 'empowerment' of people.

In an ideal world, people would be empowered. Students would be taught to be creative and how to construct something. Today's universities are all about 'deconstructing' and taking something and tearing it apart or looking at the flaws or giving 'constructive criticism'. It is about divide, divide, divide. People are constantly being programmed to think in terms of separation and division. This is opposite to constructivism, which is a concept that entails making something and building on what one already knows.

For example, in the global economy, work is being farmed out to China and India where products are made cheaper. Again, this is where a few people make money off the many. The productive part of the economy where shoes, electronic parts, widgets are made in the West has all but disappeared. The manufacturing industry in Britain, which includes huge industries such as car-making and shipbuilding, have been devastated to the point where Britain is now just a service economy.

In such an economy, law, finance and customer services (e.g. call centres) dominate. This is all about supporting patriarchal ways of being and thinking and keeping people disempowered. Constructivism is about being meaning-centred. Most children do not like school because there is no meaning to it. There is a huge gap between what they are taught and reality. In addition, the nationally prescribed curriculum of the UK, for example, neglects the creative aspiration of students.

The education establishment are not focusing on education with meaning nor are they coming from a place of meaning. It is all about fulfilling criteria as dictated to by a 'Nanny State'. One may be forgiven for thinking that the last bastion of hope for educating young people would be in a professional field such as Medicine. Think again. In the next chapter, I will reveal how Medicine has turned itself from a noble professional serving humanity to a corrupted institution propping up corporate profits.

Chapter 6: Modern Medicine - Dumbing People Down and Knocking them Out

*"Modern-day Medicine is not based
on compassion or humanity."*

A Brief History of Medicine

One of the great innovations for post-war Britain was the creation of a free healthcare service, the *National Health Service* (NHS), for all its citizens. As technology developed and the ability to detect new diseases and health conditions improved, so have the range of medicines and therapies. However, the ability to pay for ever increasing healthcare has been at crisis point for nearly two decades both in the UK and USA. It would be more appropriate to call Britain's healthcare system the 'National Sickness Service'; not just because of the systemic breakdown of the NHS, but also for the vast damage created by the 'side effects' of many of modern medicine's cures.

Modern medicine did not come into existence without leaving numerous skeletons in the cupboard. Thousands of human lives and million of animals lives have been sacrificed to yield what people enjoy as today's cures. For example, John Marion Sims (1845-1849), hailed as the 'father of gynaecology', used to perform very painful medical experiments on enslaved African women without using anaesthesia during the pre-antiseptic days. Many of the women died from infections caused by the barbaric experiments shortly after surgery.

Sims believed that the movement of a newborn's skull bones during protracted births causes *'trismus nascentium'* (neonatal tetanus). Thus, he used a shoemaker's awl, a pointed tool shoemakers use to make holes in leather, to practice moving the skulls of babies of African slaves during childbirth.

Sims was responsible for the deaths of numerous children due to his highly dubious surgical procedures. Is this the price that has to be paid for the advancement of medicine?

Another episode of extreme medicine is the case of 'prefrontal lobotomy'. This was a surgical procedure that was supposed to be used in extreme cases of psychiatric disorders. It was first performed in the 1890s by psychiatrists and became known as a 'psychosurgery'. The American clinical neurologist Walter Freeman (1895-1972) developed a quicker method, the 'ice-pick' lobotomy, which he performed for the first time on January seventeenth, 1945.

The patients were not anaesthetised, but were rendered unconscious using electric shock. The instrument, resembling an ice-pick, was inserted through the orbit and above the eye-ball using a 'hammer'. Upon entering the brain, the ice-pick was moved back and forth through both sides of the brain via the eye sockets. This procedure was favoured by clinicians as it took approximately ten minutes and did not require anaesthesia (which has a potential mortality rate). Freeman performed nearly 35,000 lobotomies during his career with mixed results that included some patients who would heal and others who were left in a vegetative state.

On 16th December 1960, Freeman infamously performed an ice-pick lobotomy on a 12-year-old boy named Howard Dull. Dully's stepmother had grown tired of the boy's behaviour and took him to numerous physicians who all concluded that there was nothing wrong with him. Finally, Freeman happily agreed to perform a lobotomy at the request of Dully's stepmother. Such behaviours have been generally accepted by the wider medical fraternity without resistance. The decline in the use of lobotomies as a surgical procedure began mid to late 1950s. Ultimately, the opposition to lobotomies was far too strong to be an accepted procedure and anti-psychotic drugs like chlorpromazine[53] (which is effectively a chemical lobotomy) became more accessible.

Today's medicine is not based on compassion or humanity. Modern medicine was founded on a desire to keep injured soldiers alive for as long as possible, so that they could function as fighting machines for as long as possible during war. If the symptoms of disease could be eliminated, soldiers were expected to fight for their cause, including to the death. Therefore, no attention was given to the side effects of synthetically developed drugs. After all, the young men were not expected to live long enough during war to protest against wrongly prescribed drugs. So why bother with side effects? To be a doctor, an individual would need to dedicate many years of schooling. This would be followed by training before they were they were qualified to practice alone as a general practitioner or as part of a specialist team.

Of course, this required a large financial investment by the student's family. As this was not a viable option for most people, medicine was usually an option for the upper and middle classes. The physician was and still is revered as an expert in all health matters and has often been treated as a demigod in many cultures. Culturally, doctors became one of the most upstanding and respected members of the community. As far as the public are concerned, what the doctor says, goes. That is true abdication of power on the part of the public.

Yes, a doctor ought to be treated with respect and dignity for his or her knowledge and experience. However, physicians lost something along the way. They believed that patients would be served best through dispassionate care. It is expected that a doctor should show professional conduct by not allowing their feelings to interfere with their clinical work. The work of doctors is based on carefully considered logic and reasoning, i.e. left brain, masculine thinking. Empathy,

---

[53] www.en.wikipedia.org/wiki/Chlorpromazine

compassion or any other emotion was shunned by the medical fraternity.

The role of the intellect and reasoning in successful healing is 20% at best. The feelings experienced by the physician and those experienced by the patient have an equal role to play in healing. Much of modern medicine has lost its way and, as with most other indoctrination institutions, too many see it as merely as a platform for their personal career development. Although most physicians are highly educated and well meaning, very few are trained scientific researchers with experience in the research labs.

The medical research carried out on new drugs is performed by scientists whose paymasters are pharmaceutical companies. The information that is released to the scientific community is held on a tight leash by the paymasters of the research scientists. Ultimately, how much physicians learn about new pharmaceutical drugs and their side effects is very much in the hands of the pharmaceutical companies.

One of my close friends, Ali, who had just finished his MBA programme at university in 1993 managed to get employed by a large pharmaceutical company to promote anti-fungal drugs. He was one of many thousands of sales professionals hired in the UK to sell pharmaceutical drugs. Ali loved his job and achieving success was a matter of a numbers game for him. To reach his sales target, he needed to visit as many general practitioners (equivalent to M.D.) as possible to 'educate' them about their latest and most innovative drugs.

He would leave samples of the drugs and marketing material and then stay in touch with the doctors on a frequent basis. The doctors were incentivised by 'gifts' and financial rewards for prescribing certain drugs. The size of the reward usually had a direct correlation to which drug the manufacturers believed could reap the greatest profits. Isn't there a specific term to describe the use of money and valuable gifts for inducing someone to make a decision or take action in your favour? Oh, yes! It is called 'bribery'.

The pharmaceutical industry, which is less than a century old, is ran by some of the most formidable illusionists with unparalleled financial and political resources to match. Even with today's incredible speed of information exchange, the pharmaceutical industry has free reign in subjugating the masses to their lethal concoctions of questionably tested legalised drugs. So what is the M.O. (modus operandi) of Big Pharma? It is a far cry from the original purpose of medicine as stated by the father of medicine, Hippocrates. *See Appendix II.*

What are the Drug Barons Targeting?

The illusionists' agenda includes more than merely misdirecting the public's attention so they can be good little worker bees. It also includes dumbing down their bodies through legally endorsed drugs. This feat is achieved by the misuse of the modern medical system and misappropriation of information and funds. The consequences are significant. The inquisitive human mind is disempowered and emotional intelligence is restricted from further growth. The masses walk around like zombies, destined to repeat the same daily routine throughout their lives without asking the question 'why?'

A forceful pawn in the illusionists arsenal is the pharmaceutical industry. Despite being downright dangerous to humans, numerous diseases have been genetically mutated to allow corporate giants to sell more of their expensive drugs. Sadly, the plethora of pharmaceutical misdemeanours is too large in number to include in this book. However, some of the major ones will be brought to light shortly.

I must add a couple of provisos first. Just because there are a number of unscrupulous individuals abusing their positions of power in the pharmaceutical game, it does not mean every person in the industry is corrupt. Likewise, just because there are numerous questionable pharmaceutical drugs being prescribed, it does not mean that all drugs are damaging. It is up to the reader to do their own research to discern between what is beneficial and what is harmful to them.

As conscious beings, humans are a constantly changing interfacing energy matrix. This matrix processes four hundred billion bits of information every second. When an individual is in a healthy life state, they have the capacity to tap into all other energy matrices in the universe where space and time are no longer variables. There is no past and there is no future. All is happening here and now. However, at the current level of human evolution, out of this vast quantity of information that is being processed by humans, the conscious mind is only aware of a very minute level.

The majority of this information that humans are aware of are related to the immediate external environment through the five senses. Imagine how much transformation could take place if individuals took steps to increase their level of conscious awareness. These statements are a massive leap for anybody reading this information for the first time. Suffice to say, when people have been conditioned to think in terms of a mechanistic universe, why would they think beyond that paradigm?

The mechanistic universe is one where any individual part has no overall effect on the sum of all parts. That individual can be replaced without consequence to the rest of the universe. Thus, survival of the individual is that person's own priority. What happens to them is not consequential. It has nothing to do with anybody else and their absence from the planet will affect nobody and nothing, right? Wrong.

Imagine a highly trained deep sea diver who swims to the bottom of the ocean. She fills an open glass container with the water from the ocean and leaves the container on the sea bed. Could it be possible that the water in the container is energetically connected to the water immediately outside the container? Could it also be true to say that the water molecules in the container are energetically connected to the water several metres or even several miles away?

The reality is all waters are interconnected with each other. Don't believe this? Watch someone doing a belly flop at a swimming pool and observe the experience of how they feel when they break that energetic connection! An energy matrix, e.g. the human body, is like water molecules in a container. It is directly connected to all other energy matrices in the universe. The physical appearance of the human body is d e c e p t i v e .

Of course, a human body is real and is composed of at least fifty-trillion cells, which are made up of many more molecules and atoms. The energetic interaction between the atoms and molecules creates a forcefield in such a way that it is perceived as a solid. The energy from the atoms and molecules are still constantly interacting with the external environment. Information exchange is taking place between atoms and molecules continuously.

The point is this. The effectiveness of information interchange and interaction is dependent on the carrier of that information. If the carrier, the human body, is corrupted, then the quality of exchange will be restricted. The more severe the corruption, the less efficient the exchange. The body is likely to misinterpret information that it is receiving. Sometimes it will 'think' it is being attacked by foreign bodies when it is not (misinformation) and the body will overreact accordingly, e.g. allergies.

At other times, it will 'think' it is being attacked from the inside by foreign invasion and the body attacks itself, e.g. lupus. In other words, if information gets to the state of 'dis'-equilibrium where there is no harmony between the cells of the body, its inner and outer environment, then it will take the actions needed to get back to a state of harmony and equanimity. The simple way to create imbalance in a body is to place it in an environment (inner or outer) that will distort information exchange. THIS is what the majority of synthetically manufactured pharmaceutical drugs do. The drugs have a direct effect on the inner environment of the individual's cells. Drugs misinform the body that they are healing the person by masking the symptoms of a 'dis'-ease. However, the cause of the 'dis'-ease remains wholly intact, which means the symptoms are likely to remain.

From Corporate Takeover to Corporal Takeover

Two of the world's leading cell and evolution biologists that I have interviewed on *The Consciousness Revolution Show*, Dr Bruce Lipton and Dr Elisabet Sahtouris, have come to a similar conclusion. The human body is not one single individual being. It is composed of approximately fifty-eighty trillion individual beings (cells) in the body. Each cell has its own brain, skin, reproductive system, skeletal system, cardiovascular system, etc.

They all work in small communities where they specialise in one function, i.e. tissue (such as fat). The specialist communities work with other specialist communities to form organs, such as the skin or the heart. All the organs interact with each other to work as one human body. When a foreign body, e.g. bacteria, enters the body, the cells concerned will do the best to manage the invasion. Whilst the body is in this state of conflict, the level of energy and attention needed for routine self repair and growth falls dramatically.

The body is in a state of survival. The greater the level of threat, the more attention and energy is used to deal with the threat. When the body is in a state of survival, the conscious mind functions less effectively and efficiently. Living beyond survival is not so important in such times. There is then a fall in the capability to perform higher level communication. The ability to tap into universal creativity is also impeded dramatically. A good example is when a teenager is sitting her university exams, but is suffering from a cold or she is dehydrated. Research indicates that such a physical state will result in her grades dropping by about 10%.

Medicine has produced some remarkable results over the centuries and has been responsible for saving the lives of millions. For example, shortly into the beginning of 2011, one of my good friends was involved in a severe car accident that left his thigh bone (femur) crushed. The doctors did all they could to help him and, thankfully, succeeded in saving his leg. Had my friend chosen to opt for something like homeopathy instead of modern medical intervention, then he would have been sent off to see a head-doctor instead. An additional benefit was that he was very satisfied with his daily dosage of morphine! Thus, I hope the reader understands that this section of the book is not about attacking conventional medicine. However, it is about contextualising the role of medicine and a humans' ability to heal.

The aim of corporal ('*corpus*' = 'body') take-over by the illusionists is easy to understand. As my friend, Randy Gage[54] says, it is to keep people sick, dumb and broke. By keeping the masses in perpetual docility, people never get to know their creativity and what it truly means. In addition, they are more likely to obey their slave masters who no longer have to be concerned about reprisals from their dumbed-down slaves. I will reveal some of the ways in which medicine has been misused for the purposes of corporal takeover. This will be done by setting the foundation for such a case by examining the biggest entity that is responsible for corporal takeover - the pharmaceutical industry.

[54] www.randygage.com/store/why-youre-dumb-sick-and-broke

The Pharmaceutical Industry is in the Business of...

...making money! Mathematics and physics have seen massive leaps in their advancement, whilst the biological and medical sciences have been far slower in adapting. The latter two sciences have not been slow in their evolution for any reason other than their personal intention. For example, there is a good degree of awareness that there are far more efficient ways to acquire energy other than burning fossil fuels. So how is it that people still burn so much oil? Quite frankly, because it is not in the interests of the petroleum industry. This industry has all the money needed to support the development of technology for the use of alternative energy sources. Even though there is access to many other forms of free energy, the oil business would collapse if they do not sell...guess what? Oil!

The story is the same here: the pharmaceutical industry sells chemical drugs. If people were to find out that they can heal themselves with their thoughts and energy, what would happen to public health? If the masses discovered the quantum mechanic principles of how energy shapes matter and influences their health, the drug companies would be in a bit of a mess. Can they sell energy? Can they sell thoughts? No! If energy healing could be packaged in a pill with a price tag, the pharmaceutical industry would jump at the opportunity.

If the drug industry cannot make a profit from these, why would they encourage it? The pharmaceutical industry is one of the most influential industries in the business world. They are tremendously cash rich and will not invest their spuriously earned money into ways of healing that lead to their profits being reduced. Essentially, they influence medical practice. The grants that research scientists receive are funded if they support the opinions of those that have the money. In this case, those that have the money are part of the pharmaceutical industry. If research demonstrates people could be healed without the use of drugs, it would be close to impossible to get any funding.

130

In October 2010, I went to visit family and friends in the USA, during which time I managed to catch up with American television culture. What I found most interesting were the commercials for pharmaceutical drugs. For example, one particular drug for arthritis was being advertised as helping alleviate the symptoms and pain associated with that condition. Approximately 15-25% of the commercial was spent on talking about how wonderful the drug was, whilst 75-85% of the commercial was talking about the 'potential side effects' of the drug, including diarrhoea, vomiting and even death! I could not believe my eyes and ears!

The pharmaceutical companies do not say these are the effects of the drug, but they euphemistically use the term 'side effects'. In their mind, that somehow ameliorates the problem. If it is a side effect, it cannot be too bad a problem, right? Very, very wrong. Here is the massive lie: these are not side effects. They are **direct** effects of the drug. The reality is that the drugs have many toxic effects because conventional biology and medicine is operating from a misunderstanding about the body's function and how the cells work. Within that environment of misinformation, they are plying their drugs.

In the USA, there is an ongoing war on drugs, which is a war on illegal drugs. So guess how many people die from illegal drugs? It would be considered a lot of people if the official drug-related deaths were taken into account. According to the US Office of National Drug Control Policy [55] there were 15,973 drug-induced deaths (which includes cocaine, heroin and, according to them, marijuana). How many people died from prescription drugs? According to Dr Bruce Lipton, in the US, over 300,000 people die every year from prescription drugs. Therefore, does it not make sense that if there is a 'war on drugs', there needs to be a 'war on pharmaceutical drugs'? Pharmaceutical drugs are more toxic than some recreational

[55] www.ncjrs.gov/ondcppubs/publications/policy/ndcs00/chap2_10.html

drugs and people are buying these under the pretext that they are good for the sick.

Mankind calls itself 'human' based on the definition of 'humanity'. The definition of humanity is based on idealistic humans who are compassionate, loving and supporting of each other and supporting of the world. As wonderful a definition as it is, most people do not conform to it. Healthcare, by definition, was a compassion process. There were healers who were compassionate about working with the sick people as their work was to bring health back. What about today's world of healthcare? It is no longer about the sick, but all about corporations - pharmaceutical and insurance.

The truth is that a corporation is about the bottom line, i.e. profits. It matters not whether they produce medicine, cars, clothes, etc. The aim is simple: to make profits. Whatever a corporation does, it is secondary to its primary mission. The primary mission of EVERY corporation is to make profits for its shareholders. Then, whatever is done within that organisation, it is part of the process of creating a profit. In the healthcare arena, people buy stocks and share in healthcare corporations in the hope of making a profit from their share-holdings.

Where is the profit coming from? The realistic story is that the profits come from sick people by charging them a lot more money than the services provided by the corporations. All the excess money that has been charged over the costs is for shareholder's profit. Therefore, is making profits from sick people humane? In my opinion and the opinion of millions of other people including Dr Bruce Lipton, it is absolutely inhumane.

The healthcare industry is an inhumane process because it is a profit-seeking industry that bleeds the poor people and the rich in more ways than one. It bleeds them of their health and bleeds them dry of their hard-earned income and savings. The USA, for example, has the sickest population amongst the developed countries of the world. Yet, despite the advanced medical technologies and medical services available, Americans pay almost twice as much for healthcare than the next sickest country.

How is it possible, with all these innovations, that the USA still has the sickest people? It is very simple. The corporations do not want to make people healthy and well. It has never been nor ever will be in their interest to make their customers well. If everybody were to get healthy and well, then the entire pharmaceutical industry would collapse. How can they profit from making people well? The healthcare industry is not for the patients. It is for the investors. The icing on the cake is this: fear and stress are the causes of 90% of the illness on this planet. The most famous king of fear-mongers in recent history was the US President George W. Bush. Anytime he got in front of the public arena his biggest mantras included:

"Be afraid. They're coming to get you and your children".

Bush scared the hell out of the people of the US as well as numerous other countries. Before Bush became President, the profits enjoyed by pharmaceutical companies were increasing a few percentage points year on year. However, after the 9/11 World Trade Centre bombings, the drug companies were making 20% profit a year, every year for five years whilst Bush was in office. The pharmaceutical industry more than doubled their sales figures in just five years. Nice work if you can get it!

In other words, as long as fear is instilled into people, the chemistry of fear shuts down the immune system and shuts down the maintenance of the body. If a person was in a sustained state of fear, the only consequence would be sickness. The pharmaceutical industry has been incredibly successful in plying their drugs for keeping the masses dumbed down. These include some of the biggest selling drugs such as Prozac, Ritalin and Viagra.

To enjoy supernormal profits, companies have also gone as far as to manufacture diseases that hitherto, nobody had ever heard of. These include Bird Flu, Mad Cow's Disease, Swine Flu and AIDS. If that was not enough, the illusionists have also turned to poisoning the bodies of healthy people by tampering with food and water supplies. The majority of people are aware that water is the single most important constituent of living organisms. When the basis of people's existence is tampered with, then their very lives will be compromised.

The Vaccination Story

Very few topics have courted more controversy than vaccinations, especially about children's vaccinations. On one hand, vaccinations have been seen as modern medicine's greatest weapon in the fight against numerous diseases which, hitherto, had been known to sicken, maim or even kill people. On the other hand, there is an increasingly growing community who are vehemently against the entire idea of vaccination as propagated by Big Pharma.

It is worthwhile looking beyond the smokescreens surrounding vaccinations. The word 'vaccination' is derived from the Latin word '*Vacca*' to mean 'cow' because the first vaccine developed was from the virus that was responsible for cow pox by English scientist, Edward Jenner (1749-1823). In 1796, Jenner tested his hypothesis on vaccination by inoculating eight year old James Phipps with material from the hands of a maid who caught smallpox from a cow. A fever and discomfort resulted but no serious illness. The boy was injected with a further dosage of smallpox to increase his immunity without a resulting infection.

Before the smallpox vaccine was developed, it was responsible for 8-20% of all deaths in Europe in the eighteenth century. French chemist, Louis Pasteur (1822-1895), took vaccination much further with his pioneering work in microbiology and was the first man to create the vaccine for anthrax and rabies. However, successive opportunists have seized on the chance to make vast sums of money by exploiting people's ignorance and pandering to the corruptibility of those placed in positions of power to protect the public.

In this section, I will give readers a peek into the world of vaccinations and how it has been exploited insofar as it not only robs the masses of money; but also how it is a threat to the health and the lives of millions of people today. As thousands of empirical data testify, the entire vaccination business is a highly complex web of deceit, statistical misrepresentation, manipulation, misuse and misinformation. Important variables have been left out of reports that are extraordinarily critical in deciding the efficacy of the vaccines.

Many diseases had been eradicated since the nineteenth century simply due to good sanitation, better education, improving diets and economic development. For example, smallpox disappeared from the USA, Europe and many other countries due to these developments alone. These are factors that are seldom taken into account when examining the efficacy of pharmaceutical drugs. Claims have been made by the illusionists in the US that smallpox was eradicated due to mass vaccination.

This is a ridiculous proposition as only 10% of the US population were ever vaccinated in the period under study. This kind of misinformation is particularly dangerous as it diverts the attention away from the true reason why damaging diseases have been thwarted and prevented. Consequently, less attention is placed on using the natural methods of sanitation, food hygiene and the vital role that water and the sun play in health.

According to Dr D. Powles (1973)[56], between 1860 and 1965, the total decline in death rate due to scarlet fever, measles, whooping cough and diphtheria occurred "**before** *the introduction of antibiotics and widespread immunisation of*

---

[56] www.parliament.nsw.gov.au/prod/parlment/hansart.nsf/V3Key/LC19921127026

diphtheria". Before the introduction of the *poliomyelitis* (polio) vaccine in 1874, its occurrence was rare. In the 1890s, however, there was a sudden explosion in polio cases with people ending up in paralysis...after receiving the vaccine! Before the introduction of the MMR (Mumps, Measles and Rubella) vaccine, deaths from measles had fallen by 99.4% in the US. The majority of the deaths that have occurred were all post-vaccination. You do the maths!

When thirteen-day old Robert Fletcher of Warrington, England, received his MMR vaccination, he suffered from fits for ten days. Subsequently, Robert suffered from severe brain damage (which did not include autism). Having taken the government to court, his mother, Jackie, received a £90,000 payout from a medical assessment panel[57]. The Fletcher family applied for compensation through the British government's *Vaccine Damage Payment Scheme*, which was turned down in 1997. However, they were successful in their appeal later on. Today, Robert has frequent epileptic fits, is unable to talk, stand unaided or feed himself. In an article by the Sunday Express, it was revealed that at least 26 families claimed their children died as a result of the controversial measles, mumps and rubella (MMR) jab.

In some cases the British government had awarded parents up to £100,000 under its *1979 Vaccine Damage Payment Act*. In some cases, postmortem examination reports concluded the MMR vaccination was the most likely cause of death. Nonetheless, the British government's Department of Health are still adamant the MMR vaccine was not the cause of their deaths! So, why does the government have a *Vaccine Damage Payment Act*?

It is not always easy for the illusionists to force people vaccinate. The weapon of choice left for governments to get people to accept vaccinations is via mass education, fear and pressure. Out of the three motivational tools, it is fear that is

---

[57] www.bbc.co.uk/news/uk-england-merseyside-11125343

the most effective tool in their campaigns. The government's real challenge is, in actuality, creating an effective marketing campaign.

A highly effective strategy induce's fear in people's minds so that they willingly take the steps to vaccinate themselves and their family. As propaganda has been the most powerful tool to proliferate the minds of the masses during war, so it is also the tool used to manipulate public opinion to suit the agenda of the illusionists. According to Peter Duesberg [58]

"Traditionally, the power of medical sciences has been based on the fear of disease, particularly infectious disease."

The Polio Scares

In the 1950s, one of the biggest health menaces to humans was polio. This is a contagious viral infection that leads to the inflammation of the spinal cord that can eventually lead to paralysis. According to epidemiological studies, deaths from polio declined by 82% prior to 1956 in England and Wales, with similar results in France. The fall had nothing to do with vaccinations. Once the vaccine had been introduced, the results shifted after ten years (1956-1966).

Polio returned to levels where it had been in the 1920s. Is it a coincidence that the rate of polio increases **after** the introduction of the vaccine? The race to find a weapon to eradicate polio was also a political hot potato. Before his accession to the US presidency, Franklin Roosevelt had been crippled by polio. However, there was one snag with polio in that it is caused by a virus and not bacteria. Therefore, antibiotics are totally ineffective against the virus leaving the medical fraternity with little to counteract such a potent disease.

---

[58] www.duesberg.com

In the early 1950s, Jonas Salk proposed that the polio virus would be grown in the labs, killed and injected into healthy children. After Salk's successful trials of 1953 and 1954, the virus was produced by five labs for the purpose of mass inoculation. In 1954, Dr Bernice Eddy, an employee of the *National Institute for Health* (NIH), received samples of the inactivated polio vaccine to certify. She and her team worked tirelessly on the brand new untested product and trialled it on eighteen monkeys.

Every one of the monkeys became paralysed leaving her team horrified that the very same vaccine was going to be injected into healthy children. When she filed the report, the director for NIH, William Sebrell stopped any further testing. Further research by Eddy between 1959 and 1960 led to the discovery that hamsters injected with the kidney mixture from which the vaccine was cultured developed tumours. Despite protestation from her superiors, Eddy presented her findings at a cancer conference with the consequence of being demoted and losing her testing facilities.

In 2011, a new agenda, the *Global Eradication Program* [59], was created to eliminate the polio virus, particularly from Nigeria, the country alleged to spread the virus more than any other. This programme, backed by the *US Centers for Disease Control* (CDC), Rotary International, UNICEF and the *World Health Organisation* (WHO), set their intention to vaccinate 74 million children across 22 African countries over the course of a few months despite widespread protestation. However, resistance to this programme was strong, particularly from influential Nigerian Muslim clerics who accused the West of using the programme for population control. Given the spurious reputation WHO had built, it comes as no surprise why such resistance is put up by Africans. Since the 1970s, WHO has been testing anti-fertility vaccines

---

59 www.polioeradication.org

that would case a woman's immune system to attack and destroy her unborn baby.

Mexican, Nicaraguan and Filipino women in the millions were persuaded to take tetanus vaccinations, which were often laced with a female hormone that could cause miscarriage and sterilization. The skepticism arose when the vaccination was recommended to women of childbearing age only. After a large number of women had vaginal bleeding and miscarriages, the cause was discovered to be the added female hormone. During an investigation, the Philippines Medical Association (the official body for family physicians) discovered that 20% of the WHO tetanus vaccines were contaminated with the hormone.

Back in Nigeria, in March 2004, a pharmaceutical scientist, Haruna Kaita[60], sent samples of WHO's oral polio vaccine to India for analysis which revealed serious contamination. Since then, there have been claims and counterclaims about a human eradication programme between Nigerian authorities and WHO. So, perhaps the Global Eradication Program was aptly named...and it had nothing to do with eliminating viruses or diseases!

Ritalin: Silencing the Next Generation

In Britain and America, a serious concern for parents and teachers are the behavioural issues of children under their care. A modern-day terminology that has become part of popular lexicon is 'ADHD' or 'Attention Deficit Hyperactivity Disorder'. This is a neuro-behavioural development disorder. It is symptomised by behavioural problems combined with hyperactivity. According to the *Diagnostic and Statistical*

---

[60] www.lifesite.net

Manual of Mental Disorders[61], the bible for psychiatric diagnosis, ADHD is diagnosed using the following criteria:

A pattern of negativistic, hostile and defiant behaviour lasting, at least, six months during which four (or more) of the following are present:

1. *Often loses temper.*
2. *Often argues with adults.*
3. *Often actively defies or refuses to comply with adult requests or rules.*
4. *Often deliberately annoys people.*
5. *Often blames others for his or her behaviour or mistakes.*
6. *Often touchy or easily annoyed by others.*
7. *Is often angry or resentful.*
8. *Is often spiteful or vindictive.*

That being the case, I estimate that I would have been doped up to my eyeballs with Ritalin (manufactured by Novartis) for most of my life as would have been the case for 90% of my friends and family. ADHD has one purpose and one purpose alone. It is a smokescreen for the mindless usage of pharmaceutical drugs as a way of controlling the behaviour of children. The indiscriminate prescription of Ritalin lines the pockets of physicians and fattens the profit margins of pharmaceutical companies. Not surprising, I discovered that there was an estimated 6-8 million American children on Ritalin in 2000. At the time of writing, 90% of the world's Ritalin was prescribed to American children.

The direct effects of using Ritalin have been glaringly obvious in both the UK and America. On 31st March 2011 [62] the coroner responsible for ten year old Harry Hucknall, cousin of

---

[61]

www.en.wikipedia.org/wiki/Diagnostic_and_Statistical_Manual_of_Mental_Disorders

[62] *Metro* newspaper published on 1st April 2011

140

Simply Red's Mick Hucknall[63], reported on the hanging of the child in September 2010. He had been prescribed fluoxetine[64] for depression and Ritalin for ADHD. It does not take a rocket scientist to figure out the reasons for Harry's behavioural problems. Harry was unsettled by moving home 14 times and was bullied at school. This included being held down and threatened with a screwdriver. I am wondering how many people in their right minds would expect such a child to think and behave normally. The coroner found the levels of both drugs in his system were above normal therapeutic level for **adults**.

The intention of Ritalin is to have the effect of depressing children (dumbing them down) so their 'behaviour' can be controlled. Studies comparing children with ADHD taking Ritalin with those not prescribed Ritalin have proved that the drug has little effect on behaviour. However, the drug is known to be unsafe as shown by numerous tests on animals. Furthermore, according to the FDA, Ritalin is classified under Section II - the most addictive class of medical drugs. This particular category of drugs includes cocaine and morphine. Stimulants like this produce pathological malfunctions in the brain, especially when given in high dosages.

In Ohio State University, Henry A. Nasrullah (1986) found that more than 50% of twenty-four young adults with hyperactivity since childhood experienced shrinkage of the brain due to Ritalin. It also disrupts children's natural growth hormone levels. When the case for Ritalin is argued with the plethora of scientifically and clinically verified evidence, the argument is overwhelmingly conclusive. Ritalin is a deadly poison that should be, under no circumstance, administered to a child or young adult.

The quick-fix mindset of modern-day carers (parents, teachers, doctors, child protection services, etc) absolves them

---

[63] www.en.wikipedia.org/wiki/Mick_Hucknall

[64] www.en.wikipedia.org/wiki/Fluoxetine

of the genuine responsibility of paying attention to the health, emotional and psychological needs of children. Although society has the right to prevent young people from dealing with drugs, it sees fit to prescribe mind-altering drugs of an extremely potent nature to children alleged to have ADHD.

Today's children are under huge pressure to conform to a military-style of education and upbringing. Yet, the essence of creativity and personal evolution is through nonconformity. When the dumbing down of children takes place through the introduction of mind-altering and physiological-damaging substances, they are being silenced. Furthermore, the new generation of humans, who are highly likely to be far more consciously evolved than any other past generations, are slowly being killed off.

Swine Flu: When Pigs Grew Wings

In the battle to have more control and power of the masses, corporations have used increasingly sophisticated strategies to gain the upper hand. The Swine Flu strategy goes back much further than people realise. In 1976, a US military recruit died from a flu that was speculated as possibly the 'swine flu' virus, a strain of virus from the 1918 'Spanish Flu' pandemic. (The Spanish Flu pandemic killed 50 to 100 million people, making it one of the most devastating natural disasters ever.)

In 1976, Donald Rumsfeld was the US Secretary of Defense to President Ford's administration and made swine flu an imminent threat. He lobbied for every man, woman and child to be vaccinated against swine flu, which resulted in vast quantities of drugs being produced. As a starter, it became policy that all soldiers would be vaccinated for swine flu. The results? Five hundred cases of *Gullian-Barre* paralysis and twenty-five deaths resulted in the military. *Guillain–Barré Syndrome is an acute inflammatory demyelinating polyneuropathy* (AIDP), a disorder affecting the peripheral nervous system.

In July 2009, government scientists were warning[65] of the impending 'Swine Flu' pandemic[66] caused by the H1N1 virus. They were advising their governments to arm themselves with vaccines to combat swine flu. Millions were spent on advertising on television, radio, printed press and numerous other forms of media warning the public of the effects of the viral infection. Massive orders for vaccines were placed with several large pharmaceutical drugs manufacturers.

On all fronts, the public were bombarded with the media campaign warning of the probability of a pandemic occurring. It was like watching the government getting on a war footing ready to defend its soil. On 1st July 2010, an official enquiry commissioned by the British government into the handling of swine flu led by Dame Diedre Hines, former Chief Medical Officer for Wales, made its findings public. In the period between September 2009 and March 2010, 457 people died from swine-flu related causes.

In the winter of 2008/9 approximately 3,700 more people than usual died due to winter-related deaths. The majority of the deaths were due to influenza-based conditions, such as pneumonia. This number has been increasing year on year. If that figure was extrapolated forward, no doubt it would be greater than 3,700 deaths in winter 2009/10. Consequently, the 457 deaths 'caused' by the H1N1 virus accounts for 1.2% of influenza-related diseases. This means that 98.8% of deaths from flu were NOT from swine flu!

Why all the fuss about swine flu? Were the public really in danger of catching this killer disease? Was swine flu real or was it imagined? Well, let the results bear out the facts or, at least, help readers to move in a direction towards reality. The British government spent £1.2 billion pounds on orders for swine flu vaccines in 2009/10. The pharmaceutical giant

---

65
www.bbc.co.uk/blogs/thereporters/ferguswalsh/2009/07/predictions_should_come_with_a_health_warning.html

66 *Pandemic* - a disease prevalent over a whole country or the world

GSK[67] (GlaxoSmithKline), the biggest supplier, turned over £883 million on their vaccine sales in that period.

The contracts between the British government and the pharmaceutical giants were inflexible. Therefore, any excess supply could not be returned to the corporations. Consequently, the British public were left with twenty-million vaccines that could not be used. Looks like the British taxpayer has been swindled by the swine flu merchants! Shockingly, government ministers were still adamant the correct cautionary measures were taken and, if it were to happen again, they would repeat such actions. The medical establishment need not have a grip on a nation's health. They will lose that influence when more people realise what miraculous self-healing powers they already possess.

---

[67] www.gsk.co.uk

Chapter 7: The Human Miracle

*"Sound is as important to
human life as water is."*

Water: Beyond Thirst

Humans are far more powerful than they have been led to believe. To understand the nature of this exquisite power, it is important to go back to the fundamentals of human nature. There are three vital elements that are critical to life - water, light and sound. In this book, the focus will be on water. It is said that a man can go without food for 30-40 days and still live, but would die without water for more than 3-5 days. Given that the human body is 70% water by volume and mass, it does not take a quantum physicist to figure out why this is so.

Earth is also composed of 70% water. If the moon has a tremendous effect on the bodies of water (tides), would it be such a leap of the faith to think the moon affects humans, too? Could that also explain why many women's menstrual cycles are affected by the lunar cycle? According to Konstantin Pavlidis, there is one fact about water that is less known by most people: humans are 99% water by molecular structure.

In other words, humans are primarily composed of H_2O, whilst the remaining 1% is made up of an array of all the other elements such as iron, phosphorus, potassium, etc. People are not so different to amoeba after all! The significance of this is beyond measure. By getting to grips with the true meaning of water to life, the first steps can be taken in understanding how powerful humans are. By taking appropriate actions, an individual's life and health states will improve, leaving little room for reliance on manufactured drugs.

What are the roles played by water in and on human life? Water is known as a 'universal solvent' because of its ability to dissolve numerous substances, including many of the vitamins, minerals and other chemicals key to good health. Water is also an important component of biochemical reactions that take place in the body. For the purposes of this book, attention will be paid to some of the functions of water that are less well known, yet are highly critical to human evolution. The next step is for readers to take the appropriate actions they feel is necessary to reclaim their own power.

Messages in Water

For thousands of years, spiritual teachers and healers have been using water as the basis of medicine in removing 'evil spirits' and bringing health back to the sick and frail. Until recently, little was known about the profound truth in these belief systems. With modern technology, it is possible to begin to see the tip of the iceberg regarding the significance of water. In natural conditions, water has specific structure and form.

This is seen when it is fast-frozen and observed under a powerful microscope. Water molecules take a crystalline shape. The beautiful shapes of the crystals can be seen on aeroplane windows in high altitudes or on windows of homes during snowfall. Each water molecule has its own peculiar shape. The geometric patterns and shapes of water were of particular interest to and studied extensively by Dr Masaru Emoto.

Emoto's experiments involve filling petri dishes with tap water and looking for crystal formation. Initially, he had little success. However, when he took naturally occurring water from numerous sources (rivers, lakes, dams, etc), the results were astounding. Each water crystal had its own unique form and shape. He exposed the water to classical music such as Beethoven's Pastoral Symphony and then to heavy metal music. The classical music led to a variety of crystalline symmetrical shapes being formed by the water molecules. The water exposed to violent heavy metal music led to malformed and fragmented shapes.

Emoto went onto exposing water to written words such as 'thank you' and 'fool'. It was discovered that words of gratitude formed hexagonal crystals, whilst 'fool' led to shapes similar to those of violent, heavy metal music. Water exposed to chanting and prayer also had well-formed crystalline shapes. This was irrespective of religion or system of faith. Emoto's most memorable experiments were when water was exposed to the words 'love and gratitude'.

The shapes of the crystals looked like a flower in full bloom. He also obtained water from different regions of the world for the experiments. Water from areas that were heavily polluted or congested were found to have little or no crystalline structure. Water exposed to heavy rock, sexually explicit or violent songs or any form of aggressive words either led to loss of shape or were distorted.

What creates such unique pattern formation? The answers come from basic physics. There are four important and relevant forces in nature - gravity, electromagnetic waves, strong and weak nuclear forces. The electromagnetic or EM waves are what people refer to as 'vibrations' or 'vibes'. Sound takes the form of an EM wave. Picture a boy throwing a pebble in the centre of a pond with the water as the 'medium'.

Ripples (the effect) of small waves will be created that reach out to the edge of the pond. Whenever a pebble is thrown by the boy (the source or cause) more ripples will result and disseminate throughout the pond (medium). When sound is created through singing (source), it will ripple out through the air (medium) and will affect all that it touches, including water molecules.

Each sound wave will have a particular vibration. That vibration will influence the likely shape and form of the water it comes into contact with. Some vibrations will have the effect of breaking up the structure of water, whilst other sounds will have the effect of building up structure. Whichever way it is viewed, certain vibrations are conducive for optimal states and others are not. The old paradigm is to focus attention on changing the effect or the symptom, however one must go to the cause or the source of the EM Waves. In this example, the cause is the boy throwing a pebble into the pond.

What are the sources of EM waves that affect people on a day-to-day basis? The answer is: there are many sources. In the case of an individual, the most important and powerful sources are: their thoughts, feelings, intentions and words. Other sources that interfere with a person's inner sources include the sounds they are exposed to - music, conversation, quality of language and how much power is placed on other people's feelings and 'silent' noises such as nature, traffic and subliminal messages.

Like sound, written words also have vibrations. The experiments that have been done on water illustrate this. These vibrations are created by the conscious intention of the writer. This is why in many healing traditions, such as Islamic medicine, charms and amulets are created to ward off illness and evil through the written word. As an eight year old child, I remember witnessing a priest writing on a piece of paper certain phrases from the Holy Koran and then placing that paper in a glass of water. That water was then given to the patient to drink over three days.

Sure enough, that person healed in less than three days. As already stated, sound can be destructive or constructive. Therefore, sound is as important to human life as water is. The illusionists know this and...now...so do you. The illusionists have infiltrated the majority of the commercial music business (as well as the movie industry). Much of the music that is commercially distributed with fanfare create harmonics and vibrations that have a destructive effect on water crystals. Consequently, listeners of such of music are affected negatively. Think of those people who are regular listeners of gangster rap, thrash metal and other such 'music'.

Does it matter if water has form or not? Yes...if one wishes to live a life with optimal health and vitality. When water is unstructured and deactivated, it is effectively sick or dead. It becomes a very poor carrier of vital energy and performs poorly in the carriage of nutrients and minerals in the human body. Therefore, the body becomes prone to disease and foreign invasion. This becomes evident when observing people who are prone to frequent illnesses.

What is the quality of the language they use? What kind of conversation do they have? Are they optimistic in their approach or are they lifelong doomsayers? What kind of noises predominate the environment they hang out in most? Here's the good news. Even when water is exposed to a negatively charged environment, it can be transformed by being placed in a healthier environment. This means that damaged water crystals can be restructured and reconfigured by exposure to sound healing, colour/light therapy and drinking structured, activated water.

Listening to music that is more in resonance with the frequency of the human body goes a long way to creating change, too. The spoken word has a very powerful affect on water, especially when done with love-based feelings and strong intention. According to the *HeartMath Institute*[68] in America, the heart has an electromagnetic field of the brain is 5,000 times more powerful than that of the brain. Thus, the true power to heal lies within each and every individual human through heart-based feelings, i.e. lovingness.

---

[68] www.heartmath.org

Memory in Water

Water molecules are simple compounds that have very complex configurations. Due to the net positive electrical charge on the hydrogen atoms and the net negative charge on the oxygen atoms, water molecules are highly attracted to each other. They are found in chain and cluster formations throughout the body. The more coherent an individual is, the greater the proportion of clusters present in their body.

Chains of water molecules are more predominant when individuals have a high degree of incoherence. The clusters may be of differing sizes and configurations. Each cluster is continuously gaining and losing individual water molecules. The bonding taking place between the hydrogen and the oxygen atoms is extremely fast at 200 *femtoseconds (1 femto-second* = 10^{-15} seconds). The bonding within water molecules are in a state of flux, which means that water clusters release individual molecules and gain new ones ad infinitum.

Why is this so important? Water molecules pick up the information created by every event they are exposed to, thereby affecting the structure of the water. Here is the most important part: the empty space inside cluster of water is where information is stored. Please reread this last statement to comprehend its importance. Water clusters are like miniature supercomputers that retain information in perpetuity. Given that human bodies are almost entirely composed of water, then it can be more easily understood that memory is not only stored in the brain, it is stored throughout the entire body. How amazing is that?

Memory and the mind is no longer the sole function of the brain but a function of the entire body. This brings a different slant to the saying 'mind-over-body'. It is more accurate to say 'mind-with-body'. The mind is not dominant over the physical body nor is the body dominant over the mind. They have never been separate but have always been as one. This means that the quality of the water people consume (drink and bathe in) is vital for both the mind and the body.

Finally, as there is a constant and rapid interchanging of water molecules within clusters, then memories and, moreover, the effect and influence of memories on a person can be also changed.

Re-membering

In December 2010, during a 'Life Encounter' course in Bali and Indonesia, I had the pleasure of receiving the best quality massages every evening. During such intense massages, the recipient experiences feelings of joy or even up-set. This is because the masseuse has 'unlocked' old memories that have been held in the molecular configuration of the body. This has important implications for behavioural therapies, such as treatment of emotional traumas, phobias, etc.

When a past trauma is present in a patient's conscious mind, the therapist may be able to manage the trauma at the level of the conscious mind. The more advanced therapists are able to deal with the memory at the subconscious mind. As memory is stored within water clusters of the body, unless the event is dealt with at the level of the body (i.e. the molecular level), then the likelihood of the patient re-membering the 'trauma' remains high.

An example of a body re-membering past memories is when an individual suppresses an early childhood trauma, such as sexual abuse, insofar as they forget the event ever took place. The subconscious mind has the ability to suppress a memory to protect the individual from potential mental or emotional breakdown. However, unless the trauma is dealt with directly, its effects will be felt by the 'victim' throughout their life without a clue why.

As the oldest child of my family on the maternal side, I received a huge deal of love and attention from my aunts and uncles. When I began to suffer from epileptic fits four or five times annually from the age of six months of age, they were horrified. It was only in recent years that I discovered the real reason why I suffered my first epileptic seizure. I was born in the northeast region of East Pakistan (now Bangladesh) in the town of Sylhet. Whilst my father was in England for most of my early years, my mother would take me to his village to visit his brothers and sisters.

At the age of six months, during the height of a hot Bengali summer, my mother took me to stay at the village. We were given a small room in the back of the house that neither had a window nor an outside door to allow ventilation. At midday, my mother popped out to get some food. The heat was so overbearing, it turned the room into a giant oven. That was when I experienced my first seizure. Then, as suddenly as it came in 1970, my epilepsy ceased after my last episode when I was eight in 1978.

Christmas of 2005 was a significant year for the bond between my mother and myself. Her lifelong dream was for me to take her on pilgrimage (*Haj*) to the cities of Makkah and Madina in Saudi Arabia. During our stay at Makkah, Islam's holiest city, we stayed at a four story budget hotel. The average temperature in Makkah was a soaring 40-45 degrees Celsius during the day and 25-32 degrees Celsius during the night. Therefore, having an air-conditioned room was crucial for the preservation of our lives.

One very hot afternoon, on my way out of the hotel, I was taking the air-conditioned lift from our third-floor room down to the ground-floor. The lift was so small that it could only carry two average-sized people at a time. As it descended with me as the sole occupier, it shuddered to a halt between the second and third floor. The air conditioning also stopped working, making the temperature inside the lift to equalise with the outside temperature and then to soar even higher.

No matter how much I shouted for help and rang the alarm, there was no help. My body collapsed in a heap as I was gulping for what remaining air was left. After, what felt like an eternity, the lift started to descend again allowing me to crawl out. Looking back at it now, I am amazed how panic-stricken I was, especially considering I had never experienced claustrophobia before that event. The three years after returning from the pilgrimage, I re-experienced the sense of collapsing on several occasions including during my visit to Sierra Leone in 2008, during several journeys on the London underground system and even in a public bathroom at a motorway service station. The childhood memory of being trapped in an oven had truly been retained in my body's memory.

I did try several methods to eliminate/overcome my phobia of tight, overheated spaces with little or zero success. All the methods involved dealing with the issue at a mental or emotional level. It was only when I began to investigate the extent to which my memory was stored in my body that I began to experience a positive outcome. The real healing took place during the two-week Life Encounter course in Bali, which helped me to identify the cause of my sufferings and then to dissolve the cause permanently.

Water equals Life

Water is an excellent carrier and transmitter of information. For example, each individual who enters a local (municipal) swimming pool leaves their information in the water and takes new information from the water into their body memory. As the water in swimming baths are rarely re-placed, the number of people sharing information becomes astronomical. Not only does the human body exchange information, it also absorbs some of that water.

How much information can be exchanged during sixty minutes of swimming? I cannot give an exact figure, but need-less to say, it would certainly be sufficient in volume to make a discernible difference over time. Water is a polar molecule, which means that it has a slightly negative charge on the oxygen atom and a slightly positive charge on the hydrogen atoms. The substance of life is a stabilising force for DNA[69] as well as being the ideal medium for DNA to operate in. Without

---

[69] Levitt and Miriam Hirshberg

water, proteins and DNA cannot form the shapes most people are familiar with. Many of the bodily functions are dependent on gene expression. Lack of water will lead to a breakdown of these functions, eventually followed by death. It is not just about the level of hydration that is important. The quality of water will make all the difference to the efficiency and effectiveness of gene activity.

2.6 billion people[70] (40% of the world) are estimated to have no access to clean water. Approximately 1.8 million children die every year due to diarrhoea, which can be prevented by using safe water[71]. Whilst such people can 'blame' Mother Nature for the lack of access to clean water, people in developed countries are having their water destroyed both through industrialisation and through sabotage, such as fluoridation and chlorination of water. Make no mistake, fluoridation and chlorination is not what they are made out to be. What the illusionists will have people believe about these chemicals is far from the reality of the situation. The reality of these chemicals will be revealed shortly.

The Industrialisation of Water

Since the beginning of the Industrial Revolution, the public have been moving away from nature to live in towns and cities where natural water is scarce. Water has to be transported across large distances from rivers, dams and lakes to people's homes. The industrialisation of water in Victorian London meant that many thousands of miles of pipes were laid so that residents in cities like London could access the water.

In nature, water does not move in straight lines but flows through curves, down slopes and in spirals. Water in nature is a living conscious entity and has structure, leading to numerous health benefits. As it has consciousness, it picks up information on its way through the planet. When water travels

---

[70] Estimated by the World Health Organisation (WHO)

[71] According World Health Organisation (WHO)

through piping systems, it flows through straight lines, tight bends and sharp angles and, thus, degrades the structure of the water.

Furthermore, as water travels through homes and neighbourhoods, it picks up information pollution through people's emotions, anger, malice and hatred. Most of the information it receives is negative. The recycling of water after domestic use and the industrial processes (includes the addition of numerous chemicals, hormones and toxins) destroys the potency of water even further. Consequently, the recycled water running through people's taps, for all practical purposes, is dead.

Tap water can only provide optimal benefits once the plethora of toxins have been either deactivated or removed and the water has been activated. One controversial subject that has left millions confused is the question of whether there are any health benefits to the fluoridation of water. How does fluoride really affect humans? Does it really have the benefits that British and American dentists are required by their professional body to propagate?

Fluoridation: Poisoning the Masses

My very first experience of visiting a dental surgery was when I as at Prince Albert Infant and Junior School in Birmingham. I had heard about the horror stories of the dentist's drill and was terrified about my encounter. Luckily for me, my teeth were healthy that day! While I was sitting in the waiting room, I was struck by the many bright, colourful wall posters propagating an 'important' theme. The message was the same. It was very important that teeth were brushed regularly and the enamel should be kept strong by using fluoride toothpaste.

The water company that supplied Birmingham, Severn Trent Water, bought into this belief hook, line and sinker. To this day, the water supply in this region has the highest content of fluoride in the whole of the United Kingdom. On the face of it, fluoridation of water and toothpastes appears to be harmless. Not true. Given its level of toxicity, its benefits are mere illusions. Fluoride in certain dosages is known to be lethal. Smaller quantities are toxic for animals as well as humans. The authorities have known this for decades.

During questioning over war crimes at the Nuremberg Trials, Nazi officials admitting adding fluoride to the prisoner's water in the concentration camps of Auschwitz. They were added to modify the moods of the prisoners and to keep them docile and inhibit them from questioning authority. This strategy had also been deployed in the Soviet Gulags in Siberia. Fluorides are classed as protoplasmic[72] poisons, which is the reason they are used in rat poisons. They kill off the rat at the deepest cellular level. Fluorides are a key component of insecticides.

Since the 1950s, with the endorsement of the American Dental Association, fluoride has been a key component of toothpaste for strengthening teeth[73]. Subsequent studies into the effects of fluoride prove otherwise. The 1984 issue of Clinical Toxicology of Commercial Products lists fluoride as more poisonous than lead and just slightly less poisonous than arsenic. The US *Centre for Disease Control* (CDC) and *The Safe Water Foundation* estimate 30,000 to 50,000 excess deaths each year in areas where there is 1 ppm (parts per million) in the drinking water, the normal added amount.

---

[72] Protoplasm' is the colorless material comprising the living part of a cell, including the cytoplasm, nucleus, and other organelles.

[73] www.ada.org/fluoride.aspx

Fluoride interacts with the bonds that maintain the normal shape of proteins. With distorted protein, the immune system attacks its own protein, the body's own tissue. Fluoride (at 1 ppm) in drinking water:

- Damages the immune system by inhibiting the migration rate of white blood cells to infected areas;
- Interferes with phagocytosis (the destruction of bacteria and other foreign agents by white blood cells); and
- Induces the release of superoxide free radicals in resting white blood cells.

The addition of fluoride also accelerates the ageing process. This acceleration occurs at the biochemical level by:

- Enzyme inhibition
- Collagen breakdown
- Genetic damage
- Disruption of the immune system

Fluoride damages enzymes which results in a wide range of chronic diseases. Fluoride as low as 1 ppm causes the breakdown of collagen, the most abundant of the body's protein at 30%. It also leads to the irregular formation of collagen which serves as a major structural component of skin, ligaments, tendons, muscles, cartilage, bones and teeth. Fluoride confuses the immune system and causes it to attack the body's own tissues and increases the tumour growth in cancer-prone patients.

Fluoride also depresses thyroid activity. Fluoride ingestion from mouth washes is extremely hazardous to biological development, life span and general health. The content of fluoride in a family sized toothpaste is enough to kill a 25 pound (12Kg) child. The side effects of drinking one to two pints of municipally fluoridated water daily includes nausea, bloody vomit, faintness, stomach cramps, tremors, constipation, aching bones, stiffness, skin rash, weight loss, and brown or black discoloration of the teeth[74].

There are a vast number of resources that are available on the internet and in books about the effects of chlorine that is highly recommended. One such book is 'The Fluoride Deception' by Christopher Bryson, whilst there are numerous YouTube videos on the effects of fluoride. However, readers are recommended to use caution and discernment when surmising one source or another as the truth.

Fluoride and Intelligence Levels

Studies show a link between high-fluoride (5 ppm) water to reduced intelligence (IQ) in children. A study of a group of Mexican children considered factors affecting IQ, including parent's education, their income and childhood exposure to lead. The psychologists used for the study were blind folded, i.e. they were unaware of which children were exposed to high fluoridation and which were exposed to 'normal' quantities. The study concluded:

"Fluoride and arsenic in drinking water have a potential neurotoxic effect in children. It is urgent that public health measures to reduce exposure levels be implemented. Millions of people around the world are exposed to these pollutants and are, therefore, potentially at risk for negative impact on intelligence. This risk may be increased where other factors affecting central nervous system development, such as malnutrition and poverty, are also present. The risk is particularly acute for children, whose brains are particularly sensitive to environmental toxins. Furthermore, it would be advisable to re-examine the benefits of fluoride given the documented health risks."

---

[74] *The United States Pharmacopoeia*

When children ingest an excessive quantity of fluoride, they are at risk of developing a condition known as 'dental fluorosis'. In its milder form, dental fluorosis produces cloudy spots and streaks on the teeth. In its advanced form, fluorosis can weaken the enamel and cause it to crumble and break. Fluoride causes these conditions by accumulating within the tooth and interfering with the tooth's normal mineralization process. By interfering with tooth mineralization, dental fluorosis represents a toxic effect of fluoride, and thereby raises the larger question of what other (less visible) tissues in the body may be similarly affected.

In 2007, the CDC released the latest national survey data on the rate of dental fluorosis amongst US teenagers. The survey, conducted between 1999 and 2004 by CDC's *National Health and Nutrition Examination Survey* (NHANES), found that 41% of 12-15 year olds, and 36% of 16-19 year olds, have dental fluorosis. In other words, over one in three American teenagers displayed a visible sign of fluoride overexposure. This is the highest national rate of fluorosis ever recorded in the US, far higher than the 1-10% range found in the 1940s, and considerably higher than the 23% found to be affected in the 1980s.

Not only has the prevalence of fluorosis increased, but its severity has increased as well. Whereas 1.4% of children had moderate or severe fluorosis in the 1980s, about 3.5% of children have it today, representing a doubling of fluorosis. Both moderate and severe fluorosis can lead to very disfiguring conditions that may embarrass and cause psychological stress to a child, particularly if present on the front teeth.

According to the National Research Council, severe fluorosis may also cause adverse effects on a child's health by weakening the protective function of the tooth's enamel. However, despite the fact that CDC is now on record stating fluoride's benefits are primarily topical, a study published in the *Journal of Public Health Dentistry* reports that most practicing dentists and dental hygienists are not yet aware of this development.

According to the study, which surveyed dentists and dental hygienists, only a small minority of dental professionals are aware of the new research. In Indiana (USA), for example, only 25% of surveyed dentists correctly identified the topical effect of fluoride, while in Illinois (USA), the figure was just 14%. According to the authors:

"Our main findings are that in 2005, four years following the release of the CDC's sentinel recommendations, a considerable proportion of dental professionals in Indiana still did not understand fluoride's predominant mode of action."

Not only were the dentists behind in their knowledge of fluoride research, but the survey also found they did not even know basic information about fluoride, such as how much fluoride is in toothpaste or high-fluoride gels. As noted by the authors:

"Another important finding was the inability of respondents to correctly identify the concentration of commonly used fluoride products."

This raises the question: if, after sixty years of water fluoridation, most dentists still do not know how fluoride works or how much fluoride is in the products they prescribe, what else do they not know? Do they know how fluoride affects other tissues in the body besides the teeth?

Chlorination: Taking Lies to Another Level

One of the most baffling illusions that I first identified as a teen was the use of chlorine in water. My basic history lesson taught me about the use of chlorine gas in war. It was first used as a chemical weapon at Ypres, France in 1915 during the First World War. It was responsible for killing thousands of soldiers. When the war was over, the use of chlorine was diverted to poisoning 'germs' in drinking water. All water supplies throughout the USA and UK were chlorinated.

Chlorine was supposed to kill bacteria and other pathogens in the drinking water. However 80-90% of bacteria in the environment and within human bodies are beneficial. Over the course of human existence, both humans and bacteria have evolved together to live symbiotically, i.e. they are mutually beneficial. The chlorine destroys all the bacteria and does not disappear itself. It is known to corrode the water pipes leaving one wondering if it can corrode metal, to what extent would it damage people's digestive tracts and arterial walls? The cause of atherosclerosis and resulting heart attacks and strokes is none other than the forever present chlorine in drinking water[75].

According to a study published in the *Journal of the National Cancer Institute, "Long-term drinking of chlorinated water appears to increase a person's risk of developing bladder cancer as much as 80%,"*. In the US alone, 45,0000 people are diagnosed with bladder cancer every year[76]. Scientists suspect that the actual cause of the bladder cancers is a group of chemicals that form as result of reactions between the chlorine and natural substances and pollutants in the water such as organic matter that include algae, vegetation, leaves and twigs. These byproducts are considered as 'mutagenic' and/or 'carcinogenic'.

---

[75] Science News, Vol. 130

[76] St. Paul Dispatch & Pioneer Press, December 17, 1987

"Although concentrations of these carcinogens are low...it is precisely these low levels which cancer scientists believe are responsible for the majority of human cancers in the United States."[77]

According to Dr J.M. Price (MD), the risk of cancer is 93% higher for people drinking chlorinated water than for people who drink non-chlorinated water. So far, drinking water has only been considered. What of chlorine in swimming pools and showers? The largest organ of a human is the skin. Its functions includes excretion of water and salts (sweat) and absorption, too. Thus, absorption of chlorine through the skin is high. Readers may have noticed that after using a swimming pool the skin smells of chlorine for many hours afterwards. Is this a coincidence? I do not think so.

"Studies indicate the suspect chemicals can also be inhaled and absorbed through the skin during showering and bathing."[78]

A long hot shower can also be very risky. The toxic chemicals are inhaled in large doses. The chlorine and some of its byproducts evaporate out of the water to be taken in by the lungs.

"House holders can receive 6 to 100 times more of the chemical by breathing the air around showers and bath than they would by drinking the water."[79]

Showering is suspected as the primary cause of elevated levels of chloroform in nearly every home due to the chlorine in the water.[80] Chloroform is potentially fatal if

---

[77] Report Issued By *The Environmental Defense Fund*

[78] *New Scientist,18 September 1986*

[79] Black, B. *Chlorine and Your Shower*

[80] Brown, H. PhD *American Journal of Public Health*

swallowed, inhaled or absorbed through the skin. Children exposed to large amounts of chlorine especially in their early years have the increased risk of developing upper respiratory infections as well as asthma. These risks apply to individuals who work in an environment where chlorine is present, such as swimming baths. It is vital that in such situations, there is plenty of ventilation.

There are several viable alternatives to the use of chlorine, particularly in drinking water and swimming pools. Due to the anaerobic nature of many of the waterborne bacteria, i.e. they breathe without oxygen, such bacteria die when they are exposed to oxygen. Adding ozone gas (ozonating) water does precisely that. A molecule of ozone is composed of three atoms of oxygen, which is an odourless, colourless gas and is unstable. Consequently, it is a very reactive agent and oxidises iron, manganese and sulphur rapidly.

As it is so unstable, ozone degrades within a few seconds up to thirty minutes. It certainly is more effective at destroying viruses and bacteria than chlorine without the harmful effects associated with chlorine. Ozonating water is as viable for drinking water as it is for swimming pools. A further natural alternative is sea salts for swimming pools. Oh, of course! If water can be 'cleaned' in nature through the use of salt, maybe it is not such a bad idea using it in swimming pools. The challenge for the illusionists is that there are little known harmful effects in swimming in sea water. Doh!

The Great Water Crisis

By the late 1980s, I had seen so much negative news around the subject of water that I realised that Earth's most abundant substance would soon be the most scarce. Why? Primarily through the exploitation and poor management of natural resources. Although the planet is abundant in water, only 1% is fresh water. How effective have people been in managing this minute amount? One of the great tragedies in nature is the presence of arsenic, a deadly poison, on the Earth's crust. Much of this is found in deeper levels of groundwater. Approximately seventy countries of the world are affected by the arsenic. The region most affected has been West and East Bengal (Bangladesh). Before the 1970s, Bangladesh had the highest infant mortality rate in the world due to the arsenic in the water. Subsequently, tube wells were built, which cut that number by half. Now, however, 20% of the tubes are contaminated by the arsenic.

884 million people in the world do not have access to safe water, which is approximately one in eight of the world's population. 2.6 billion of the world's population do not have access to adequate sanitation, which is 38% of the world's population. Finally, 1.4 million children die every year from diarrhea caused by unclean water and poor sanitation. [81] However, when looking at the big picture, 29,000 children die every day due to other preventable diseases. That is one child death every three seconds. Tick. Tock. Tick. Tock. Tick. Tock.

When will people wake up? If mankind truly wishes to see a change in these figures, people must begin to start the process of getting to know the most vital element to their universe - themselves. As humans are 99% water, surely they need to be extraordinarily mindful of their own water intake.

---

[81] Source: www.wateraid.org

Where does one start to begin the transformation for their body through the use of water? There are several key guidelines in determining the quality of water you consume:

1. Drink water that is activated, i.e. either from natural sources or activated through specially designed devices that can be purchased.
2. Drink water with low *Total Dissolved Solids* (TDS).
3. Drink water that is contained in glass vessels. Plastic bottles have a tendency to leach dangerous hydrocarbons into the water, especially when they have been stored above 25C (77F).
4. Drink water in a calm, peaceful and loving manner.
5. If there is little choice but to use municipal tap water, ensure you get yourself a water filter jug as a minimum.

These are just the very basic guidelines for the consumption of water. Nonetheless, do not believe a word I say. There is so much research available about water that it is difficult to avoid getting sound advice. Once the nature of water as part of life is understood and relevant adaptations are made to lifestyle, then it is highly recommended to address the issues of the second most important area of consumption - the food people eat.

Chapter 8: Playing God

"The line between today's politics and profits is not blurred. There is no line."

Food: the Desperate Race for Mass Control

Whilst the intake of good quality water is vital to human existence, attention needs to be paid to the quality of food eaten, especially as consumption is unnecessarily excessive today. It is another highly important area that some of the most despicable illusionists have targeted. During its heyday, the German industrial giant, IG Farben, was the world's fourth largest company after General Motors, US Steel and Standard Oil. IG Farben worked closely with the Nazis during the planning stages of the invasion of Czechoslovakia and Poland. They were the single largest sponsor of Adolf Hitler's Nazi party and were the greatest profiteers when the Nazi's got into power.

The web of corporations and illusionists working in collusion with the Nazis before the war is nothing short of mind-boggling. In 1941, there was an investigation into the cartel agreements between J.D. Rockefeller's Standard Oil and IG Farben, but it was later dropped as industrial attention was required for the 'war effort'. During the 'IG Farben Trials', which were part of the Nuremburg Trials (1947-48), thirteen of its directors were convicted and imprisoned for between one and eight years for their part in World War II.

IG Farben held the patent for the gas, Zyklon B, and were involved in the production of this toxic gas used in the gas chambers to murder thousands of prisoners. They were also the producers of synthetic oil and explosives used in the war. Furthermore, at their peak, IG Farben used up to 83,000 slave workers in their factories, including their factory in Auschwitz built by Fritz ter Meer. After the trials, IG Farben was split up into smaller companies of which the ones that survived in include Bayer, Hoescht and BASF.

However, IG Farben was not dissolved until 2003. What is most interesting is how individual directors of IG Farben had direct associations with respected US household names such as the Ford Motor Company, Bank of Manhattan, the Federal Reserve, Bank of New York and Standard Oil. One of the board members of IG Farben, Fritz ter Meer, had a far-reaching affect after the Nuremburg Trials. He was heavily involved in the brutalities that took place in the concentration camps which included him building the Monowitz concentration camp.

Having had his sentence quashed from seven years to only two, Fritz Ter Meer[82] (1884-1967), was reinstated as a member on the board of Bayer AG. During the Nuremberg Trials, he commented:

"Forced labour did not inflict any remarkable injury, pain or suffering on the detainees, particularly since the alternative for these workers would have been death."

Ter Meer's natural flair for creativity led to him being appointed as one of the designers and chief architects of *Codex Alimentarius* (Codex) which is Latin for 'Food Code'. Why would a convicted war criminal suddenly be interested in the health and safety of the masses through food? Simple. He who controls food, controls the world! Codex was created by the United Nations as a trade commission installing the *Food and Agricultural Organisation* (FAO) and the World Health Organisation (WHO) to oversee the new organisation.

The fact that it is a **trade** commission makes it clear that Codex is about creating and protecting profits. In 1962, they announced the total global implementation of Codex by December 31st 2009. Numerous commissions (27 committees)

---

[82] www.en.wikipedia.org/wiki/Fritz_ter_Meer

were set up to manage the change with over 4,000 regulations and guidelines being created. These guidelines oversee everything that humans consume with the exception of pharmaceutical drugs, which is overseen by the FDA.

When the WTO was formed in 1995, it accepted Codex and it aimed to harmonise member states with the rules laid down by Codex. If there is a dispute between two member states regarding food, the case is automatically won by the member who has accepted Codex rules, regardless of the merit of the case. Consequently, every country in the world is actively seeking to become Codex-compliant. Codex only serves the interests of corporate interests with the consumer being least served.

Codex operates under the Napoleonic Code law system, which means that anything that is NOT permitted is forbidden. Naturally occurring herbal remedies or other medicinal plants or any other food product that has not been overseen by Codex are considered illegal. One of the two committees that *Codex Alimentarius Commission* (CAC) has set up is called *Codex Committee on Nutrition and Foods for Special Dietary Uses* (CCNFSDU), which is headed by Dr Rolf Grossklaus. He is on record stating:

"Nutrition is not relevant to health."

In 1994, Dr Grossklaus declared nutrients to be toxins! He followed this up by initiating the use of Risk Assessment (toxicology) to prevent nutrients from having any impact on those taking supplements. This is because, as they are considered poisons, the public have to be protected from them through 'risk assessment'. This is done by testing the toxin on animals with an increasing dosage so that 50% of the animals are killed. This is known as the LD_{50} test ('LD' is short for 'lethal dosage'). They extrapolate what the LD_{50} will be for a human being.

Micro-dosages are given to animals with increasing concentration until the maximum upper limit is reached **before a discernible impact** is shown. This dosage is divided by 100 which gives us the recommended safety limit, i.e. the dosage (1/100th) is scientifically determined to have zero effect on a human being. Under other Codex rules, every cow on the planet must be treated with Monsanto's *recombinant Bovine Growth Hormone* ('rBGH'). There are serious questions linking rBGH to cancer and udder infections. The infections are treated with antibiotics which are thought to directly affect humans through the mixture of milk and pus in the milk! Every animal that is eaten (bird, fish, mammal) must be treated with sub-clinical antibiotics and exogenous growth hormones.

All foods must be irradiated unless it is eaten locally and raw, including organic food. The standards for organic farming are very low. Organic farmers are allowed to use hormones, antibiotics, etc but then can reclassify the animals as 'organic' for the marketplace. Paradoxically, Codex sets incredibly high limits for the dangerous industrial chemicals that the public can have in their foods. For example, the limits set by Codex for the presence of arsenic in virgin olive oil is 0.1mg per Kg[83]. Yet, the World Health Organisation set the upper limit at 0.01mg per Kg!

In May 1995, the international community composed of 176 countries, including the USA and the European Union, decided to take action on 'Persistent Organic Pollutants' (POPS). These are twelve chemicals that are deemed to be so bad that everybody agreed that they had to be banned world-wide. Nine of the twelve are pesticides. Since then, Codex has brought back seven of these nine forbidden POPS. Border control has no power to prevent the importation of such contaminated food as this is considered as a trade violation.

---

[83] www.codexalimentarius.net/web/standard_list.do?lang=en

Codex themselves estimate projections[84] of a minimum of three billion deaths from just the vitamin and mineral guidelines alone. One billion of these will be from simple starvation alone. Two billion will die from preventable diseases through under-nutrition, including cancer, cardiovascular disease, diabetes and many other diseases.

The Genetic Modification of Food

The subject of genetically modified (GM) food or Genetically Modified Organism (GMO) has been the centre of controversy in the first decade of the twenty-first century. The first company to commercialise genetic-engineering (GE) was Genentech[85] when they created a new strain of E. Coli to produce insulin in 1978. Although it is easy to see the numerous benefits of GM plants, it is still an area shrouded in mystery, deceit and misinformation.

The five key areas of political controversy related to genetically engineered food are food safety, the effect on natural ecosystems, gene flow into non-GE crops, moral/religious concerns and corporate control of the food supply. Whilst European producers agreed to remove GM ingredients from their products, GM crops are not even labeled in the USA. In the USA, it is forbidden by law to label food as 'free from GMO' or 'containing GMO' - a law enacted under the auspices of George H.W. Bush.

As the USA has a virtual monopoly on GM seeds, the GMO industry is treated as a national issue equivalent to National Security by the US government. That is why they apply tremendous pressure on the EU and other nation states to accept GM crops. According to a CBS/New York Times poll carried out in May 11th 2008, 53%[86] of Americans said they

---

[84] *'Diet, Nutrition and the Prevention of Chronic Diseases'*, a report of joint WHO/FAO Expert Consultation

[85] www.gene.com

[86] www.cbsnews.com/stories/2008/05/11/eveningnews/main4086518.shtml

would not eat products that contained GMO. Yet, 90% of all US soybean crop are genetically modified.

In 2007, 56% of the world's soybean crop was genetically modified[87]. This crop is primarily used as feed for livestock (poultry, swine, and cattle). The main GM crops produced in North America are soy (91%), corn (85%), cotton (88%) and canola[88] (80-85%). All four are used as vegetable oils. The largest share of the GMO crops planted globally is owned by the USA corporation Monsanto[89]. Its Indian subsidiary, Mahyco[90], developed Bt[91] Brinjal (aubergine) and claims it is resistant to natural pests. However, huge controversy was aroused in 2010 and production was brought to a halt on the grounds of food safety[92]. On the subject of GMO, the FDA appear to be applying double standards. On one hand, they say that:

"...the agency (FDA) is not aware of any information showing that foods derived by these new methods (GM) differ from other foods in any meaningful or uniform way."

Based on this testament, they decided no testing was necessary. These assumptions are used to turn a blind eye to GM crops without testing them. In fact, they are completely satisfied with food producers selling their products with NO FDA approval! Leaked FDA documents state that FDA scientists are concerned about GMO creating nutritional problems, new diseases, allergens and toxins. Despite the

---

[87] www.gmo-compass.org/eng/grocery_shopping/crops/19.genetically_modified_soybean.html

[88] Canola is the product from rapeseed.

[89] www.monsanto.com

[90] www.mahyco.com

[91] Bt is the abbreviation for Bacillus thuringiensis, which is a spore-forming bacterium that produces crystal proteins that are toxic to many species of insects.

[92] www.news.bbc.co.uk/1/hi/8506047.stm

pleadings of scientists to the senior managerial team, they have been systematically ignored.

The FDA policy documents were effectively political documents with no scientific evidence or results being mentioned. The Head of Policy, Michael Taylor, overturned the policy proposals presented by the scientists. Interestingly, Taylor is Monsanto's former attorney who later got promoted to the role of Vice-president. In laboratory tests and non-laboratory tests alike where rodents are given a choice between GM crops (e.g. corn) and naturally seeded crops of the same variety, the GM crops are untouched whilst the natural food is always eaten.

When rats were force-fed GM food, several developed stomach lesions whilst others died within two weeks. Even though scientific tests have been carried out that demonstrate the damage done to rats using GM crop, the entire subject is a political hot potato. Anyone caught whistle-blowing has had their credibility devastated and lost their jobs instantly such as eminent scientist, Dr Arpad Pusztai of the Rowlett Research Institute[93].

GM crops do not undergo the thorough testing that other synthetically manufactured products are required to undergo. The tests are limited to one or two nutrients. Currently, there are far too few published results that identify any direct effects of GM food on humans. How do they affect human bodies? How do they affect people's genetic makeup? From the tests done in his esteemed labs in San Diego, immunologist Professor David Schubert[94] of Salk Institute, says GM soy produce a natural insecticide, *rotenone*, which may be responsible for causing Parkinson's Disease in humans.

Schubert has also criticised the unnecessary genetic alteration of numerous crops, including Bt Brinjal. Brinjal is

---

[93] www.abdn.ac.uk/rowett

[94] www.salk.edu/faculty/schubert.html

not under threat by insect infestation nor poses a threat to native plants in the environment. It will become increasingly more expensive to use Bt Brinjal and it will lead to social and political dependence on corporations. Most worryingly, Bt Brinjal poses a serious health risk to those eating it, including increases in allergic reactions to the crop[95].

In fact, hundreds of farmers in India who have been exposed to Bt cotton by simply touching the plant have been reporting allergic reactions. Bt has properties of known allergens and causes sneezing, runny nose, itchiness, red eyes, fever as well as eruptions and discolouration all over the body. Even Monsanto's tests have shown that Bt corn damages test animals. Rats that ate Bt corn suffered a variety of conditions, including diabetes, liver and kidney toxicity, high blood sugar, anaemia, high blood pressure, allergies and infections.

According to reports, entire shepherd communities have endured the deaths of approximately 25% of their flock of sheep[96]. In other cases, animals as large as buffaloes have been reported to have died within days of grazing on cotton. Not only have livestock been killed by GM crops, but so have humans. Having been enticed by the promise of untold riches by the producers of GM seeds, Indian farmers unwittingly took out vast sums of loans to invest in their future wealth. Once they realised it was going to be near impossible to repay their debts, approximately 125,000 farmers committed suicide. [97]

Another important observation are the results of using Monsanto's *Roundup* herbicide. Adjunct professor in the Division of Plant Sciences at the University of Missouri authored five papers in October 2009 in *The European Journal of Agronomy*. Since 1997, he has been studying the

---

[95] www.gmwatch.org/latest-listing/1-news-items/11871-david-schubert-on-bt-brinjal

[96] www.i-sis.org.uk/MDSGBTC.php

[97]
www.dailymail.co.uk/news/worldnews/article-1082559/The-GM-genocide-Thousands-Indian-Farmers-committing-suicide-using-genetically-modified-crops.html

effects of glyphosphate, which is the main ingredient in Roundup. Microorganisms were seen to be colonising the roots of soybean roots that had been subjected to Roundup. This led to a root fungi problem and led to sudden death syndrome[98].

This herbicide is creating toxicity in the soil and killing off important bacteria that are vital to the health of plants. The entire farming system is under threat from the increasing concentration of weed-killers being used year on year. There is also the distinct possibility that the glyphosphates enter the water table and into streams and rivers. Although viewed as low risk to humans, they do inhibit certain enzymes in animals. The affect on humans begins to get pretty serious when combined with certain other chemicals[99]. These include skin irritations, respiratory distress, impaired consciousness, pulmonary oedema, shock, arrhythmias, renal failure requiring haemodialysis, metabolic acidosis and mild conjunctivitis.

A further concern about GM food is that the DNA of products do not get destroyed by the digestive process. In fact, tests on volunteers eating soybean products have been found to have GM food DNA integrated into the gut bacteria of the volunteer. Until there are long-term definitive studies with large enough samples, it will be difficult to conclusively prove how GMO affects human DNA. However, waiting around to see how multiple thousands of people react through their physiology is a step too far. The illusionists do not care for the health and wellbeing of people. The best ways to deal with them are to NOT eat GM foods. To reduce or eliminate GM foods from your diet:

1.   Start buying organic foods and/or grow your own food.
2.   Buy products labeled 'non-GMO'.

98

www.non-gmoreport.com/articles/jan10/scientists_find_negative_impacts_of_GM_crops.php

99 www.ncbi.nlm.nih.gov/pubmed/15862083

3. Avoid 'At Risk' items (soy, cotton, corn and canola).

If a large enough group of people refuse to buy GMO foods, then retailers will withdraw such food from their shelves. In this case, the customer truly is still king!

Microwaving Food: Distorting the Body Balance

Food is far less important than water as a prerequisite for life. For millennia, food consumption have become a socialising process where a family or tribe would gather to celebrate life through wonderfully prepared food. As humans have advanced and become more 'civilised', this act of celebration has been gradually eroded. The act of eating food has become more of a conditioned response like the 'Pavlov's Dog Effect' whereby, the moment lunch hour strikes, humans psychologically and physiologically prepare for the meal by salivating.

Eating food, particularly in developed countries, has taken on an addictive nature where far more food is consumed than is required energetically by the body. Consequently, obesity along with the dieting industry has been one of the fastest growth areas across the world. So now, not only do people eat too much, they eat too much of the foods that are empty of nutrition and vitality AND they prepare them in a manner that is detrimental to their physical condition.

To fill their insatiable appetites, humans have been conditioned into resorting to quicker and cheaper methods of consuming food. The proliferation of fast-food restaurant chains and TV dinners are testimony to the despondency towards food. In the rushed twenty-first century lifestyles, one of the most used devices to help cram more into their 24-hours is the microwave oven.

There is no doubt that a microwave oven saves significant amounts of time in food preparation, especially if it is a ready-made frozen meal overloaded with e-numbers (additives and preservatives) to keep the food lasting much longer than nature intended. After all, why bother having a freshly cooked gourmet meal that may take 60-90 minutes to prepare when a frozen meal can be thrown into the microwave and in 7 minutes...ping!

"Honey, dinner's ready!"

There is a tradeoff between cooking modalities and the state of human health. Microwaves are one of the greatest sources of introducing free-radicals into the body. A free radical is an uncharged molecule with an electron looking for another electron to pair up with. It is like the ball in a pinball machine that has been fired off with a bang, desperately trying to find somewhere to settle. The internal machinations of the human body become unsettled whilst the immune system tries urgently to 'knock out' the abundant supply of free radicals present in the microwaved food. Using a microwave is a sure-fire way to create severe imbalances in the evolution of an individual human.

Aspartame: the Sweet Lie

A consequence of eating too much food without a proportionate burning of the calories is obesity. One of the biggest growth industries since the 1980s to gain from the human desire to overeat is the multibillion dollar diet industry. Many people have a genuine concern about managing their weight and appearance. Unfortunately, all rationality seems to go out of the window in a desperate attempt to lose weight in weeks and months that they originally gained over many years. Corporations know this and have exploited the vulnerability of dieters.

One such method of exploitation has been through one of the deadliest products to be developed in 1965, *Aspartame*. It is now synonymous with sugar and is widely accepted by the masses. This is an artificial sweetener that is viewed as an alternative to sugar, is made by the Monsanto Corporation and is marketed under the brand of 'NutraSweet', amongst other names. Aspartame is two hundred times sweeter than sugar and is often found in 'diet' products.

It is a synthetic drug that dupes the brain into thinking that the food being eaten is sweet. For those looking to lose weight using aspartame, there is a double whammy. First, it increases cravings for carbohydrates and, second, it is poisonous to the human body. With the high temperatures of the stomach, aspartame breaks down into three toxins: aspartic acid (40%), phenylalanine (50%) and methanol (10%).

The aspartic acid is an 'excitotoxin' in the brain and creates such a high level of stimulation of the neurons (nerve cells) that the nerve cells die. Methanol (wood alcohol) is considered as a severe metabolic poison and narcotic. It quickly breaks down into formaldehyde which is a preservative that is used in biology labs. It is a derivative of benzene, a known carcinogen, i.e. causes cancer. According to the FDA's own data, aspartame is the common denominator for over 92 different health symptoms, including memory loss, seizures, vision loss, coma and cancer.

It is also known to worsen conditions such as fibromyalgia, MS, lupus, ADD, diabetes, Alzheimer's, etc. Consumers of aspartame may wish to consider moving on to an aspartame detoxification programme. Aspartame can be replaced by natural alternatives such as honey, fruit sugars or 'stevia'[100]. Originally aspartame was rejected for approval by the FDA. In 1985, the CEO of Searle Laboratories (manufacturers of Aspartame, which was later taken over by Monsanto), Donald Rumsfeld, was on President Ronald Reagan's transition team. A day after taking office, Rumsfeld appointed a new FDA commissioner, Arthur Hull Hayes.

The new commissioner approved aspartame on the market despite it not having been allowed by any other commissioner in the previous sixteen years. Of course, readers

---

[100] www.stevia.net

may be familiar with Rumsfeld as he was one of President George Bush's closest advisors and the US Secretary of Defense under Bush's presidency. The line between today's politics and profits is not blurred. There is no line. The connection between corporate economic interest and national leadership, even at the expense of lives, is inextricably linked. This is the most fundamental principle of fascist rule.

The Onslaught on Vitamins

It is worth reminding oneself what the intentions of the illusionists are: power and control over the masses by greatly diminishing freedoms. In 1982, when I read George Orwell's novel '1984', I sensed the book had more truth in it than fiction. The thought that there would be CCTV camera everywhere sounded far-fetched. In March 2011, I was having a business meeting in a cafe at Waterloo train station, London. When I was waiting for my orders at the counter, I was stunned to see there were 6-8 CCTV cameras located just in the bar area of a very small cafe. Big Brother indeed is in full swing!

The onslaught on corporal takeover by the illusionists knows no bounds. Growing up in 1970s England, we got most of our nutrients from naturally grown fruits and vegetables. Part of these nutrients included vitamins, which are organic compounds that are needed by the body that cannot be synthesised internally. Hence the need to acquire them through food sources. The absence of certain vitamins led to different ailments and conditions.

For example, scurvy was a wretched condition experienced by many sailors on prolonged voyages until Scottish surgeon, James Lind (1749), discovered it could be prevented by eating citrus fruits rich in ascorbic acid (vitamin C). The use of lemon and lime by the Royal Navy led to them being given the nickname 'Limey'! Another example is the deficiency of vitamin A, which leads to night blindness. The ancient Egyptians helped sufferers recover by feeding them liver.

With the ever expansive use of mass-farming methods within tighter time frames many of the vitamins and minerals vital in the metabolic activities of the human body are lost before reaching dinner tables. The continual growth of the multibillion dollar vitamin supplement industry is not a surprise. As many of the vitamins are produced from natural sources and do not test positive as toxins, they cannot be considered as a pharmaceutical drug.

Thus, they cannot be monitored and, what is more important, controlled by the big pharmaceutical companies. What does this mean to these illusionists? No fat profit margins, for starters. Even more important, people who are enjoying better health and wellness with little or no sign of sickness. Pharmaceutical companies cannot make money if people are not sick.

I am sure readers would have guessed by now that, given the billions of dollars at stake, the pharmaceutical illusionists will seek out ever-more cunning ways to circumvent such obstacles. They will seek out the individuals who can be most manipulated and corrupted to carry out their wishes through any means necessary. Enter the world of politics. Ask why individual politicians and entire political parties have such strong relationships with large pharmaceutical giants? Why do Big Pharma pump so much money into political causes? Why has there been a collaborative effort between a United Nations committee and the European Union to curtail the public's ability to use alternative health remedies and vitamins?

The pharmaceutical industry is particularly determined in eliminating the readily available high dosage vitamin supplements. Here's the thing about naturally available vitamins - when higher dosage are taken than a person needs, the body eliminates most vitamins through its natural excretory mechanisms. For example, when a high dosage of vitamin C is taken, what colour does the urine become? Orange, right? Is that not a way of eliminating excess vitamins?

Step by step, illusionists are stealthily conditioning the public to think and behave like their bodies are useless without outside intervention from products that are mass produced by them. And, the masses are falling for it. New policies and laws are being formulated by unelected officials under the banner of the European Union with little or no mention in the mass media. Whilst this attack on the public's freedom of choice is old news, it is important for the public to wake up and learn to make better health choices as well as learning that food does not have to be an opiate but can be medicine for the mind, body and soul.

When the real benefits of food have been eroded by modern farming methods, awareness has to be raised about what helps human function most effectively. Food and food supplements are part of that critical equation. The more knowledge one has, the better chance they have of re-membering how powerful they really are. As many of the master teachers throughout millennia have said,

"There is only one sin - ignorance"

Not knowing is no longer an excuse that is viable in the New Universal Order. Becoming a victim of circumstance is also not going to cut the mustard in an age where transparency, responsibility and accountability will make up a highly important foundation. This will include the dissolution of myths and fables that have been used to trample on people's freedoms. One such area that is being increasingly exposed is the area of human genetics and its relevance to human life and health.

Chapter 9: Breaking the Genetic Myth

"The conventional story that medicine operates from is that a human is controlled by their genes."

Genes Do NOT Determine your Biology[101]

Cutting edge science, such as quantum physics, is viewed as 'new science' by certain quarters even though they may have been around for more than a century. Skeptics of new propositions and new ways of thinking conveniently forget the history of science, calling anything they disagree with as being 'pseudo-science'. One such science that is still relatively unknown is *'epigenetics'*. Although formalised in 1995, Dr Bruce Lipton (cellular biologist), had been working in this field since the 1960s.

During his experiments, he would isolate a stem cell and put in a culture by itself and observe its division every ten or twelve hours. By the end of two weeks, there would be thousands of cells in the petri dish. The cells were genetically identical because they came from the same parent cell. He then took the cells and broke the population up into three different groups by putting them into three different petri dishes. The only difference was that he changed the composition of the culture medium, i.e. the environment, by a small amount. In one dish, the cells formed muscle, in another dish they formed bone and in the third dish, they formed fat cells. So what controls the fate of the cells? Since they were all genetically identical to start off with, the only different variable was the environment.

The only conclusion was that the environment controls the genetic activity of the cell, which was contradictory to what

---

[101] This chapter is taken as a direct result of the author's interview with Dr Bruce Lipton on *The Consciousness Revolution Show.*

Lipton was teaching at the time. He concluded that by teaching genes controls the cell, he was inadvertently creating a victim out of people. Individuals do not pick the genes they received at conception; nor can they change the genes if they dislike the traits that they have, whilst all the time they are controlled by their genes.

The conventional story that medicine operates from is that a human is controlled by their genes. People cannot control their own genes, i.e. people have a set of genes that controls them and they cannot and do not regulate the genes. This makes the individual a victim of their hereditary. If they have some kind of illness (such as cancer, Alzheimer's disease, diabetes, etc) running in their family, they will believe it is a trait that they have and, therefore, will suffer from it at some point in the future.

On discovering the role of the environment on humans biologically, it turns out that this whole notion of victimisation is totally incorrect. As the cells in the petri dishes reveal, if the environment is changed, then the fate of the cells will change, too. So, what is the mechanism that controls cells in the human body? Some people may say that this is really just about cells in a plastic petri dish. So what does that have to do with the human body?

When one looks into a mirror, they see themselves as a single human being. However, that is a misperception. Humans are made out of fifty-trillion cells. That is 50,000,000,000,000 cells! It is the cells that are the living entities. So when someone says 'me', then they are talking about a community of cells. As Bruce Lipton puts it,

"Human beings are skin-covered petri dishes with fifty-trillion cells inside".

When a critique talks about the 'culture medium' of the petri dish, Lipton contends that this represents the blood. In his experiments, he changes the composition of the culture media in plastic petri dishes, which leads to a change in the fate of the cells. What controls the chemical composition of the blood? The answer is the brain. The brain is the chemist and it releases chemicals into the blood that control the fate of the cells. The kind of chemicals the brain releases is dependent upon what the mind perceives. That perception is then turned by the mind into chemistry.

A simple example is this. If someone is in love and they look at the world with eyes filled with love, they release chemicals into the blood such as oxytocin, dopamine, endorphins and serotonin. These are chemicals that enhance the health of the body and give vitality to it. That is why when people are in love they feel like they are on top of the world, healthy and excited. This is all because they have got great chemistry running through their blood. This chemistry is feeding the cells and making such people healthy.

What happens if something scares people? The chemical composition is totally different here. Stress hormones, inflammatory agents, histamines, etc, are released. This composition also has an effect on the fate of the cells and prepares the body for a protection response at the expense of growth. When a person is in a sustained state of protection, they use their energy to guard themselves and not to maintain themselves.

When the plastic petri dish is taken from a healthy environment and put into a less than optimal environment, the cells immediately start to sicken, die and the culture begins to crash. The response might be to ask what medicines can be used to make the cells better. Here's the thing: humans do not need medicine. What they do need is to take the petri dish and put it back into a good environment. The moment this happens, the cells regain their health. The change of environment for a petri dish is exactly the same as a skin-covered petri dish (humans).

In other words, if people put themselves in a bad environment or a non-supportive environment, then their cells are going to get sick. So many people are taking drugs because the environment they live in is not supporting them. The cure will not come from taking drugs. The only thing that will help people get well is returning them selves to a healthy environment. The body is a complement to the environment. When observing a sick person, it is easy to think that person's body is sick. The truth is that the cells in that body are reflecting their response to being in an environment that is not supporting them.

What is the Role of Genes?

There is great misunderstanding in the role that is played by genes. People commonly use terminology about genes like "a gene turns on" or "a gene turns off" or "a gene controls this or that". Every one of these thoughts assumes that the genes are actively making the decision as if a gene decides to turn on or a gene decides to turn off or a gene decides to give a person cancer. Not true. A gene is a chemical blueprint and is like a linear message. DNA is like a ticker tape[102] because it has a sequence of chemicals that are blueprints to make proteins of the body. The proteins are the physical building blocks that give shape to the body.

So the physical shape and the function of a body are controlled by the proteins, but the character of the proteins is in the blueprint of the DNA. Thus, DNA controls a person's traits. Here are two important factors to consider. First, do blueprints turn themselves on or off? The answer is no. They are blueprints. For example, if an architect was asked if her blueprint for a building was on or off, she will wonder if the person inquiring had gone nuts.

There is no 'on' or 'off'. It is a blueprint. A blueprint or a gene does not control itself. A gene is the equivalent of an actual piece of paper with a blueprint design on it. This is so

---

[102] In the old days a ticker tape was a long strip of paper with words printed out in a roll giving a message and used for transmitting information.

important to understand because, otherwise, the blueprint will be given self-actualisation. The blueprint decided to turn itself on? The blueprint turned itself off? Plllllease! If blueprints were self-controlling, then an architect will only have to drive by a building site, throw the blueprints inside the yard, drive away and come back in a couple of months to find a self assembled building.

Saying genes control things, such as the development of the human being from conception, is like saying the blueprints are controlling the erecting of a new building. If genes are blueprints, then how do they work? A contractor is needed and someone to select and organise the blueprint. Genes neither control nor activate themselves. They have no idea what is needed by the body and have no idea what is going on in the world so that they can adjust the biology. It is the 'contractor' who does all this. In this case, the contractor is the mind. The mind, in its perceptions, releases chemistry into the blood. It is through the act of thinking that the chemistry is released, the blueprints are read and the blueprint that create the body's life and functions is selected.

It may be argued that the blueprints are inherited from parents. However, the way someone responds to the environment can modify the readout of those blueprints. For every gene in the body, the way a person responds to the environment (and consequently, the chemistry that is released from the brain) cannot just select the gene and read it, but it can modify the gene. Therefore, a human can create 30,000 different variations of proteins from the same gene blueprint...just by the way they respond to the world. This is important because over 95% of humans arrive on the planet with a perfectly adequate set of gene blueprint to have a healthy, happy, prosperous life.

If it is the case that every person has a healthy genome, then how come there are so many sick people? Well, the genes were not responsible. It was the perceptions of the individual that read a healthy gene and modified it to the extent that the protein that was created from the healthy gene became detrimental. For example, it is claimed by some people that cancer is caused by genes. In truth, only 10% of cancer is connected to heredity genes and 90% of cancer is due to an individual's lifestyle. It is the way they respond to the world, the food they eat and drink, the condition they live in, the stresses, the fears as well as their beliefs that are not supporting them. These are the things that change the chemistry released by the brain, which in turn, selects the specific gene and then modifies their readout which then results in the cancer.

Researchers started looking at the fate of children that were adopted into a family that had cancer. They found that the adopted child would get the same familial cancer with the same percentages as any of the other natural siblings. But, how could this be if they came from totally different genetic stock? The genes were not responsible for the cancer. It was the behaviours and the manner in which the person learnt how to respond to life from the parents they grew up with. It was from having inappropriate responses to deal with life's stimuli that led to modifying the genes that cause cancer. It was never the gene that caused the cancer. That is why people with terminal cancer have a very profound change of belief about life and all the stresses.

The majority of people go into panic mode about a person with terminal cancer and are left in awe when they see this person have 'spontaneous remission' (*an unexpected improvement or cure from a disease which usually is taking a different course*). What has happened is that they changed their belief system so profoundly that the new chemistry released by the brain returned the cell to the healthy environment. Just like the culture in the petri dish that was moved from a bad environment to a good one, the cell immediately recovered its health.

The Human Genome Project

During my time as a biology student during the late 1980s, I remember the excitement brewing up around the *Human Genome Project*. Scientists would finally be able to discover all the key genetic coding that make-up human beings. They were going to decode the genetic makeup of the most complex of animals, the human, and were expecting to find approximately 120,000 genes present. It was these genes that were expected to coordinate the functioning of a human being. However, by the time the human genome was mapped out, it consisted of less than 20% of genes than expected, i.e. just 23,688 genes!

That being the case, what was coordinating the multiple functions of the human? As the results proved inconclusive, scientists have begun to explore other possibilities. They have been asking questions such as what activates and deactivates genes? Why is it that the environment is also known to turn certain genes on or off? These new explorations bring into question the concept of Darwinian genetic determinism, i.e. human genes do NOT determine human biology.

Scientists have discovered that a significant amount of genetic activation is due to a person's subjective experience and how they manage these experiences. Veteran cellular biologist, Dr Bruce Lipton [103], has emphatically demonstrated how individual cells of the body behave as individual entities and the state of health and functionality of that cell strongly correlates with its immediate environment. This is composed of the internal environment (biochemical, energetic, mental, emotional and spiritual inner map) and the external environment. Researchers estimate that,

---

[103] Lipton, B. *The Biology of Belief*

"Approximately 90% of all genes are engaged...with co-operation and signals from the environment."[104]

What does it mean to have 90% of genes being affected by the environment? A child growing up in an environment with stress factors such as dysfunctional families including parental alcoholism, regular arguing and fighting, separated or divorced parents has 500% greater chance of being depressed compared to one raised in a 'normal' family. Those who had multiple stress factors have a 300% chance of becoming smokers. If an individual had a high level of dysfunction, they had a 3000% likelihood of attempting suicide.

Clearly the implications are very serious. There were also other severe health implications such as heart disease, diabetes, hypertension, hepatitis and obesity, etc. When a child grows up in such conditions and is mistreated during their early years, they are more likely to be violent when they grow up. When the stress hormone Cortisol is produced, the body moves away from repair and growth to fighting the cause of the stress. When Cortisol is produced in large quantities, it kills brain cells.

Needless to say, much more attention needs to be paid by adults when it comes to interacting with children. The 2011 riots in London and other parts of the UK is evidence enough to show the lack of attention given to British youth. Will real lessons be learnt by the British establishment to prevent a recurrence or will the establishment lash out in anger and revenge? Maybe, if they revealed to the public that the youth were already powerful entities that have phenomenal abilities to heal, be creative and define their destiny, then such people would no longer feel like victims. However, there may not be so much profit in it if too many people knew this!!!

---

[104] Astin J.E et al *The efficacy of 'distant healing': a systematic review of randomised trials. (Annals of Internal Medicine)*

Chapter 10: The Human Pharmaceutical Machine

"Placebos do not sell."

The Placebo Effect[105]

One of the most intriguing subjects for the medical fraternity is the *'Placebo Effect'*. A placebo is an inert substance or a procedure that is given to a patient to make them think they are being cured. The placebo effect is the result of a patient having the perception they are being or have been cured by a medical or therapeutic intervention. It is the result of the mind's ability to heal the body through the belief that one is being cured.

Even though numerous clinical trials have overwhelmingly proven the efficacy of the placebo effect, the allopathic medical fraternity have not accepted the effect fully. One of the arguments given is that it contradicts the Hippocratic Oath because it creates tension between an 'honest' doctor to patient, relationship. Although, the placebo effect is as real as healing from pharmaceutical or surgical intervention, the medical fraternity dismiss it out of hand.

During clinical trials, the patients with the same conditions are separated into primarily two groups - those who receive the intervention and those who do not (the 'control group'). These are blind trials where neither group know whether they are receiving the medication or just dummy pills, for example. Then there are double blind trials where not even those who administer the medication know which patient is receiving the actual medicine. Numerous trials have shown that the individuals not receiving active ingredients in their

---

[105] Much of this section is taken from the *Consciousness Revolution Show* interviews with Dr Bruce Lipton and Dr David Hamilton.

treatment have healed nearly as much as those receiving the medication. However, the results have been ignored.

Here is an example. The Baylor University Medical Centre in Texas published in the *New England Journal of Medicine* in 2002 the results of the work carried out by Bruce Mosely, MD, an orthopaedic surgeon. He wanted to find out which of two surgical procedures produced the best cure rate for osteoarthritic knees. The two possible procedures were 'debridement' and 'lavage'. Debridement involves incising (cutting) on both sides of the knee cap and scraping off strands of cartilage off the surface of the kneecap. Lavage involves injecting water at high pressure through the knees to remove all old material. During the trial, Mosely had a third control group who only received incisions on the skin. No surgery was done at all. The results were nothing short of astounding. The control group did as well as the groups receiving lavage and debridement. In some cases, the control did even better than those who received surgery.

In *'Soul Medicine'*[106], Dawson Church PhD, cites that, given the number of debridement and lavages performed in the USA, over three billion dollars a year are spent on procedures that achieve little more than pretending a procedure works. The question arises who really benefits from this enormous expenditure? The placebo effect is most predominant in the pharmaceutical industry.

A more widely regarded reason why the placebo effect is not taken seriously is the implications it has for the pharmaceutical industry. If a person could be healed without paying for medical intervention or medical insurance, how will big pharma make money? The pharmaceutical industry is in the business of making money. Lots of money. Amongst the top 48 companies in the world[107], this ranges from $1.5 billion by H. Lundbeck to $70.7 billion by Pfizer. One of the best-

---

[106] www.dawsonchurch.com

[107] www.en.wikipedia.com/wiki/List_of_pharmaceutical_companies

selling pharmaceutical drugs in the USA is Prozac. Irving Kristol, PhD, a psychologist at the University of Connecticut carried out a meta-study of 47 studies of antidepressants from the FDA database. He analysed the overall results of several studies carried out by other scientists.

The results showed "an average of 80% of the effect of drugs was due to the placebo effect." This ranged from a low of 69% (Paxil) to a high of 89% (Prozac). The study showed that the drugs were clinically insignificant compared to the placebo. Yet Prozac still remains the most prescribed drug in the US. Is it likely Pfizer or any other drug producer is going to give up their cash cows without a fight? Furthermore, are drug companies going to let those legally plying their drugs know how ineffective most of their products really are? Probably not.

What are the Side Effects of Placebos?

The answer is simple: the placebo has no side effect! On the other hand, prescription drugs have significant effects. According to the *Journal of the American Medical Association*, 250,000 a year die every year from the negative effects of prescribed drugs, unnecessary surgeries, infections they pick up from hospitals and other doctor-caused illnesses. When all factors are considered, on average 783,966 people die a year[108]. For example, in 2009, there were 30,797 motor car-related deaths in the US[109]. This places doctors, hospitals and the pharmaceutical industry as the leading cause of death in America.

The horrific tragedy of 9/11 left nearly 3,000 people dead from the bombing of the Twin Towers. The victims were Americans as well as many others from different nationalities. The aftermath led to the invasion and occupation of two countries. Draconian and unconstitutional laws were passed

---

[108] Church, D. *The Genie in Your Genes: Epigenetic Medicine and the New Biology of Intention*

[109] www-fars.nhtsa.dot.gov/Main/index.aspx

without the inclusion of the voting public in so-called democratic countries. This included the USA Patriot Act[110]. Some of these laws enacted by the US government have trampled on the civil rights of all American citizens to counter-act 'terrorism'.

Yet, every year 260 times the number of people are killed by the Medical fraternity without the government so much as batting an eyelid. What is missing from this equation?

Facts:

1. Placebos do not sell.
2. Nobody is able to make money from its effects.
3. The pharmaceutical industry will never be interested in advocating the placebo effect (unless it suits their cause).

The Nocebo Effect: the Darker Side of Medicine

The placebo effect is responsible for anywhere between 50% and 66% of any healing. It may be higher for certain processes. 50% to 60% of all healing in the medical arena is not due to the medical practitioner, but due to the belief of the patient that whatever the practitioner is going to do is going to heal them. If positive thinking has such a powerful consequence, what about negative thinking? It turns out that negative thinking is equally as powerful as positive thinking, but as one would suspect progresses in the opposite direction. In other words, with negative thinking not only can people make themselves sick, they can kill themselves.

In essence, thinking influences health. Positive think-ing gives a health advantage and negative thinking causes disease. Therefore, it can be stated that the power of thinking affects our health. Psychologists estimate that 70% of every individual's thoughts are negative and redundant, which is the nocebo effect. The average person is leaning much more towards illness because of the way they are thinking. The

---

[110] www.en.wikipedia.org/wiki/USA_PATRIOT_Act

human psyche is based on what the mind perceives, which changes the chemistry of the body through the blood. Then the chemistry of the blood changes the fate of the cells. So thinking adjusts chemistry.

Beliefs control the ultimate composition of the chemistry. When people are young, they were programmed with a simple belief that, when it comes to health, they are not the professional. When it comes to personal health, one turns to a professional like a doctor. In childhood programming, they learn that when it comes to issues about their health, they buy the word of the professional as truth. Consequently, if the doctor tells their patient they have cancer and they believe that, whether they have the cancer or not, then we will generate a chemistry that will create the cancer.

If a doctor says a person has three months left to live, in truth, what they are doing is setting a time clock in the patient's head that counts backwards. By the time approximately three months are over, their clock will shut them down and say:

"Now you are supposed to be dead."

The thought process will release the chemicals that will kill the person. That is the worst nocebo effect a person can get; not that they believe they will get sick and die, but when the professional tells them that they will die. THAT is the ultimate nocebo effect. So, how much power do people wish to give to their professional medical expert?

Chapter 11: From Survival to Creativity

"Having the knowledge of one's true personal power conflicts with the interests of those who choose to maximise their control over them."

The Impact of Thoughts on Reality

There are two basic kinds of thought processes: *familiar* and *experiential*. 'Familiar thoughts' are those that are based on the intellectual and theoretical realms that one experiences when learning something new. 'Experiential thoughts' are those which have an emotional component. These are connected to events related to the outer world. This type of thinking is based on duality - right/wrong, up/down, in/out, etc. This is known as linear thinking.

When a thought is sustained with concentration, focus and clarity, the frontal lobe is kicked into action. As the frontal lobe is activated during a thought, the brain organises itself to classify that event as an experience. The end product of the experience is a feeling or emotion. The moment a thought is created in the mind, the body creates the experience through feelings and emotions ahead of the event.

Whilst thoughts are the language of the mind, feelings are the language of the body. When these two are combined, a person is in a state of being. The quantum field responds to who they are 'being', i.e. when their actions match their thoughts. Konstantin Pavlidis takes it one step further. When thoughts, feelings and intuition are aligned, one enters a state of 'knowingness'. This is why so many people who watched the blockbuster DVD movie, *The Secret*, failed to understand the true meaning of *The Law of Attraction*.

Consequently, very few people achieved their biggest dreams, such as becoming a millionaire, through thoughts or feelings alone. When the part of a person, the subconscious, which accounts for 90% of the mind, is ignored during the process of conscious manifestation, it comes as no surprise that the mantra 'thoughts become things' does not work.

Can People Control their Thoughts?

It is the mind that controls the chemistry of the body, which then controls the chemistry of the cells and the genetics. There are two parts to the mind - the 'conscious mind' and the 'subconscious mind'. There is a profound difference. The conscious mind is the latest evolution of the brain just behind the forehead and is the part that is connected to personal identity, spirit or source. The conscious mind is creative and has no time limitation. That is why the conscious mind in a person's head says:

"What am I going to do next Monday?"

"What happened two months ago?"

The conscious mind can go to the future, to the past and can go into a person's head and solve a problem whilst daydreaming. There is no limitation to which direction the conscious mind can move. The subconscious mind is time-bound. It is always in the present moment. Here is the difference. The conscious mind is creative because if one can say what they are going to do next Monday based on some-thing they have not done yet, then it has created a future event. The conscious mind holds a person's wishes, desires, aspirations and what they want from life. The subconscious mind is the 'habit mind' that learns the behaviour and then, when one pushes the button, it replays the behaviour. It is like when a person puts money in a juke box. As soon as they press a certain button, the same song is played verbatim. The primary programme of the subconscious mind gets downloaded into humans before they are six years old.

Conscious brain processing does not become predominant until after six. In other words, for the first six years of a person's life, the brain is in a hypnotic-like state, which is a beta EEG ('*Electroencephalogram*') state. This is the state of imagination. That is why children particularly between two and six years live in the imaginary world, all the time mixing it with the real world. This is because it is in a theta state where imagination predominates. It is during that state one gets downloaded with programmes by observing how their father and mother behave, how the family and the community works. It is at this age that we learn all the rules of society and behaviours by observing other people.

The primary programme of the habitual mind comes from a person's family and their parents. The creative and conscious mind comes from thoughts of creativity, which are affected by a person's wishes and desires. The habit mind arises from the programmes learnt from other people. Herein lies the problem. Neuroscientists believe people use the conscious mind in creating their personal lives about 5% of the time. 95% of the time people are operating from the programmes of the subconscious mind.

Just as a reminder, the word 'subconscious' means below consciousness. So when someone is working from subconscious programming, they do not see this. For example, a person may have had a close friend that they knew very well. They would have known their friend's behaviours and may have noticed the behaviour patterns of this person's parents. It is not unusual for both the parents and the child to exhibit similar traits in behaviour.

If, however, it is suggested to the friend that they behave just like their father or their mother, then the first person to go ape-shit at being compared to their parent is the close friend. During my childhood, my father was continuously stressed from the poverty conditions we were living in. As he somehow felt like he was failing us, he became an angry man who would lose his temper over trivial matters in moments. When I was eight years old, one of his sister-in-laws would frequently tease me over my own reactions. If I chose to react/respond to her, she would accuse me of being temperamental just like my father. Can you imagine that? I would fume with rage and would totally refute her accusation...at the top of my voice!

There are two profound points to recognise here. The first point is everyone else could see I behaved like my father, except me. The reason is I had downloaded the programmes of his behaviour patterns into my subconscious mind. When I played out these behaviours, I could not see them. The second profound point is all humans are constantly playing programmes they do not see. They are not that person's beliefs, but they were downloaded from their family. People are invisibly acting from these beliefs, even though frequently they do not support them. People try to go through life with the following idea in their minds:

"I am creating my life with the desire to be healthy and happy."

Then, they ask why it is not working. It is because humans only work with 5% of the mind, whilst 95% of the time they work with the beliefs they acquired from their parents. Psychologists advise that these beliefs are very disempowering and extremely limiting. As these downloads cannot be seen, people end up moving through life wanting to be happy and healthy, yet they end up struggling and suffering never knowing why. Then they conclude that the universe must be against them, fate is against them, or that it is simply not on the cards for them to experience good things. It turns out, however, that none of this is true. They had inadvertently sabotaged themselves because their thoughts were operating without attention being paid to subconscious programming. These programmes do not belong to them. They came from their parents. The Jesuits understood this and they were proud in their saying:

"Give me a child until it is seven years old, I will show you the man."

Or they would say,

"Give me a child until it was seven and it will belong to the Church for the rest of its life."

What the Jesuits were able to distinguish was that if they could programme a child for the first six or seven years, that programming would determine the rest of their life, in spite of the child's conscious wishes or desires. In principal, a person's life is not theirs as long as their subconscious is re-playing the old programmes. Life becomes a struggle in many ways. This is due to the invisible self-sabotaging behaviour that a person picked up from their parents. Therefore, there is a tendency to feel like a victim when, in actuality, one is creating this reality.

Most people can think of a time when they created heaven on Earth. At this time, they were the healthiest they had ever been, had more energy than they ever experienced and life was so beautiful that they could not wait for the next day. That was the very first time they fell head over heels in love with somebody. Dr Bruce Lipton calls it the 'honeymoon' and suggests people go back to such a state of being. That honeymoon was not an accident. It was created by the individual concerned.

The honeymoon is the time a person becomes so self-conscious, they begin living in the present moment. They keep their focus on the present moment. If one keeps their mind focused on the present moment, then their conscious mind will control their life. If the conscious mind is allowed to travel continuously, which it always does, the power that is associated with being present is lost.

There are numerous stories of individuals driving along in their car, reaching their destination and, not being able to figure out where half the journey went. As they were driving, their mind wandered to the future or the past, maybe trying to work things out in their head. Their mind was not paying attention to the road ahead of them or even the traffic. Every time they were thinking, they were not being present. The subconscious took over by taking over the driving of the vehicle.

In the honeymoon, the subconscious was not allowed to take over and one was living in that present moment. Guess what? All the wonderful thoughts a person has when conscious, e.g. their aspirations and desires, are what were running the mind when they were in the honeymoon. It was a personal creation. However, the honeymoon ends when life gets so busy that the conscious mind starts to wander all over the place.

At that moment, little or no attention is being paid and the subconscious mind kicks in. That is when the honeymoon ends. The subconscious is not even the programme of the individual, but it leads the person to behave like their mother and father. Then, the honeymoon partner, on seeing the person start operating from these programmes, begins to wonder who they are!

Let's Face it: We are all Addicts

I remember the first time I played on a computer game in the summer of 1981 when I was living in Birmingham. Every child my age was either hooked on the alien war games, 'Space Invaders' or 'Vanguard'. I would stay on the machine at the local cafe for hours until either my money ran out or I got kicked out. That was escapism for me in the 1980s. Today, the choice of entertainment and ways of escaping day-to-day reality is staggering. The annual turnover of the gaming industry now significantly outstrips the Hollywood movie industry. Technological advancement has made games more interactive and lifelike. Much of what I could only imagine in the 1980s has become today's reality.

Escapism is prevalent in all aspects of twenty-first century society. As an example, the average Briton spends two hours a day, every day of the year watching television. That equates to just over thirty days of watching television back-to-back without taking a break. Put another way, the average Briton loses more than one full calendar month just watching television...and some people say they have no time!

The average American, on the other hand, watches anything from four to six hours of television everyday, which equates to three months of back-to-back television! Television is just one form of escapism, but it is the most prevalent and highly addictive. Hence, it is known as the 'opiate of the masses'. The most popular television series in the first decade of the twenty-first century have been the reality, fly on-the-wall shows that follow the lives of ordinary people such as Z-list celebrities desperate to make a comeback in the entertainment world.

Many of these shows have become world-wide hits and they give an indication as to where mass appeal lies. They include programmes like 'Big Brother', 'Survivor, 'Britain's got Talent', 'American Idol' and variations of these shows. With little value to offer the viewer, television acts as a strong distraction from the real issues affecting people's lives. However, there is a more sinister side to the 'escapism' industry. Those who have instigated these distraction tactics are usually higher up on the pecking order.

During the time of the Roman empire, public dissent was rife because many people were out of work and had very little to eat. With the impending threat of rioting, looting and civil disorder, the Roman leadership under the rule of Emperor Vespasian began the building (70-72 AD) of one of the major Roman engineering feats in history, the *Colosseum*.

This gigantic stadium that seated 50,000 people acted as a theatre as well as a place of execution for gladiatorial combat. Spectators would not only be entertained, but would be thrown loaves of bread to pacify them. The use of the Colosseum for the purposes of distracting the masses from their true plight is likely to be the model used by illusionists to distract people from the true brutality that is taking place around them.

Modern day entertainment such as major sporting events (e.g. the Superbowl, World Cup Football, the Olympic Games, etc), royalty and celebrity events (e.g. Prince William and Kate Middleton's wedding), computer console games (made by Sony, Nintendo, etc) are mere smokescreens for the blatant corruption that goes on beyond the awareness of the public. Today, the distraction strategies implemented by the men in power are numerous and they permeate all levels of society.

Simply put, it is of interest to certain people for the public to hand over as much of their power to outside authorities. Clearly, no sane person would give up their power knowingly. If everybody had knowledge of their true personal power, it would conflict with the interests of those who choose to maximise their control over the masses. Since time immemorial, authorities of all denominations and interests have tried to control their respective population. However, due to the current level of people's heightened awareness, the degree of control is more subtle.

Consequently, the escapism industry is of immense importance to the illusionists. The subtle methods of control is through manipulation of the mind and body. One of the biggest differentiators between humans and animals is a person's emotional system. When a person feels there is something missing in their life, rather than look within for the cause of this feeling, they seek answers outside themselves.

Occasionally, it is possible to find something external that gives a sudden rush of pleasure. Biochemically, this rush is caused by a release of endorphins and other hormones. On the next occasion this individual wishes to enjoy the same pleasure, the body needs a greater release of the same hormones to achieve an equivalent level. Each time this repeats itself, the achieved gain is less and less and the associated pain is more and more. So begins the addictive cycle of behaviour.

The addictions may take the form of biochemicals (e.g. narcotic drugs, marijuana, alcohol, pharmaceutical drugs, etc), sexual pleasure (e.g. pornography), sporting tribalism (e.g. soccer, basketball, etc) and even violence or incitement to hatred and violence. When a person is hooked, they pass over total control to those who choose to manipulate them and, therefore, become enslaved. All modern economies implement control strategies through escapism. When asked about why someone chooses their form of escapism, the usual answers include *it gives me something to do* or *it helps me relax*.

In actuality, escapism does nothing but suppress the 'negative' feelings individuals are trying to get away from. Eventually, unless the root cause of the feeling is dealt with, they lead to dis-ease of the body and/or the mind. The manifestations of this are a wide-range of illnesses such as cardiovascular diseases, cancer, digestive system disorders and many more conditions. Of course, extreme cases of addiction of any type leads to death.

In the 1960s, the backlash from decades of racial tension and oppression of the African-American was felt throughout America. On one end of the spectrum, inspired by Mahatma Gandhi's success in India, Martin Luther-King successfully united a large section of the Christian African-American community into the civil rights movement. On the other end of the spectrum, the more radical Malcolm X (later known as 'Malik El Shabaaz') was creating his own wave of civil disobedience with the support of the *Nation of Islam* [111].

---

[111] www.en.wikipedia.com/wiki/Nation_of_Islam

The *Black Panthers*[112] were a militant group who were also at the forefront of civil rights movement through their more radical form of organisation. Black America was on the move. They expected their equal rights and they were not going to accept 'no' for an answer.

It was during the 1960s when there was a sudden proliferation of crack cocaine within the black communities across America. To this day, many believe the drugs were introduced by the American secret services to dumb down the black community. They claim that no black man or woman owned a plantation from which to make cocaine. This drug infestation was the perfect way to create community break-down and internal rife. Effectively, the African-American community were silenced almost completely for the next four decades.

The supply of narcotic drugs to any community begins a chain reaction of other associated crimes, which includes burglary, prostitution, gangland violence and murder. Since these drug-related crimes are most abundant in urban neighbourhoods with social deprivation, the people who are most affected are usually those who are poor or who have no education and little means of combating the crimes without heavy external intervention.

Much has been written about addictions particularly by scientist, Dr Candace Pert in her book, *Molecules of Emotion*[113], as well as the wonderful work by chiropractic, Dr Joe Dispenza[114]. Both of these eminent experts appeared in the movie, *What the Bleep: Down the Rabbit Hole*[115], with Jayzee Knight[116] who also speaks widely on the addictive nature of

---

[112] www.en.wikipedia.org/wiki/Black_Panther_Party

[113] Pert, C B. *Molecules Of Emotion: The Science Behind Mind-Body Medicine*

[114] www.drjoedispenza.com

[115] www.whatthebleep.com/rabbithole

[116] www.ramtha.com

people. The bottom line is this: the human condition includes having an addiction(s) to certain chemicals that leave them feeling in a state of ecstasy. Such addictions become a problem when the desire to experience ecstasy is so great that they look to external sources that are either harmful to them, other people or the environment.

The illusionists are notorious for propagating addictive substances to the masses. After converting those with weaker dispositions to addicts, they introduce a different strategy. In the next phase, they ban these highly addictive substances, imprison the suppliers and chastise users. Yet those substances that directly or indirectly take many more lives, such as tobacco, alcohol, pharmaceutical drugs, are used as revenue generators for governments of developed countries. I would love to hear an explanation for this, especially from a person in a place of power.

In the next chapter, the game is taken to another level as we discover how one's personal evolution has a direct relationship to the health and wellbeing of the entire planet and beyond. The lack of understanding of this simple concept is perhaps, in itself, a tragedy. In learning the role every individual plays in making a difference to the world, there will be a much greater probability that peace and unity will exist and persist.

Chapter 12: From Personal Evolution to Global Transformation

"By understanding the cause that leads to one's current reality, they have a strong opportunity to change that reality one step at a time."

Reclaiming Individual and Collective Power

Many people are dissatisfied with the state of the planet and have a desire to make the world a better place. The issues are numerous and far reaching. They include, but are not restricted to, reversing degradation of the planet, stopping pollution, preventing endangered species from going instinct, stopping war, getting people out of poverty, stopping child abuse, caring for the elderly and the disabled, giving everybody a chance to have a roof over the head and so on.

This is symptomatic of human conditioning and programming - to look externally for solutions when the cause of all suffering begins on the inside. Let's face it, if everybody was like you or I, then the world would be a better place. There would be no more theft, rapes, murders, war, destruction, pollution, child abuse or any other tragic human behaviours. By the way, I am making a serious assumption here: I am hoping that the reader is not a thief, rapist, murderer, abuser, etc!

The fact is that not everybody is as highly conscious as the readers of this book. Most are in a state of survival. These behaviours are purely effects of deeper underlying causes, which are run by even deeper programming and patterns. Despite all good intentions to make the world a better place, the challenge is to awaken each individual. This begins with removing the inner conflicts that become personal suffering. Yes, Gandhi did say, "be the change you want to see in the world", but do those who are inspired by his words know what it means? What is it that one needs to change? How is it possible to change something that one does not know? The human condition is to believe that if change can be intellectualised, then the job is more or less done. All the necessary actions for change will just flow thereafter. Not true. It is no longer about creating change. It is about making a difference.

For that to happen, one must be conscious of what it is that they are trying to make a difference to through the five faculties of the mind. One must consciously think it and believe it. There must be a feeling of the difference being made. A certainty or knowingness that a difference is happening needs to take place in a person's mind. The difference must be experienced through physical sensations as if it has already taken place and via the observer without judgement, criticism, elation or resentment. There are no shortcuts.

Taking shortcuts means the difference will be temporal and disappointments will follow. However, the process can be fast-tracked. Once the change process begins from within, its manifestations will begin to take place in the outer world. Numerous studies have been carried out by a several organisations to observe the changes that can be instigated through the process of meditation, for example.

One particular experiment was designed by quantum physicist, John Hagelin PhD, from 7th June to 30th July 1993 in Washington State[117], USA. Then, Washington State had one of the worst rates of violent crime during the height of summer, which included assault, homicide and rape. Hagelin's experiment involved 4,000 experienced TM ('*Transcendental Meditation*') meditators and the experiment was monitored by key organisations, including the police and several universities.

Important variables were taken into account, such as the varying environmental temperatures and changes in police activity. The aim of the meditation was to increase coherence

---

[117] www.istpp.org/crime_prevention

and reduce stress in the District of Columbia. During that time, crime rates fell significantly and dipped by up to 23.3% in the final week when the numbers of meditators were at their highest. Based on the results of the study, the long term effect of the 4,000 participants in the TM meditation was calculated as a 48% reduction in HRA (homicide, rape, assault) crimes in the District.

Such a phenomenon of creating change through meditation is known as the '*Maharishi Effect*' after the founder of Transcendental Meditation, Maharishi Mahesh Yogi. When the square root of 1% of a given population meditate and are entrained (focused attention like a laser beam) on one area, e.g. peace, then the change will affect that entire population. Thus, to bring an increase in peace to the UK (61m), USA (311m) and even the world (6.89b) requires 781 and 1,763 and 8,300 meditators entrained on peace, respectively.

Numerous other studies have been carried out to demonstrate the potency of meditation. That being the case, why is there a lack of peace in the Middle East and other conflict zones throughout the world or even in many neighbourhoods in urban areas across the world? First, reconsider the *Washington Experiment* of 1993. The 4,000 meditators were paying attention to coherence and the reduction of stress (i.e. inner peace) in the neighbourhoods.

In order for them to be able to affect change externally, they themselves must have been coherent and at peace with themselves. This means that the simple act of meditation alone does not suffice. The meditator has to attain inner peace before they can affect outcomes externally. Gandhi was right after all! One MUST be the change from within. This implies that relying on people in places of power and authority like politicians, judges or police chiefs is a waste of time. They must be at peace and integrated within themselves before seeking to change the external environment.

Second, based on studies into altered states of consciousness, not everybody who thinks they are meditating are actually meditating. Proficiency in meditation requires guidance from meditation masters. Third, and equally importantly, the correct actions must be taken to support the peace that is sought. So, for example, if the American, European and Arab governments wish to create peace and reconciliation in the Arab-Israeli conflict zones, one of the first steps to take is to stop financing or supplying arms to both parties.

As an example, the US has been the biggest suppliers of arms to Israel despite publicly denouncing the slaughter of civilians in occupied territories. As one can imagine, having their families killed will mean peace is the furthest thing from the minds of the Palestinians. On the flip side, certain Arab governments have been accused of supplying ammunition to the Palestinian guerilla fighters. The Arabs have on numerous occasions used suicide-bombing as a tactic of choice in causing maximum casualties to the Israeli population.

Transforming communities, neighbourhoods, nations and the planet will only begin to take shape once people begin reshaping their inner cosmos. As a stand-alone process, meditation is certainly one of the most powerful ways to begin inner transformation. To supplement this with action means much more can be achieved. It is never too late to learn and practice nor has the need for peace in the world been more needed. Later on in this book, I will share some of the most profound results I have encountered about meditation that have certainly rocked my world.

If I ruled the world...

My close friend, David Hyner[118], is probably one of the most talented motivational trainers in the UK. He has built his reputation through his goal-setting system and transformational work with thousands of teenagers. I have been fortunate enough to assist in delivering several of his workshops in many schools. An exercise that I found revealing about the mindset of young people involves them preparing a presentation beginning with the statement:

"If I ruled the world, I would..."

The participants state how they would change the world to make it a better place for everyone. Their presentations are nothing short of remarkable. Most of them want to overhaul prohibitive laws, introduce a holistic set of rules and create freedom. Given the practicality and the profound nature of their responses, it is a sad state of affairs that young people are not respected for their wisdom and foresight.

Instead, the public abide by the rules, regulations and bureaucracy of psuedo-illusionists (those aspiring to be illusionists) who are more interested in their pension pay-outs than the future of human civilisation. To reclaim one's own personal power and, ultimately, freedom, one needs to understand not just who they are, but what they are. By beginning to understand one's true nature, it is possible to begin to understand the nature of the Cosmos and all that lies within Her...

---

[118] www.davidhyner.com

The New Universal Order

For the longest time, humans have understood external phenomena by the process of comparing and contrasting one thing with another. For example, how black is something compared to white? How tall is something compared to short? How deep compared to shallow? How masculine compared to feminine? This is typical of the kinds of questions people are indoctrinated into asking from an early age. Remember the questions given in the school exams?

"What's wrong with this approach?" one may ask.

Fair enough. By asking to compare and contrast, the assumption has been made that there is separation. There is no interrelationship between the phenomena being looked at. This is fundamentally a mechanistic view of the world and does not take into account that there are multiple layers of complex relationships between all matter and non-matter. For example, it is very easy for a person with a mechanistic world view to say all natural herbs are risky if they have not been tested by a pharmaceutical company; or a natural health fan may bitterly argue that all allopathic medicine is wrong. This is the old world order of thinking. Perhaps a more realistic approach would be to ask questions like:

'How much black is there in white and how much white is there in black?

'How much small is inside big and how much big is inside small?'

'How much masculine is inside feminine and how much feminine is inside masculine?

'How much weak is inside strong and strong inside weak?'

Scientist, movement artist and spiritual master, Konstantin Pavlidis makes the distinction:

"How much of the perceived opposite is, in fact, complementing each other?"

When this is taken to its conclusion via the last of the apparent comparisons, the question asked becomes:

"How much of me is inside you?"

This is the true essence of the *inner process* or the *yin* process. This is also known as the 'Feminine Principle'. For example, it takes seconds for sperm to fertilise an ovum, yet it takes nine entire months for that to grow into a human being. The *yang* process is the final product, i.e. what is on show externally (in this case, a baby). However, the yin process may take months or even years to develop to have that final show.

The exhibition or demonstration of the end result is merely the tip of the iceberg. The majority of the iceberg is where a huge amount of time, energy or money has been used up in the creation, preparation, integration and presentation. The New Universal Order is not just about seeing oneself in other humans, but also in all other beings. This means seeing oneself as an integral part of Nature and Life.

In many cultures across the world, especially in Africa and Southeast Asia, the youth are encouraged to follow the pathway of their ancestors through culture and heritage. When they grow old enough, they understand the true significance of the cultural programming. There is such a stranglehold on their lives that they are left feeling they are not even breathing for themselves. For the first thirty years of my life, I was content with the Bengali and Muslim culture I grew up in.

The younger generations from such communities were expected to continue the traditions and culture of the parents. Regardless of a completely different lifestyle in Britain to

Bangladesh, I was expected to continue my inherited lifestyle whilst living and earning in Britain. Furthermore, there was an expectation to maintain an Islamic culture, which, in many parts, conflicted with Indian Subcontinent traditions...whilst I was living amongst Westerners. No pressure there then!

Although such a cultural heritage is supposedly family oriented, it was not until I got divorced that I saw the lack of compassion that existed for those who 'broke' out. Islam is accommodating towards divorce, but the reality on the ground is far from compassionate for rule-breakers like me. Yes, of course there were lots of pitying and sympathising about my separation, particularly as it involved my children. Even young, educated professionals of the opposite sex from a similar background were viewing single fathers as 'damaged goods'.

The mix of Islamic and South Asian culture is a volatile concoction that, if left unchecked, can and does lead to disempowerment of the highest degree. This includes severe mental breakdown, emotional volatility, a sense of hopelessness and even suicide. It is now possible for me to begin to imagine how difficult it may be for Indian/Muslim women who separate from their spouses and extended family.

Not too long ago, I remember having a 'conversation' with my own mother. Her shame and sense of cultural embarrassment because her son no longer followed the religious tenets of Islam was astounding. I was not adhering to her subjective view of the world. The most common way to 'punish' such an individual is using a form of 'emotional blackmail' through the tried and tested emotions of fear, shame and guilt.

Is it a surprise that young men and women from the Indian Subcontinent living in the West cannot wait to break away and live their own lives? In reality, there has been a powerful pendulum swing between living the life of the ancestors and our own lives. Very few people realise that there is something out there called 'Life'. This is something people seem to miss in their existence. What most call 'my life' is nothing more than a set of programmes that they have inherited from their parents. This is the matrix that most people are stuck with, which is the ultimate cause of their sufferings.

Comparing, Contrasting and Competition

The very nature of comparing and contrasting incorporates and engenders criticism and judgement. It is difficult to compare and contrast without having a critical eye. It is even more difficult to hold back and maintain neutrality and say:

"In the process of comparing and contrasting, I see a pure difference between these two objects or qualities that I have been comparing and contrasting."

This behaviour also engenders separation. Over many millions of years of evolution,[119] humans have developed the mechanism for 'survival' and the 'survival instinct'. Unless, a person has a mentor or a parent (biological, spiritual or even someone from outside) to guide them on what that 'survival' means, it is very difficult to navigate their way through this existence. One needs a sense of survival to be on the planet long enough to live and go through some process of evolution as well as to have a life. Otherwise, they are at the disposal of external sources that may cost them their life. External sources include predators, pathogens and, now, other humans.

Being complementary or harmonising is about maintaining a level of neutrality and seeing how much of one-self is in the other. A person sees their strengths and weak-nesses without the necessity to see the other as a potential threat, but rather a reflection of themselves. Competition does have its place with humans - as long as it is not abused. For

_____
[119] *Homonids* - a primate of a family ('Hominidae') that includes humans and their fossil ancestors.

example, knives are an absolutely imperative tool in a kitchen in order to cook. However, out of jealousy and competitiveness, an individual can easily lose their temper or self-control.

In an instant, the knife can become a weapon of death. This is a simple example of something that can be abused very effectively for a destructive purpose. Technology has improved so vastly that today there is interconnectivity with four billion mobile phones on the planet. This has been a catalyst in causing the dissociation between the reality that existed before to a situation which creates even greater illusions.

In recent times, the disease that caught most people's attention was cancer. This was surpassed by the fear of contracting AIDS. Then, a very new disorder was introduced to society called 'consumerism'. As a result of this, people ended up buying things that they did not need. The interconnection between the financial services with their goods and services, so that the masses can buy without having money, has become like a runaway train.

Going Beyond Illusions

To surpass the paradigm of comparing, contrasting and competition, a decision needs to be made about achieving brilliance in line with one's own potential. The first step in achieving brilliance is to get to know one's SELF. How can a part of a person shine without that person knowing which part already shines? People have many layers that keep them in the dark regarding their true nature.

On many levels, they have to become explorers, like an 'Indiana Jones', but the exploration is of their Self. It is like a miner going deep into the belly of the Earth and finding the naturally created stone that has been under extreme temperature and pressure. They then bring it up to the surface. Once it has been brought to the surface under the light of day, they must learn to facet it so that it has faces that are equal to each other. That way when that part receives light from nature, i.e. the Sun, an interaction takes place via their facet and the light of life.

The light of life reflects the light that is within them. The first step of getting to know one's Self can only happen if the person is willing for it to happen and willing to be in touch with their true self. This means daring to have the courage to find out what really lies inside without the additions and subtractions that humans have put onto their perception of their being. Once they have found it, the second step is to raise the diamond so that it can be looked at. This means to start looking at themselves and going through a deep inner contemplative process to research and understand their particular nature. What has made them what they are until this time? What has brought them into this reality? What makes up the person they see in the mirror?

The third step is the transformation process or the faceting stage so that the individual can catch pure light and reflect it 360 degrees, 24/7, 365 days of the year till the end of their life. When a person goes through the process of development, they open up faculties that all humans innately have. The focus is on developing themselves in such a way that they amplify their ability to function effectively and efficiently.

One of the most important aspects is the way in which thoughts interact with feelings; then interact with knowingness (also known as our 'centre of gravity', 'sea of energy', *pranic centre*', '*dan tien*'); then interconnecting that with the physical body and then developing the observer. The observer gives the ability to watch half a metre from above the body to, not just understand thoughts, words and actions, but also desires, the need behind the desires and the motivation behind the need.

Fundamentally, behind all of this is the reality that humans are an 'energy matrix' that are lying dormant and waiting to be activated. Most people's bodies are like light switches that have been partially turned on. As long as there is resistance, there will be impairment to the harmonic flow of the life force through the body. When resistance is reduced, there is a heightened life force throughout the body. As a result of the electrical impulses through nerves, the body has the 'body electric'. As a result of the fields created, there is the 'body magnetic'.

There is the 'body mechanic' (physical) as a response to the sympathetic and the parasympathetic nervous systems. There is the 'body sound' as a result of the waves of sound being created. For example, the heart is the source of the greatest sound in the physical body. Finally, there are the electrons that have been set free, travelling through a tunnelled effect as a result of light (photonic) emissions within the body when the body is exposed to a light source (be it the Sun or another source of light).

All of these energies interact in such a way that, when the mind is developed, the heart, the kundalini or the chi that interconnects the subtle and the super-subtle levels of energy, they create a very profound and complex, interactive matrix of energy. One supports the other like a chain reaction. There is an expansion of the ability to, not only send the mind beyond the limits of the physical body or a short distance, but, any-where on the planet and into the Cosmos. It is about the development of consciousness.

Breathing techniques are at the very fundamental level of any type of energy development in the body. It is said that the 'chi' (energy) rides on the back of breath like a cork rides on a wave. Developing correct breath is a good place to start in the establishment of calm in the emotions. Another step is to learn to calm the thoughts. Thoughts are like the molecules of a gas. At any time, there are many thousands of them flying about at very high speeds in a large space.

Instead of trying to control the thoughts, the space is held to allow them to be there without being overtaken by them. As one descends from the faculty of thoughts in the head through deep breathing, allowing gravity to take them into the heart, they begin to observe that the emotions are like a stream or a current of water that is flowing. They walk towards that stream or river and watch the emotions. They can pick the water up in their hands, but within seconds, it will trickle through.

Emotions are more substantial than thoughts in many ways. They are 'e-motions', i.e. 'energy in motion'. They are the most powerful part of the energy complex in the body. From the heavens, energy enters as a thought into the mind and descends towards the Earth. From the Earth, energy ascends into the body and houses in the first chakra and continues its ascension into the heavens. The meeting point of the ascending and descending energies is the heart. When the heart is open to receive these two energies, as well as becoming a receptacle, it becomes a chalice. In many spiritual practices, that chalice is a 'Eucharist' or the 'golden cup of gratitude'. Trying to harmonise erratic emotions is filling the cup and allowing excess to flow so that one does not feel like they are losing something.

Cause and Effect

The conventional approach in dealing with suffering of any nature is to deal with the symptoms or effects. Given the multitude of symptoms and effects each individual may experience at any one time, would it not prove more prudent to deal with the reason for the suffering, i.e. the cause? There are many ways to look at 'cause and effect'. Some people call it 'blame' because they are looking at who or what is responsible for what has happened.

The most important aspect of cause and effect is understanding that the more neutrality that can be established and maintained, the more clearly the cause to an effect will reveal itself. If a person is programmed to believe that there is always something outside of themselves that causes their suffering, they end up becoming either external blamers or internal blamers. In other words, they either blame other people or other 'things' or they blame themselves.

Unless an individual looks at what cause led to a particular effect that they are involved in, then their situation remains something that is like hearsay to them. An example would be if there was a war in a certain country or a famine in another country or a flood in another country. Unless a person is a part of it or inside the country in question, it is not their 'predicament'. It is something they have just heard about.

When it becomes their predicament, they are experientially a part of that reality, not just mentally. At that time, unless they can open up to try to understand what created the predicament, they immediately fall into victim mode. This can happen very easily and, consequently, they start looking to blame someone or something. Cause to effect is what Sir Isaac Newton talked about in the *First Law of Motion*, which says 'to every action there is an equal and opposite reaction'.

Imagine something manifesting that cannot be understood. One could try to work it out intellectually or get attached to it emotionally. By creating the space for the effect to have its own life, it will reveal what truly created it in the first place. As a result, a series of events will be witnessed that led up to that final product, which can be called an 'effect'. It will then be understood where it fits in its own life and how it effects everyone. It is usually the explanation and overall blueprint of why things are the way they are, where they have come from, how they have been created and what can be learned for future interaction with them.

Some call this cause and effect 'karma', but for many people, karma is associated with mysticism and Hinduism. Therefore, it is less well accepted as a concept. On the other hand, one does not need to be a mystic or a rocket scientist to understand that cause and effect takes place at multiple levels of vibrations. These include vibrations from thoughts, words, feelings and actions. By studying cause to effect, a logical sequence to everything can be seen. Rather than get confused by the world of the mystical, it is more practical to understand the cause of different situations by logically retracing the steps to its origins. By understanding the cause that led to the current reality, a person has a wonderful opportunity to change their reality.

What is Reality?

At a fundamental level, there are natural laws, such as the law of gravity, that govern the universe that cannot be refuted. There are celestial bodies in the universe that exists whether a person accepts them or not. The Sun is the celestial body that radiates light at different levels of frequencies to Earth. Whether someone chooses to believe this body of light exists or not matters not one bit to the Sun. It does not care what a person thinks or chooses to believe. It will keep on being what it is, doing what it does and having the effect that it has.

The next level of reality is that of an individual's own making. There is an old saying: 'seeing is believing'. However, consciousness research is coming to the conclusion that what a person believes is what they see and, therefore, what they believe is what they experience, i.e. 'believing is seeing'. Ultimately, individuals create their own reality and co-create a collective reality through all the multidimensional and vibrational levels of awareness. As an experiment at the University of Chicago in Illinois, researchers videoed a basketball game and part way through the game, they got someone in a gorilla suit to walk across the court in full view. They put volunteers in front of the video and asked the volunteers to count how many times the basketball was moved between the team.

The vast majority of the people who were viewing this video were so focused on the number of times the ball was passed between the players they did not see the gorilla[120]. Even when the gorilla was pointed out to them afterwards, there was

[120] Try this out for yourself by visiting: www.youtube.com/watch?v=vJG698U2Mvo

still a significant proportion that could not see the gorilla because they did not expect to see it. They did not have a sense that the gorilla should be there. They did not believe the gorilla was there and so they did not see the gorilla. This is a straightforward and easily replicated experiment.

There are many other experiments that demonstrate that if a person does not believe something, they do not see it. This has important implications for scientific research. As there is no such thing as objective reality, then even the best intentioned scientist or experimenter of any background will affect the outcome of their experiment based on their own intentions and their own beliefs. This is well known even though experimental scientists do not always like to acknowledge it. It is known as 'the Lab effect'.

What is Co-Creation?

Whilst some religious teachings are based on spiritual understandings, they are often interpreted by different people who live and follow the great teachers. Rarely do the followers open up the teachings to evolve alongside the rest of humanity. Surely, it would help to go forward and to continue to explore what it means to be human, who we really are and our place in the Cosmos. Instead, they are propagators of the religion and end up forcing dogmatic views onto people that say they are this or they are not that.

Most religions are to some degree into the view that humans are a creation of God and, somehow, they are lesser. Evidence from all ancient spiritual teachings and evidence from cutting-edge science and spirituality coming together is saying something different. They are saying ordinary humans are extraordinary. What they put forward is that humans have been giving their power away so often and for so long that they have forgotten that they are divine beings.

It is time for humanity to literally grow up to be their own inner guru, honoured the teachings, and honoured the spiritual path. No longer should individuals give power away to the human interpretation of those higher teachings. Every person is a co-creator of their own life at many different levels of awareness, including at the subconscious level, through cultural conditioning and inner beliefs. If one takes a breath out and goes to the collective psyche, goes beyond that to archetypal levels of awareness, then their reality is as co-creators from all of those levels of awareness.

As humans are waking up and the shift is gathering pace, many people are having experiences of telepathic connections, synchronicities and going beyond the perceived limitations of space-time. Scientists call this 'non-local' connectivity, which is linking humans with their own guides and their highest guidance. In this way, humankind is essentially raising the vibration. As they move increasingly to the energy of love and beyond the limitations of fear, then they are able to become ever more conscious co-creators of their reality.

It is a bit like the energy of 40, 60 and 100 watts light bulbs that light a room. Those light bulbs are radiating light of different vibrations, wavelengths and frequencies around themselves. If all those frequencies of visible light became a single frequency and a single vibration and were radiating in one direction, then the energy of the light bulb would become the energy of a laser. Instead of lighting a room, the same energy could cut through steel. The more humans become conscious co-creators of their reality, the easier they move from being a light bulb to becoming a laser.

As people attune themselves and align themselves in love with their own highest guidance, then what flows through them is ultimately in service to the highest purpose and divine intention. That may mean someone wins the lottery, but it may also mean that they are happier and have greater well-being. There is a Zen saying:

"Before enlightenment, chop wood draw water. After enlightenment, chop wood, draw water"

It is not that the world necessarily changes. It is that an individual's entire attitude to their experience has been transformed.

Chapter 13: Separation Consciousness, the Beginning of His-Story

"The ego is reliant on a mindset that empowers separation of one person from the other."

The Ego: The Real Adversary

The 'ego' is that part of an individual that takes a mechanistic and individualistic view of the world. The ego is most present in the logical and rational left side of the brain. It sees itself as separate from the creative centre of the right brain and even further removed from the rest of the body. The ego can operate from either the victor, dominating over other parts of itself and other beings; or from victimhood, fear and isolation.

In modern day spiritual practices, the ego gets bad press. The ego is composed of the thoughts, feelings and desires that all individuals possess. It plays a vital steering mechanism for humans. However, a different story unfolds when the ego overtakes all other functions. It works from fear-based emotions such as apathy, lust, anger, pride, guilt and a myriad of debilitating feelings. These emotions are triggered by the survival instinct shared by all animals. The survival instinct is a critical element in human existence. Without it, there would be no end to the times individuals endanger their own lives.

The survival extinct is pretty useful if an individual was about to scald their hand with piping hot water. It cannot be denied that the survival mechanism is darn useful when a speeding car gets a bit too close to a person as they are about to cross the road. Needless to say, having an alert survival mechanism is very useful if one is in the middle of a safari in Kenya and they find themselves toe-to-toe with a hungry hippo. At that moment, the person will probably not be thinking about the best tactics to negotiate their way out of the lion's main course. They are more likely to run like hell and hope the person with them is a slower runner than they are!

This may be everyday reality in the animal world of Kenya. Given the nature of, well, Nature, it is not surprising that animals have super-developed senses. On average, animals can spend up to 3-5 minutes a day in the fight or flight survival mode to avoid being killed. Then they just forget about it and carry on with life. Humans, however, are the only creatures who will spend up to 95% of their time in the survival mode by reliving a 30-second fight or flight incident repeatedly. Sometimes, they may even spend many years or decades in that mode. THAT is victimhood.

As the desire to survive is not just a learnt process, it does not mean that a person has to play hostage to their genes. A person's environment and their beliefs are major players in the potency of their survival mechanism. The ego is reliant on a mindset that empowers separation of one person from the other. It polarises the intellect, the emotions, the knowingness, the energy body, the spirit and the interconnection between material and nonmaterial world. It thrives on creating scarcity, lack and void.

The person who lives in a fear-ridden world is susceptible to control, manipulation and deceit. For example, take any dictatorial leader. How do they operate? He (it is usually a man) will use propaganda to agitate the voting public by showing how terrible the opposition leaders are. Some leaders have won unprecedented levels of public support by targeting a common threat to their homeland security and the prosperity of their country. The possibility of the danger is blamed on immigrant communities, religious groups, 'terrorists' or just plain ethnic minorities.

If such a leader is in power, then shock and awe tactics are used to get the backing of the country's citizens for the government to introduce draconian laws. When the masses have an overarching reliance on their ego, there is a collective victimhood. This makes them highly susceptible to manipulation and very gullible to propaganda. This creates the perfect cocktail for the agenda of unsavoury people in places of power, such as Hitler.

The Ego's Fight for Survival

When the ego overrides a person's decision-making faculties, they become a constant worrier about their survival in areas such as job security, debt, housing issues, health concerns, relationships and much more. In his book 'Power versus Force', psychiatrist, author and spiritual teacher, Dr David Hawkins[121] cites how the level of awareness has a direct correlation to the dominating emotions and a person's ability to discern truth from falsehood.

When an individual operates at lower levels of awareness, their primary driving emotions are fear-based. Hawkins has assigned numerical values to different levels of a person's awareness. He has mapped these values out in a logarithmic scale, which he has coined as the 'Map of Consciousness'. The Map of Consciousness has been devised using kinesiology or muscle testing[122]. This test leads to a scale of consciousness/ energy level, which is calibrated from 0 to 1000.

There are seventeen different levels of consciousness demarcated by specific points on the Map. From 0-199, a person's world view is primarily fear-based. This progresses to a more predominantly love-based world from 200-1000. Hitler, often cited as 'the most evil man in history', was at the level of 70, which approximates to the consciousness level of a Komodo dragon. This animal will kill its prey for one reason...to eat it. Hitler, on the other hand, killed for a different reason. Pleasure.

---

[121] www.veritaspub.com

[122] For more information on muscle testing for the *Map of Consciousness*, see *Power versus Force* by Hawkins, D.

The fear-based emotions are below the level of 200, the minimal level for integrity to exist. As individuals can be measured for their level of consciousness, so can entire nations and humanity as a collective be tested. Throughout history, up to the late eighties (during the time of the Harmonic Conversion [123]), Mankind was below the level of 200 and, therefore, constantly at the brink of self-destruction. At the time of the great avatars like Jesus, Buddha and Mohammed, the planetary consciousness was at 100 only.

What does it mean being below the level of integrity? Simple. Do not expect to trust the word and actions of someone below the level of integrity. Even though Neville Chamberlain, the Prime Minister of Britain in 1938, was at 195 at the time of his negotiations for peace with Hitler (70), the dictator had absolutely no intention of keeping his side of the bargain. As a collective, humanity is now at 205. That means there is hope for the human species surviving a nuclear holocaust or worse.

Nonetheless, any individual, organisation or institution at lower levels of consciousness than 200 will seek to achieve their objectives through the manipulation of the fear-based emotions. Think about it. How do most 'democratic' leaders engender support from the public? In many of the countries I have observed, it is through stoking up fear of what the opposition may do if they got in power. That has been the modus operandi for most political leaders across the world. Is it surprising that politics all over the world, civilised or otherwise, is rife with corruption?

---

[123] *The Harmonic Convergence* is the name given to the world's first globally synchronized meditation and which occurred on August 16–17, 1987, which also closely correlated to an exceptional alignment of planets in our solar system.

Ego at the Workplace

With a few notable exceptions, most corporations operate at levels below integrity. How can they be spotted? Observe how they treat each other within the company, particularly between different levels of the hierarchy. Look at the companies whose leaders' heads have been on the chopping block, such as Andersons and Enron. In the mid-nineties, I used to work for a company that enjoyed consistent year-on-year sales and profit growth. It was even voted as one of *Sunday Times Top 200 Companies to Work for*.

Granted, they were highly respected by the competition and other industrialists alike. What outsiders were unable to see was the degree of dictatorial rule and how little trust was engendered by the MD of the company towards the 200+ staff at the time. When an employee is worried about their job being on the line, perhaps because they forgot to wear their tie, questions must be raised how conducive such an environment is for the health of its workers. For many employees, it felt like Big Brother was constantly watching them.

I was field-based and I did not feel the heat so much. However, shortly after I had left, all company cars were fitted with tracking devices to monitor the whereabouts of staff always. It was not just employees who were troubled by the leadership. The final straw for the financial director was when he was asked by the MD to sit in the security hut to watch out for individuals who came in late or left too early. That director resigned in disgust.

The implications of a rise in consciousness is damning for those who choose to use fear as a manipulation tool. In the last two decades, particularly in Britain, growing numbers of people have chosen to opt out of employment. Some follow the path of self-employment, others take time out to do voluntary work, whilst millions choose not to work at all. The ego-manipulation strategies of politicians and big company leaders do not bode well for the future of major world economies.

However, are there any redeeming features of the ego? Actually, yes. Not everybody in the world will be or is expected to be in a high state of personal consciousness. The ego is responsible for helping people to stay grounded. If humans are spiritual beings having a physical experience, how can one condemn their own physical experiences? The ego has a desire to procreate and have sexual relations. It has a built-in mechanism to avoid danger and to move towards growth and development.

As the ego stabilises the functions of creating a stable home base and gathers resources for life (such as food), it tends to become less dependent on other people. It chooses to make its own mark through personal success and by standing out from others. As it develops further it adapts the values of relationship with others through teamwork and personal relationships.

However, if an individual is to evolve beyond the ego, it must learn to move away from fear-based emotions through the daily practice of being in a state of lovingness, forgiveness, compassion and surrender to a power far beyond their comprehension. No amount of logical or rational thinking can ever explain this power. The nature of the ego is to separate and pigeonhole information. That way, it is easier for the brain to understand new information and to arrange it according to existing patterns and information.

People have a tendency to compare and contrast all information to serve this purpose of separation. Except for a few communities during a few fragments of time during the majority of known history, humans have been living in a dog-eat-dog paradigm. Fear has been the big stick to motivate the masses. As long as a person cannot discern their thoughts, feelings, actions and intentions from those that are fear-based and those that are loving-based, then they are likely to continue their ongoing suffering. Expanding the ego means contracting the consciousness, which leads to increasing the self-imposed enslavement to the illusionists. Raising one's consciousness means letting one's ego play a lesser role in daily living and being.

The Value of Stress to Illusionists

Living life from the perspective of separation and survival of the fittest places people under huge stress. This puts the sympathetic nervous system into a habitual response. For example, anxiety is one of the most common conditions in the West. The cause of anxiety is because people stop breathing properly. Stressors can be very useful as excellent motivators, e.g. deadlines for getting projects done.

Stress becomes a problem when the stressors exceed the level that a person can handle. If the tools to overcome anxiousness are not developed, a person becomes stressed. Therefore, being well-equipped with the correct tools is a necessity for people who gravitate towards stress. When people get stressed, the main issue that bothers them is their lack of control. They really want to control the situation, but they feel they have a lack of control.

So, they look into parts of their life where they can gain more control. One of those parts is breathing because people think they are in control of their breathing. When a breath is taken in, it feels like air is being sucked into the body. However, this is not the case. When a person breathes in, they are letting go as the diaphragm relaxes. The lungs expand to equal the pressure of the planet. This is why it is also known as 'Nature's Breath'. It is the Earth breathing a person in. This is also why a person cannot kill themselves by holding their breath.

The atmosphere is composed of many gases including oxygen, nitrogen and carbon dioxide, which create a certain pressure. When there are high pressures and low pressures, wind is created and moves to equalise it. The universe moves to equalise the pressure. When the diaphragm is relaxed, a vacuum (empty space) is created. Consequently, the atmosphere of the Earth (air) rushes in to equalise the pressure on the inside (the body) and the outside.

Although it seems like air is being sucked in, the individual is doing nothing at all. In fact, what they are doing is letting go. When a person breathes out, they are pushing the muscle back up and they are pushing the air out. Paradoxically, breathing out feels psychologically very relaxing. In other words, breathing in is about a physiological relaxation and breathing out is a psychological relaxation. When people have control issues in their life, they will look for areas that they can try to gain control. Breathing is one such place. So they start to hold their breath because somewhere in their mind, they have decided that they are the ones who are going to choose to inhale and they are not going to be invaded by the air. This stimulates the solar plexus chakra where the diaphragm is situated, which itself is connected to the adrenal glands.

These glands pump out the hormone 'adrenalin' which gets a person excited. As they are holding their breath to gain control, they are getting panic or anxiety attacks. Unfortunately, it gives them less control, which makes them more anxious and completely out of control. People with a persistent pattern of hopelessness from stress are prone to certain kinds of disease. The cumulative effect of living in hopelessness and despair leads to differences between people who are healthy and emotionally adjusted. This can be an average of 35 years in the difference in lifespan [124].

Thomas Oxman claims that a positive social network can add up to 13 years to a lifespan. Identical twins offer the most remarkable findings. They have identical genomes (genetic make-up), yet their ability to manage their mental, physical and emotional health can create a difference of up to 10 years of lifespan. Stress leads to biological ageing. Stress is

---

[124] Church, D. *Genie in your Genes*

an epigenetic driver of ill-health. By taking control of this, life span can be expanded and health span can be increased.

In the 1950s and 1960s, Norm Sheahy correlated hopelessness and despair with cancer, whilst anger and resentment correlated with heart disease. A study group looked at Vietnam veterans. Even though some of them had no symptoms of any disease, some of them had an elevated level of a protein called 'C3'. This is a marker for future heart disease. It takes a while for such diseases to show up in the body. Having a gene for a disease is not problematic. It is when the gene is expressed or activated that problems arise for the individual. Exercise alone lowers the level of stress for depressed people. Movement and any kind of vigorous exercise will shift the pattern of gene expression.

Stress and Ego

Stress is the single biggest reason why people take time off work. Stress is caused by the gap between a person's true self and their ego. The greater the separation between the two, the greater the level of stress. Each person is a different permutation of the energy matrix that operates slightly differently to another. When the thinking, feelings and behaviours at work, for example, do not correspond with a person's essence (energy matrix), they put downward pressure on themselves which is called 'stress'.

From stress comes anxiety, which manifests into physical form, such as having panic attacks. According to Eastern traditions, the solar plexus of a person is the seat of the ego. The solar plexus is like a film projector. A movie is being projected out and that movie is about that person. The movie is representational of the balance between a person's ego and their true self. The good news is that a person does not need to change anything about themselves because their story is dependent on how good their individual projector is.

There is no correlation between the high quality of a home TV screen and the poorly made television program aired by the local cable company. What a person needs to do is to be true to themselves. This means to breathe a deep breathe in through the nose down into the belly, paying attention to the breath going as far as two inches below the navel. Breathe so that this area expands out and embrace the true essence. Nobody can tell a person who they are. A person just has to be true to themselves. When the habit of holding breath is dropped, anxieties will go. When anxieties fade, so does the grip held onto an individual's life by their ego. Then, the space is created for individuals to realise that there has never been or ever will be separation and that we are all part of a much greater Infinite Mind.

Chapter 14: The Infinite Mind

"Consciousness is seen as the creator of the mind."

Beyond Human Awareness

The most profound personal experiences take place when a person is in an altered state of consciousness. These experiences include prayer, healing, meditation, shamanistic states, mediumship, channelling as well as high states of arousal and ecstasy. Even something as simple as a mother breast-feeding a child involves her going into an altered state of consciousness. At that point in the child's development, it is not possible to communicate with the child using the usual modalities such as listening and responding. Therefore, the communication takes place at an intuitive level.

Altered states of consciousness also take place in certain types of movement work such as classical ballet, traditional Martial Art forms like Qui Gong and Tai Chi. These are often described as out-of-body experiences or near hypnotic states. The practitioner is physically awake and moving, but the body feels different to when they are in a conscious state. It becomes lighter and more expansive. The Taoist and Tibetan Tantra traditions describe this as being an 'energy matrix' that can perform numerous physical and psychic feats.

In Western competitive sports, physical exercise and movement tend to be performed for the purpose of winning. Therefore, the focus is on external, masculine (or *yang*) energy with little attention being paid to inner development. The sympathetic nervous system responsible for voluntary actions is predominantly used in Western sports. The objective is for the athlete to get the body to follow his desire.

The movement arts are, on the other hand, about undergoing a journey to find one's self. It may be said that the goal is self-development and the raising of self-awareness. For some people, it may even be a desire to achieve enlightenment. True movement arts and authentic music tend to be less about competition. Therefore, the parasympathetic nervous system is utilised more.

Until recently, there have been very few scientific studies carried out to research the altered states of consciousness during movement arts and sports. Konstantin Pavlidis is a pioneer in this field and has been looking into the effects of altered states of consciousness on performance, health and well-being using several quantum-based diagnostic and therapeutic devices. This includes the observation of brainwave patterns, oxygen uptake, heart rate variability, energy states, chakra alignment, heat transfer in the body and the brain and the effect on blood in real time. The devices include the use of the EPC (*Electro-Photonic Capture*) developed by Professor Konstantin Korotkov of St Petersburg University, Russia.

Before and after entering an altered state of consciousness images are taken by the EPC. The images reveal any discernible difference made by the healing, trance or movement work. Thereafter, it can be stated whether the form practised (such as *Qui Gong* or *Reiki Healing*) has any effect, if at all. The inner journey of the movement artist has been turned into something that is scientifically verifiable and explainable.

Every human being is born with the desire to search using their inner inquisitor and to ask questions like how, what, where, when and why. Pavlidis calls this inquisitor the 'inner scientist'. It is natural to get inspired by something that is internal or external and have a yearning to communicate with that. This is combined with a wanting to share it by expressing it with words, by painting it, or by performing it through movement or by song. This creative process is called the 'inner artist'. Regardless of one's faith or beliefs or being agnostic or atheistic, at some point everybody asks:

"Where did we come from?"

And,

"What is out there beyond the physical ('metaphysical')?

Some call it 'God', others call it 'spirit', whilst others call it 'consciousness'. These three - the scientist, the artist and the metaphysicist - make up the foundations of all human beings. The interface of the three allows one to experience themselves in a full and total manner. Unless there is an equal development of the inquisitor and the artist unified with the metaphysicist, there is disharmony and imbalance.

Spiritual teachers have observed, for example, that if an individual tries to connect direct to source using solely the left-brained inquisitor, it just does not happen. This is seen particularly today in certain sects of Islam where the Holy Koran and its traditions ('*Ahadith*') are taken literally using intellect alone. When this is taken to the extreme end of the spectrum by groups such as the Taliban, there is a fanatical desire to replicate the existing conditions of seventh century Arabia.

Therefore, the content of the teachings are taken completely out of context of time, space, technological development and civil liberties. What was right and absolutely correct in seventh century Arabia may be wholly incorrect and inappropriate in twenty-first century London or Lahore or Laos. Surrendering to Universal Consciousness or God through writing, calligraphy or movement alone has also been observed as an imbalanced process with little success. The right hand and the left side of the brain represent the scientist, whilst the left hand and the right side of the brain represent the artist. They are like the two sides of a pyramid that, when developed, integrate above the head and interface with the Cosmos or Universe. They work as a trilogy.

What is the Conscious Mind?

Conventional Western mechanistic thinking dictates that consciousness arises from the brain and is called the 'mind'. In the East, consciousness is seen as the creator of the mind. The mind has its root in the word '*mente*' which is the 'realm or domain of awareness', rather than the intellectual process that uses the firing of neurons in the brain to gather data. It is then stored in a logical sequential manner in order for the person to revisit that particular information as and when they need it.

That, at best, becomes knowledge. The other level of mind exists in the entire being that, when awakened in every cell, organelle and subatomic particle within a person, is called 'knowingness'. This is the main delineating factor between knowledge and knowingness. The mind is composed of five key faculties - thoughts (intellect), feelings, intuition (which includes instinct), sensations through the physical body and the observer.

Each faculty is an equal partner in the constitution of the mind. Developing solely one aspect of the mind, such as the intellect, as is done in the West, leaves imbalance and dis- harmony. Even if an individual was at the highest level of intellectual development, it is still 100% of 20% of the total mind. If developing the intellect was enough to evolve an individual completely, then the most enlightened beings on the planet would be all university professors. This is not the case.

Unfortunately, educators in the modern schooling system are adamant in developing the intellectual brain, the left brain, to the detriment of the children. Yet, it is the other four faculties that, when harmonised with each other, create a balanced individual who could access true creativity and personal power. Developing the intellectual mind alone is putting more fuel into the collective fire. It only serves to create more ego-based individuals.

The illusionists were so keen on hijacking every tool at their disposal to achieve their purpose that nobody was spared. The original purpose of the IQ ('intelligence quotient') test, created by Alfred Binet, was to support the learning process for children with learning disabilities. However, its mass use in the USA had darker motives. The IQ test was developed further and was seen as a mechanism with which to separate out Hispanic and African-American communities from mainstream Anglo-European communities. If a person is able to learn a new piece of information using their thoughts, feelings, sensations, intuition and observer, then they become consciously aware of that information.

Otherwise, they are just paying lip service about the new information either because they are gathering information with their thoughts alone (schooling system) or because they have some emotional resonance with the information. It is like learning music. Knowing how to read music or listening to music does not make a person a musician. It is in the understanding of that music, feeling it through the emotions, playing the music, intuiting it and observing the whole dynamic from a neutral stance that makes someone not only a musician, but a musical genius. All humans innately have this ability, yet few recognise their presence, let alone use them.

How do Thoughts and Feelings Affect Reality?[125]

Research shows that humans have 60,000 thoughts every day. Wherever these thoughts come from, they have a profound effect on a person's day-to-day reality. Each thought that occurs in the brain has an electrical charge. This sets off emotions (= energy in motion) in perpetual flow throughout the body. When attention is paid to a particular thought, an associated emotion triggers off a feeling that then creates a magnetic field.

---

[125] This section has been taken from *The Consciousness Revolution Show* interviews with Dr Joe Dispenza, Konstantin Pavlidis and Dr Jude Currivan

The more frequently a thought is repeated, the more powerful the magnetic field it creates. Therefore, the more attention that is given to a thought, the stronger a feeling becomes. When a feeling is played out for a protracted time, it is known as a 'mood'. When a mood is repeatedly replayed, it becomes a 'temperament'. When a temperament is demonstrated over a long time it becomes known as a 'personality trait'.

When the brain replays a thought over and over, it adjusts the brain's shape and structure to accommodate that mode of thinking. By definition, this leads to the type of feelings this person will demonstrate. In the quantum world of infinite possibilities of local and non-local positions of subatomic particles (energy), when one pays attention to one of those possibilities, the infinite possibilities become one probability. In other words, when a person has an infinite choice of thoughts that they can experience and they focus on just the one thought (and hence feeling), that thought and feeling becomes their reality.

In a person's transition from childhood into adulthood, their pattern of thoughts become so repetitive that they enter the subconscious mind as their reality. Therefore, it takes little more than a thought to trigger off a feeling of, say for example, unworthiness. This happens in a fraction of a second as the subconscious mind has decided that THAT thought could only mean one thing - unworthiness. If humans are to evolve in any manner in their lives beyond the current reality, they must ask ourselves this:

"As I have a series of personality traits, which personality traits serves me and which ones dis-serve me?"

If a person is to make a radical change in their lives, they need to make a radical change in their personality. As Dr Joe Dispenza [126] says,

'We must change our personality in order to change our personal reality'.

Thus, the actions one must take begin with noticing which thoughts receive one's attention and, therefore what feelings are created. Nobody can ever make a person feel one way or another. No man, woman or child can make another person happy, sad or angry. Feelings can only be created by the one experiencing them. And, it is done from the inside. If someone says or does something that 'makes you feel sad', the speaker has simply triggered an emotion that was already attached to the words internally. The speaker did not make someone sad. The sad person made themselves sad.

Likewise, a person can never make another person happy. Happiness can only be experienced by someone who chooses to be happy. As long as a person allows themselves to experience feelings due to external events, then they will remain a 'victim of circumstance'. No matter what someone thinks or says, every individual chooses to feel the feeling they want. As Larry Crane [127] puts it,

"What someone thinks of me is none of my business."

Thus, should one choose to accept that they have the power to change their reality, they must first learn to recognise where their feelings arise from and how to manage them. The simplest way not be affected by feelings is to just let go of them. The alternative is to suppress the feelings or express. Both courses of action lead to disharmony and dis-ease.

---

[126] Dispenza, J. *Evolve your Brain*

[127] www.releasetechnique.com

The Intuitive Mind[128]

Intuition is nonlinear knowledge that does not come through the analytic mind. It comes through as gut feelings or hunches or flashes of knowing or dreams or a sense of energy. Intuition is experienced when a person is in a receptive mode. The analytical mind is linear where A + B = C and is the mode of operation. The big illusion particularly held by conservative groups such as psychiatrists tend to consider intuition as C. Intuition is multidimensional and, therefore, cannot be measured through a linear manner.

In the past, people who claimed to have a connection with God or to be in communication with other beings or being able to predict the future were often locked up and dosed up with drugs in mental hospitals. There was a connection associated with psychosis and intuition which led to American psychiatrists considering such people as psychotic. As a physician and psychiatrist, Dr Judith Orloff[129] has spent much of her time explaining to doctors and healthcare professionals that intuition is not a sign of psychosis. According to her, medical doctors must develop their intuitive sense to diagnose and treat patients as well as to teach their patients to develop intuition. Held within the word 'intuition' is 'inner tuition' or 'inner teaching' or 'inner guidance'. The brainwave patterns formed when using intuition is quite distinguishable and can be seen from the flow of energy in movement work such as Tai Chi and Qigong (or Chi Kung).

Athletes tend to use the left-brain sympathetic nervous system and are oriented towards achieving very specific goals. People involved in the movement arts use the right brain more and the parasympathetic nervous system. Rather than be concerned with goals, the movement arts are oriented towards

---

[128] The information in this section on intuition through to the end of the chapter has been taken from the author's interview with Dr Judith Orloff and Konstantin Pavlidis on *The Consciousness Revolution Show*

[129] www.drjudithorloff.com

a state of being and harmony. That being the case, the entire process has to have guidance from inside. This could be called 'intuition' and provides knowledge about themselves directly from the body rather than the intellect. The intellect is more about setting up linear parameters with action and time. For example,

"I will learn how to meditate in order for me to learn how to relax and connect with somebody."

It is possible to take a left-brain, linear approach for achieving things, but that is not how it happens for most. It requires numerous years of using traditional ways, meaning that it is the way that it has always been done, such as in the Far East and other parts of the world. Nearly every practice involves learning about oneself as well as the processes of one's body and mind. It takes a long time with the practitioner working from an inner level and not so much a rational linear level. This leads to the individual receiving messages directly from the environment, translated via the senses, through the lower brain ('*Medulla Oblangata*') and then into the midbrain.

That information is then translated and sent to the two higher brains ('*corti*') via the '*corpus collosum*'. About 90% of this inner learning process is as a result of an inner knowingness. This is intuition. Intuition has been a difficult concept to grasp for the medical community. Furthermore, energy is not a terminology that they can get their heads around as it is not a concept that they are familiar with, i.e. the flow of 'subtle energy' (*chi, ki* or *prana)* along meridians.

It does not fit into their context for seeing reality. The term 'psychic' is emotionally charged and despite the compelling evidence available proving its existence, it causes many professionals to shut down. Surprisingly, there is little resistance to the term 'gut feeling'. They can identify with their gut feeling when deciding to go ahead with a particular treatment or they have a gut feeling if something is not right with the patient. In the process of helping medical professionals to trust their deep inner guidance, it matters not what terminology is used.

The Importance of Dreams[130]

A very important altered state of consciousness that affects everybody is dreaming. Dreams are made up of potent intuitive information that can guide lives and help to make decisions that, when conscious, may have been ridiculed and important opportunities neglected. There are different types of dreams, such as psychological dreams, which are important in helping the dreamer to understand their fears, insecurities and anxieties that may plague them.

Dreams help to drive a person and shine a light into their dark recesses and help a person to awaken from the darkness, leaving them in a much freer state. For example, seeing a dark man in a nightmare may be representational of an abusive father or spouse in someone's life. When these dreams are interpreted with a qualified and experienced therapist, they can be worked through to lead to a solution instead of retaining the nightmare within themselves.

There are times where it is very important not to have intentions or to have any concentration. Instead, let life spontaneously unfold, especially in dreams. Intentions do not need to be set for dreams. One can simply use the technique of asking a question before they go to sleep. A person can ask the dream to give an answer for the next morning. It is beautiful to play in these realms of consciousness and to trust them without trying to control them or to intend anything. Just see what comes in the dream in a totally improvisational and spontaneous mode.

Over the last 120-150 years, the majority of science has become far more left-brain, goal-oriented and it tended to rule out anything that did not fit the paradigm that they decided to

---

[130] The section on dreams was taken from *The Consciousness Revolution Show* interview with Dr Judith Orloff and Konstantin Pavlidis

follow. The pioneering scientific minds, including Albert Einstein, have made their greatest breakthroughs as a result of intuition and creativity. There is a powerful correlation between science, art and metaphysics. The inner scientist is as a result of asking what, where, who, how and why. The inner artist is a response to the innate creativity and capacity to respond to the spontaneous unfolding of what one sees and considers to be life, and the interface between that and the universe.

The metaphysical element is that particular point, like the apex of a triangle, which unifies both the inner scientist and the artist. It takes one beyond the physical to an aspect of trying to reconnect with what may be considered as Source. The unification of the scientist, artist and metaphysicist takes one beyond the normal mode of operation and the normal paradigm and experience of life. Dreams are signposts that are very potent guides to people's lives.

In Western society, most have lost touch with the power of the dream and they have abandoned the natural power that is within. Dreams are a result of a process that enables a person to go through a portal into their unconscious via the subconscious. Dreams can also reveal what is happening in the collective unconscious. There are various types of dreams. The first type is one where a person sits and watches the dream, but they are not in it.

In this type of dream, it is as if they are watching a movie. Much activity is taking place, but the person is not taking part in that particular scenario or series of scenarios. The second type of dream is where the dreamer is a part of it and they are in a major, a secondary or even tertiary role. The entire series of events is leading them to a particular message. It is like watching episodes of a TV series with a little message at the end. The end message is the peak of the dream.

The third type of dream is one where the dreamer sees themselves in it. They are the lead player and, whatever is happening (being chased, killing someone, choking a snake or fighting a sixty-foot monster), the symbolic message of the metaphor is very important. This is the main message of the whole series of events representing another type of peak. The fourth type is when the dreamer is in the dream, but it is not seen as something that is separate from them where they are not sensing or feeling. In actuality, the series of events become that much more real as they smell, touch and taste as if it is happening in their real normal physical environment.

The fifth type of dream is when the dreamer transcends experiencing themselves and moves out of their body into space. What would appear to be separation is no longer separation. This is often known as an 'out of body experience'. Such an experience happens in two different ways. The first happens unconsciously, unwittingly or without their intention. The second is something they practice and the dream happens at will whenever they require. Dreams are a reflection of the subconscious and the unconscious aspects of one's existence.

The other type of dream is when a person is 'portending', which means they are prophesying. They see events that they are not necessarily part of but they do not know where, how, why or when. There are times where all those series of events, after a period of time, fall into place. Such dream states were experienced by people like Edgar Cayce[131], who made numerous predictions for healing and for the future for humanity that have more or less come true so far.

Dreams are like clues and part of a detective story. For example, Dr Gary Schwartz[132] interviewed Christopher Robin over a series of dreams for a documentary. The documentary was made on the basis of the way Robin would receive information through different dreams, piece them together after a period of time and then go into different locations to witness the prophecy come to life.

---

[131] www.edgarcayce.org

[132] www.drgaryschwartz.com

What is Intention?

Intention is goal-directness that one wishes to happen and attention becomes angled or spun in such a way that one reaches out for it. In terms of an organism, it wants to go towards the goal. Internally, the way that one's intention is translated, e.g. to pick up a glass of water, is not known exactly how that works. It is possible to have the internal intention, but translating it to the actual movement is still somewhat of a mystery especially regarding the neuroscience behind it.

Most neuroscientists would probably agree that some-day they will probably figure out the circuitry that connects the mental intention to movement. The deeper level of intention, i.e. in a meditative state where one gets to that point of silence and stillness inside, is where one can still have intention. Intention is not expressed in terms of body movement but it is just there. In a sense, it is there to act as a gravitational attractor as a metaphor for pulling a certain future event towards a person.

Experiments by IONS[133] (*Institute of Noetic Sciences*) have been undertaken to see if it is possible to do purely mental intention and see whether humans can literally pull a certain future towards themselves. This has been done using RNG's ('Random Number Generators') to test pure intention expressed by the body. The results of these experiments suggest that in some way, it appears that intention and retro-causation may be related to each other.

Some of the negative press about the idea of intention is that it is too easy. If a person thinks about something enough, such as a car, it would appear. This kind of thinking has been widely propagated by books and movies on the *Law of Attraction*. Some of the seminars also teach how people can be wealthy and healthy just by wishing it. Clearly, having a thought or intention alone is not that strong nor does it have that level of power.

---

[133] www.noetic.org

I have yet to personally meet a person who has become a millionaire from watching the movie that bought mass attention to the Law of Attraction, 'The Secret', by applying just a few seconds of wishing or thinking. However, the basic idea is correct that through intention and powerful concentrated and repeated intention, one does the equivalent of becoming a gravitational source. They pull things towards them that they wish to get.

On the other hand, there is a New Age guilt that takes place when someone becomes ill, for example. Typically, they do not wish to become ill. One of the problems of this New Age guilt is that people do not know yet how an intention scales up from individual intention to large scale collective intention. Few know how to make that connection very well. There is certainly plenty of room for random events in the universe. In the next second, the world could disappear because the planet gets hit by an asteroid. Nobody intends that either.

The collective intentional effect would be akin to all humans being on a small raft on a large river with a very strong current. They are going to get pulled along with that current no matter what they do, but the capacity to paddle a little bit to help steer the raft is there. The collective personal intention helps steer the boat. With enough persistence, the human species could steer it reasonably well even if they are caught up in a large current. However, if the end of the river is a waterfall, unless they are paddling like crazy to get onto the shore, they are still going to go over with everybody else.

In the case of being caught in a tsunami, like the one that took place during December 26th 2005, some people were paying attention to a presentiment that maybe there was something wrong with the water that day and they decided not to go near the water. Maybe those people did save themselves from being swept into the ocean. People who were at the wrong place at the wrong time perhaps were not paying as close attention. Most of the animals sensed the tsunami beforehand and, consequently, migrated inland.

An 'intention' is 'something that establishes or sustains tension'. In this case, the tension is action. For example, there could be a specific action in a specific direction for a specific goal to be achieved. However, an intention made is hugely subjective to the individual's own personal level of evolution. Factors affecting a person's intention depend on where they learn from, the way their inner process is established through belief systems based on patterns.

Most people are incapable of maintaining, an openness, on multiple levels to receive information directly like a photographic plate does. When the aperture is open in that moment, it receives light in a whole or 'gestalt'[134] perception of what is there. Depending on what their mindset is, what their beliefs are, what mood they are in and where they are in that moment, they will be receiving that information in a different way and will respond accordingly. That information initially becomes a catalyst. Then there is a response and, if the individual does not go to deeper levels, they usually just react initially.

Nobody conducts research without there being an intention. To carry out research just for the sake of it is an action without a goal. Thus, an intention is about a specific focus and attention. There may not be an expectation of what the outcome has to be, but there has to be focus and awareness. So if one does not focus, there is no attention. If there is no attention, they cannot concentrate. If there is no concentration, there will be no awareness. If there is no awareness, one will not be able to achieve a set or specific outcome.

---

[134] *Gestalt* - an organized whole that is perceived as more than the sum of its parts

Chapter 15: The Cosmic Connection

"...when activities, such as meditation, are practiced and attention is paid to what is going on deep inside the mind, a person can become aware of virtually anything they wish to."

Going Beyond the Five Senses

All humans are taught about the five senses of sight, sound, touch, smell and taste. However, there are numerous other senses that people are far less aware of, including a kinaesthetic sense, sense of pain, balance and nausea. Mind experts such as Dr John Demartini[135] and Dr Dean Radin[136] suggest there are at least a dozen senses beyond the usual five. 'Psi' is a kind of sense but has no specific anatomic structure associated with it.

The reason scientists scoff at the notion of a sixth sense is because they are not dealing with a tangible organ, such as an eye. There is no specific part of the brain that is responding to that sense. Psi phenomena, is rather a reflection of the fabric of the universe itself, whilst humans are part of that fabric. Humans have access to this information because they are embedded in the information and the information is embedded in them.

It is a holistic way of seeing the relationship between humans and the rest of the universe. Psi gives the impression of being a sense because it feels like a movie is being watched inside the head. So where does the movie come from? It is a similar process to evoking mental imagery, which is related the brain. However, the reason the imagery comes about in the

---

[135] www.drdemartini.com

[136] www.deanradin.com

first place is because, at some deep level, the physical brain itself is coexisting with the rest of the universe.

For at least a century, momentum within psychological research and the neurosciences has shown that conscious awareness of the world is a very thin slice of what humans are actually aware of. So, the word 'awareness' seems strange in this context. There is a paradigm in psychology called 'implicit learning' or 'implicit awareness' where behaviour can be strongly influenced by things that a person is not consciously aware of at all. This means that there is a large portion of cognition that is simply not at the level of awareness.

It means there is pre-processing, subconscious processing and there are all kinds of things going on inside the head that humans are unaware of. The same idea came about from psi research carried out over a 100 year period. People knew that most of their psychic awareness were occurring at a level where they were not consciously aware of. If it were possible for one to observe changes in skin conductance or heart-rate variability or changes in brainwave patterns of people without their awareness, it would be considered that people were responding unconsciously to things out there in the world that were not coming through the five senses.

At an unconscious level, humans are aware of everything that is taking place within their own environment as well as beyond the environment. More attention is usually paid to things that are in the direct vicinity. It takes strong influence or attention or motivation to pay attention to the other senses consciously. Experiments have been carried out in a laboratory by Dr Rupert Sheldrake where someone looks at another person indirectly through closed circuit television (CCTV)[137]. So, the watcher was not actually close to them. They were at a distance.

---

[137] Sheldrake, R. *Journal of Conscious Studies,* **12**, No. 6, 2005, pp. 10–31

The watcher could only see them through a TV camera. Instead of asking the person being stared at to consciously report that they were being stared at, their skin conductance was measured, this is where micro amounts of sweat on the palms and the fingertips are measured. Those experiments showed that when someone is staring at another person, the sympathetic nervous system is aroused.

When people are asked whether they are aware of it, most of them say 'no'. This means that, at an unconscious level, people know they are being stared at. One of the things that can happen with long-term meditation is that the meditator becomes more aware of what is happening inside their own head. They acquire a deeper and greater reach in the supposedly unconscious parts of their mind. Consequently, the unconscious becomes conscious as a result of meditation. Perhaps this is why meditators experience more synchronicities and more psi events because they are more aware of what is going on inside their heads.

The Spooky World of Psi

Cynicism around the study of psi phenomena is due to a worldview developed by science over the last two centuries, which is a 'mechanistic' perspective. They see the world as a big machine as though a human's ability to sense how things work is the same way a clock works. Gears intermesh, which leads to explaining how causality works. The assumption is made that space and time are absolutes. Time moves at a certain rate. All things that are more or less common sense, i.e. what the fives senses are saying, violates that world view.

The first reaction of most people, including scientists, is that the thing that violates the worldview simply does not exist because it is outside the framework of how humans think things work. The reason so many people are so cynical about psychic phenomena is not so much that the phenomena cannot be demonstrated. Most people have, at some time, had an unusual experience. The reason there is so much resistance is because, within the prevailing worldview, there is no way to explain how these things can exist.

The worldview that most believe, which has been termed by Dr Dean Radin as the 'common sense worldview', is incorrect. Much of the advancement in science in the twentieth century has pretty much demolished all human ideas about the fabric of their reality. Thus, if one needs to start building up a new worldview, what is a more accurate one than from a scientific perspective? It turns out that the new worldview, which is not so new (nearly a century old), is not well received.

The new worldview is not more compatible with the fact that psychic phenomena are real, but that they have been predicted and, therefore, they must exist. This is a real dramatic change towards how it is thought that the universe holds together. The systematic study of psychic phenomena and other unusual mental capacities has been going on since 1882 starting at the *Society for Psychical Research in London*[138].

Psi is a neutral word that is the letter 'p' in the Greek alphabet and it stands for roughly the word 'psyche', which is the Greek word for 'mind and soul'. It is a convenient way of describing the nature of these phenomena without assuming that an explanation for how they work is required.

The following are considered as psi phenomena:

1. *Telepathy* - exchange of information between two minds.
2. *Clairvoyance* - reception of information from objects at a distance either in space or time.
3. *Precognition* - a form of clairvoyance where information comes from the future - and *Retrocognition* - the information comes from the past.
4. *Psychokinesis* - a direct form of mind-matter interaction.

---

[138] www.spr.ac.uk

These four categories sound like they are different, but they are likely the same kind of phenomenon that simply manifest in different ways.

Bridging the Gap between Science and Spirituality

Thanks to the advancement of the scientific understanding of the Cosmos through quantum physics, there are highly plausible theories that bridge science and spirituality. These include string theory and the concept of entanglement. *'Entanglement'* is the English translation of a German word that means 'enfolded', whereas in English it suggests a tangled ball of string. 'Enfolded' is better because it suggests that, at some deep level of physical reality, objects appear to be separate and isolated, but they are actually not. They are enfolded among each other.

This was predicted by the mathematics of quantum theory at least thirty or forty years after the mathematics was discussed. Then, physicists did not think this was a real property of matter, but only a theoretical one which was probably an artefact of the mathematics. In 1964, physicist John Bell[139] figured out a way of testing whether the entanglement might be real or not.

Starting a few years later and continuing until the present, there have been more and more experiments that have been looking at the possibility of objects being entangled. It has been found with those that have been looked at so far that they are entangled at every level. The physics explanation of entanglement only works at the microscopic, atomic and subatomic world. Nonetheless, they work very strongly. In everyday reality, humans do not seem to recognise that everything is connected, but see all as separate.

Objects do not blur into each other very well. Time and space are seen as separate. Fundamentally, it is known that the

---

[139] www.en.wikipedia.org/wiki/Einstein-Podolsky-Rosen_Paradox

fabric of reality is not built that way. At some deep level, human concepts of space, time, energy and matter are all relative. There are relationships that exist between each other. They are not absolutes. What is more important, especially concerning psi phenomena, is things appear to be separate, but they are not.

Experiences exist at the level of the subatomic world that are completely compatible with the quantum world. What one experiences as *"I know what is happening at a distance"* (like in lucid dreaming), should not be too surprising because one should know what is happening everywhere all the time. In this case, the mystery is turned on its head. It is no longer the case of how did the information get into a person's head? However, how was it that only this information came to mind then?

In reality, people have access to all information any-where in space and time. From that perspective, minds throughout the universe coexist. The mystery of the brain is: how does it act as a filter that only presents the things that are of interest to an individual? People can access any information in time and space, not because they are reaching out to get it, but because it is already there. The mind and the universe co-exist at some level. It is likely that the brain and the nervous system act as a kind of a filter and only present tiny bits of the universe to people.

Most of the information is coming through the accepted five senses. But when activities, such as meditation, are practiced and attention is paid to what is going on deep inside the mind, a person can become aware of virtually anything they wish to. This is not just the realm of mystics, psychics and spiritual masters. Every human has these capabilities.

Chill Out: It's Already Happened!!!

According to Albert Einstein, the speed at which light moves is constant (186,282 miles per second), as shown by his formula $E = mc^2$. Nothing can travel faster than the speed of light. Nothing, that is, that has mass. Today, cosmologists have developed the maths further and argue that the speed of light is indeed at a constant...within the human perception horizon. However, beyond the perception horizon, light travels at infinite speed. As it slows down, and at the point it enters the perception horizon, it splits up in to two parts - *matter* (that which can be measured with the senses) and *antimatter*.

The matter region (C region) is the universe in which humans reside[140]. The antimatter region (C^2 region) is the region that is the exact equal and opposite to the universe that we reside in. This means that there is an exact antimatter version of everything, including you, in this region living the same reality that you live. There is one important difference between the two universes - time. Whilst the perception of time moves in a forward linear motion in this universe, it moves in a negative timeline in the antimatter region. This is significant. It means that every event that is ever going to take place in the current universe has already happened in the antimatter region!

Thus, the idea of destiny has a new significance. Everything that will happen has already happened in the antimatter region. One may ask that, if everything that will happen has already happened, is it possible to change destiny? The answer is an emphatic 'yes'. When one becomes attuned to their inner reality, it is much more likely to attune to the outer cosmos and the antimatter region. Everybody is born with this ability, except most tune themselves out through their programming and conditioning. This is why truly evolved psychics and mystics are able to 'predict' the future. They

---

[140] See *Genius Groove* by Dr Manjir Samanta-Laughton MBBS

'tune' into their counterpart in the antimatter region and see the reality there.

What they are saying is that what has not happened here as yet, has already taken place in the antimatter universe! This is the place where déjà vu, precognition and other futuristic predictions take place. There is no magic to it. Magic and miracles are just facts that cannot be explained by the current mode of thinking. The key to transforming one's reality is learning how to be present. As Master Oogway from 'Kung Fu Panda' wisely puts it:

"Yesterday is history, tomorrow is a mystery, but today is a gift. That is why it is called the 'present'."

The Phantom DNA Effect

Conventional science has primarily been based on Newtonian physics that believes in a universe based on separation and non-connection. Throughout the past hundred years, evidence have been produced that have been contrary to this belief. In 1985, Dr Peter Gariaev was working on DNA at the *Institute of Physics/Techniques Problems at the Academy of Science* of the USSR. He saw an effect that shook up conventional scientific thinking.

In 1995, Dr Vladimir Popinon and Dr Gariaev published their findings in the USA after Gariaev had already discovered this particular phenomenon a decade earlier (1985) and subsequently published them in 1991 [141] and 1994 [142]. They were investigating the relationship between human DNA and the smallest particles of light, i.e. photons. They took a glass tube and withdrew all the air and particles they could to create a vacuum, which meant that the tube was completely empty.

---

[141] Gariaev P.P., Chudin V.I., Komissarov G.G., Berezin A.A., Vasiliev A.A., 1991, *Holographic Associative Memory of Biological Systems, Proceedings SPIE - The International Society for Optical Engineering. Optical Memory and Neural Networks.* v.1621, p.280- 291. USA

[142] Gariaev, P.P. *Wave based genome*, Ed. Obsh. Pl'za, 279p

Nonetheless, photons of light, which the universe is made of, will still remain dispersed throughout the tube.

As expected, they found randomly scattered particles of light. They then introduced human DNA into the tube and witnessed something very interesting. The photons of light aligned themselves around the DNA forming a precise spiral around the DNA. It was as if the DNA had a magnetic attraction to the photons. The scientists then removed the DNA and expected the photons to resume their original random distribution. Surprisingly, the photons were still behaving as if the DNA was still there and retained a perfect alignment.

Conventional physics had no way of explaining this phenomenon, which became known as the 'Phantom DNA Effect'. This showed that communication takes place between DNA and photons of light through a medium or a 'field' of energy. This may explain why people such as former soldiers, who have lost part or the whole of the arms or legs experience the 'Phantom Limb Effect'. Approximately 60% to 80% of individuals with an amputation experience phantom sensations in their amputated limb and the majority of the sensations are painful.

The discoveries do not stop there. Having pioneered a series of experiments on intention, Dr Cleve Backster designed a new experiment for the US military in 1993 to study the effects of human emotions on their DNA and over different distances[143]. A sample of DNA was taken from a volunteer's mouth and was placed within equipment to measure it electrically. The volunteer was taken to another room within the building a few hundred feet away. This was a sealed chamber where no form of communication exchange could take place, including EM (electromagnetic) waves and radio signals. The volunteer was shown a series of video images that were designed to stimulate different states of emotions.

---

[143] Motz, J. *Everyone an Energy Healer: The Treat V Conference* Santa Fe, NM, Advances: *The Journal of Mind-Body Health,* vol. 9 (1993).

The movies included ranged comedy, erotica and violence. In the meantime, the volunteer's DNA was being monitored in the first room through electrical responses. During times of high emotional arousal for the volunteer, there were peaks and troughs in the graph depicting the reactions of the DNA. Despite the distance, it seemed that the DNA responded instantaneously. There was no separation and both the DNA and its owner behaved as if they were one.

After a short time, the military ceased their experiments and Backster continued the investigations with his team to study the results at greater distances up to 350 miles. Despite the distance, the effect of the volunteers' emotions on their DNA was instantaneous. These experiments demonstrated that there is an 'invisible' quantum field through which all things are connected.

Given these results, it is worth considering experiences that one has on a day-to-day basis. For example, how many times has a story been told of a mother's instinct about an impending (often negative) event that was about to happen to their child? From the age of six months, I suffered from episodes of epileptic seizures every year until I was eight. Each time, just one to two hours before a seizure, my mother would unexpectedly experience strong panic attacks and heart palpitations. Somehow, she was receiving warning signals in preparation for the impending event...ahead of time.

Consider this: in the process of touching someone else (e.g. shaking hands, kissing, etc), an exchange of DNA is taking place with that person. No matter how many times the parts of the body where the exchange took place are washed after-wards, the Phantom DNA Effect will still take place. Most people have emotional highs and dips. What would happen if this person that was touched experiences emotional extremes? Would the person pick up on the information through their DNA?

Whether one picks up on the emotions experienced by their 'friend' will depend on a number of factors including their emotional connection to the 'friend' and their level of conscious awareness. The former explains why it is possible 'pick up' on the highs and lows of close family and friends more easily than total strangers. Could this explain why people sometimes experience sudden emotional upsurges out of the blue? Something to think about.

Chapter 16: Tapping into your True Power

"In the ever continual pursuit of happiness, many have lost sight of what happiness really is."

The Infinite Power of Meditation

There is no subject that has been researched in more depth than meditation, by both scientists and spiritualists. It used to be seen as an Eastern tradition, whereas there are numerous Western forms of practices, too. The key to meditation is the training of where one places their attention. Attention is not ordinarily thought of as something that can be trained, but it can. People are entrained to pay attention to the television, to electronic video games, to music, sports, etc.

People's attention can also be trained on themselves and around their minds. The meditative process is a way of training how to allocate attention and to focus it. There are thousands of years of tradition, especially in the yogic traditions, that show if one begins to train their mind to focus attention onto their internal experience, one of the first things they begin to come across is clairvoyance. It is a natural fall out from the action of paying close attention to what is going on inside.

Neuroscience suggests that long term meditation changes the functioning and the structure of the brain itself. It does not just change the circuitry of the brain, but it literally changes the shape of the brain! Reshaping the brain is very similar to exercising the muscles in the gym. When someone keeps working out their biceps, they will literally change the shape of their arms. The same thing happens through paying attention to the brain.

If an enormous amount of time is invested on paying attention as a musician, for example, that portion of the brain related to music will be enlarged. There will simply be more to bring to bear in terms of the ability to process that information. Likewise, if much time is spent on meditating, which involves paying attention, the frontal lobe, which is the portion of the brain that is allocating and directing attention, will change.

Approximately 1% of a population in any domain, be it in music or meditation, will have a natural talent for it. They will excel in their chosen field. The rest of the 99% will make improvements through training, but some people would never quite get to the level of the Olympic athlete. I can practice doing the long jump all day, but I would never reach 29 feet (8.95m), which was the current world record in 2011. However, not everybody needs to be at the level of the Olympic athlete. 99% of the population will need to build the skills required for meditation.

Before the 1980s in the West, meditation was considered as some kind of Eastern mumbo-jumbo. Now, it is on the cover of major magazines and it is covered by medical insurance and prescribed by doctors. It has come a long way to become mainstream and has become widely accepted by the western world. The 1% of people referred to above, through meditation, will develop their ability to perform psi phenomena, especially clairvoyance, by using a substantially different level of technique.

Most people will have some degree of clairvoyance, but some people will experience this at will and are able to control it. Unfortunately, most people are not talented enough to do this without a huge amount of practice. In some cases, even with much practice, they can only go so far. Regardless of the types of meditation there are, one of the major things that happen is the rhythms of the heart begin to change in a very positive way. The heart begins to produce nitric oxide, which dilates the arteries. This is why meditation can have such a good impact on the heart initially.

Many studies show how meditation offsets neural decline caused by the ageing process. As ageing begins, some part of the brain, particularly above the eyes called the 'prefrontal cortex', begins to decline in thickness in much the same way as muscle does. If a person exercises a muscle, then the muscles start to grow and become denser. If a person stops exercising that muscle over a time, then the muscle becomes thinner and thinner.

The same happens with the brain. Neuroscientists often use the analogy that the brain is like a muscle. If a person does not exercise the brain, it begins to decline. As they mature, the prefrontal cortex gets thinner and thinner, year on year. However, it does not have to become thinner as fast as it does. Meditation offsets this process by slowing down the decline. In many studies, the average 50-60 year old who has been meditating regularly has thicker frontal cortex than a twenty year old. Instead of the muscle declining, it gets thicker. Their brain is healthier, more active and more connected than the average twenty year old.

The third major discovery was when a group of novice meditators were given a simple meditation to do for twenty minutes a day for eight weeks. Meditation affected 1,561 of their genes. Picture a person's genes as little light bulbs on a Christmas tree. Humans have 25,000 genes represented by the light bulbs flashing on and off in a seemingly random pattern. The overall effect of meditation is better health and an overall slowing of the ageing process.

What are the Consequences of Not Meditating?

A profound effect of having little frontal lobe development from a lack of appropriate exercise, i.e. meditation, is stress. The effect of chronic stress (high levels of cortisol in the blood stream) over a long time leads to osteoarthritis, acceleration of skin wrinkling, loss of muscle mass, low bone density, poor digestion and lower levels of sexual performance, to name a few. Meditation powerfully placates stress. According to Dean Ornish MD[144], men had a fall in prostate cancer markers and an overall improvement in their health once they learnt to meditate, exercise and practiced corrective eating. The benefits of meditation are many, but the consequences of non meditation are, quite frankly, quite dire. These include:

- A lack of frontal lobe development leading to being driven more by survival.
- A reduction in conscious awareness of the internal and external environment.
- More frequently experiencing the feelings of being frustrated, irritated and stressed.
- Increasing likelihood of cardiovascular disease, cancer and other life-ending conditions.
- Being easily affected by 'negative' events, circumstances and people.
- Having a lower level of emotional intelligence.
- More reliant on achieving happiness and joy from external conditions.
- A reduced ability to harness one's intuition.
- Reduction in life span.
- Less able to consciously manifest goals and desires.
- Increased ageing.
- More prone to brain related conditions, such as Parkinson's disease.

---

[144] www.pmri.org/dean_ornish.html

The Pursuit of Happy-ness

In the ever continual pursuit of happiness, many have lost sight of what happiness really is. Most people are happy because they are avoiding sadness. They do this by trying to achieve 'things' like acquiring material possession or getting the highest sales figures. They may be associating happiness with the content of their wardrobe. If they did not achieve that thing, they would not be happy. This happiness is all about duality and makes up only a very small part of the mind.

The whole story is about left and right, up and down, black and white, yin and yang. They work in opposite pairs. A person would not know what 'hot' was unless they had 'cold' to compare it to. The mind that is associated with a person can only be in a state of duality because the brain and the mind can only understand things that have edges. There needs to be a beginning, a middle and an end to something.

In order for someone to touch something, there needs to be a place where the finger ends and the object begins. If there were no ending or beginning, a person could not touch anything. This is why the whole anthropomorphism of God is ridiculous. Humanising God makes absolutely no sense. God is given human qualities and is sitting somewhere on a throne observing everything. If God is one thing everywhere (omnipresent), which almost everyone agrees God is, then where does God sit to have something outside of Him to observe it? It is impossible.

There is the happiness of the mind where one is constantly seeking achievements and rewards from their actions. These are some of the most miserable people on the planet. They are never satisfied and seek more and more and more. They will never be satisfied because they are always moving the goalposts. Being in the moment is where all the glory and where all true satisfaction is. The problem arises from the mind pulling a person either into the past or the future, but very rarely into the present moment. If one could be in the moment, they would realise that all satisfaction, contentment and happiness will be experienced there too.

Meditation and Manifestation

The key benefit of meditation is that a person can become like a laser-beam. They become focused and attuned. Throughout the day, most people become engaged in multiple tasks whereby they may be distracted by other tasks. However, a meditator's attention is much more focused and they are much less susceptible to distraction. This also means they will be more efficient at their task and will perform it quicker, easier and better with enhanced results.

However, it is important to note that meditation is nothing to do with someone doing the right sort of task. A person may be doing a task and falling into a habitual response of self-sabotage, which means they are doing an action that only confirms what they think they know about themselves. For example, they may believe they are worthless or have no possession or that they cannot earn money.

As humans, there is a strong desire to be right. So, when an opinion is being held by a person, they constantly look to the outside world for confirmation that their opinion is correct. If they have an opinion that they cannot earn any money, then they will constantly look for evidence to support that. Lo and behold! They will find it. There is a phenomenon of 'cause and effect', but it is such a complex one that it is beyond a person's ability to calculate. However, there is no harm in a person manifesting things by spending time thinking what their desired outcome is. Then, they observe whether the actions they are carrying out support the desired outcome or not. If they do not support the outcome, then they stop taking those actions and do something else. Meditation helps a person make better choices in what they do.

Who wants to Live Forever?

Even with the highly advanced medical technology in the USA, it has the highest number of sick people in the world. It is also amazing to learn that one of the most remote countries in the world from technology, Georgia [145], has some of the longest living people in the world. However, it is not a question of how long one can live, but what quality of life do they have? One may live for a hundred years, but if the cells of the body age quickly, they are more likely to be a cripple than to age with grace.

Meditation counteracts the ageing process in a number of ways. One of the immediate things to happen is the reduction of blood pressure. Having high blood pressure is associated with accelerated ageing. Not having enough nitric oxide in the body is also associated with the ageing process. There are a handful of things that cause ageing. The lack of nitric oxide is considered by scientists as one of them. This contributes to muscle tone of veins, arteries and capillaries.

When a person exercises their muscles in a gym, they get muscle tone. Likewise, when a person meditates, then the release of nitric oxide into their bloodstream leads to the toning of their cardiovascular system. A Harvard study found that some of the genes (light bulbs) that were switched off were producing stress hormones in the body when they were switched on. Thus, stress hormones are also a major factor of ageing in the body. By reducing stress hormone levels, meditation directly slows the ageing process.

During meditation, certain genes are switched on that produce natural antioxidants, which act like sponges by absorbing free radicals. Free radicals are another one of the major ageing factors and play a significant role in causing wrinkles. This is why so many anti-ageing creams try to eradicate free radicals. Free radicals, can be reduced directly

---

[145] Georgia was formerly a part of the Soviet Union (USSR)

through meditation. Regular meditation is certainly better than botox![146]

The average life expectancy of humans has been increasing gradually over the past century. There is a direct correlation between a nation's wealth and life expectancy. Whilst Britons and Americans have an average life expectancy of 80 years (Britain: 77 for men and 81 for women; US: 75 for men and 80 for women), the poorest country in the world that I visited in 2008, Sierra Leone, has an average life expectancy of 40 years.

Therefore, as a country evolves more into a wide range of areas, such as better education, improved healthcare, so does the life span. Most people may not wish to live forever, but it is certainly worth having a fulfilling and enjoyable experience with the time that one does have. Meditation helps in achieving that experience. According to the work of Dr Andrew Weil[147], an individual's negative perception of ageing can shorten their lifespan, whilst someone who has a positive outlook on ageing can outlive the former by approximately $7\frac{1}{2}$ years.

A study of nearly 1,000 older adults followed for nine years showed that individuals with a high positive outlook had a 23% lower risk death form cardiovascular disease and a 55% lower risk from all causes compared to those with a pessimistic outlook on life. Norm Shealy M.D. PhD[148] found that "75% of people who die of heart disease and 15% of those who die from cancer are members of the Lifelong Anger Club".

---

[146] Botox is a toxin produced by the bacterium 'Clostridium botulinum' and is used in cosmetic surgery for reducing frowns and wrinkles. Effectively, it causes paralysis of the target tissue.

[147] Church, D. *The Genie in your Genes: Epigenetic Medicine and the New Biology of Intention*

[148] Shealy N. *Life Beyond 100*

Chapter 17: Breaking out of the Shackles

*"Whenever attachment to an emotion is created,
one is holding onto a feeling that is redundant
the moment it is created internally."*

Fear: the Barrier to Personal Evolution

Achieving freedom is about setting an intention to not lead a fear-driven life, but to lead a lovingness-based life. This very basic intention adds colour to a person's entire life. It is important to make it an intention to overcome any fear no matter what shape or form it appears in. Otherwise, the 'negative' activities taking place on a global scale in the immediate environment will suck a person in, chew them up and spit them out. Unless an intention is set to use intuition and other faculties, fear will inevitably get to a person and keep them further away from the process of creativity.

Learning to work with fear, learning to not go under with it, knowing what one's top five fears are and knowing where one's buttons get pushed gives a certain consciousness and awareness. Consequently, when the buttons do get pushed, it gives a clear indication of the issues that one needs to work on rather than going under with them. This gives a person incredible empowerment when it comes to intention and intuition. Knowing how not to be drawn down by the most toxic feeling - fear - can be one of the most empowering and liberating experiences.

The next step is to work with this information and, eventually, become a master of different energies, one of which is emotion. In December 2005, I was nominated for *British Junior Chamber's*[149] *Most Outstanding Trainer of the Year*.

---

[149] www.jciuk.org.uk

This was a coveted prize that I had already been awarded in 2004. As the winner was being announced, the National President built it up in such a way that I assumed she meant me. How wrong I was! It was awarded to my friend and colleague, Tony Brook, and deservedly so.

Nonetheless, I was really upset and very angry. My ego was severely bruised and, in my head, I was screaming blue murder. When I jumped into my car to drive back home, I was fuming with rage and thinking of all sorts of reasons why, after such a dedicated year to the development of my organisation, could I lose this award at the last minute? Yes, I became a victim of circumstance. As soon as I hit the motorway, I knew I had better calm down.

The road back home was long and dangerous at that time of night. I decided to use a method of letting go of my anger that my friend Jon Boys had taught me. I was in awestruck. After only 4 minutes of releasing my anger, I no longer had any negative feelings toward the whole episode at the awards ceremony or the people involved. One of the biggest causes of human suffering is people's unassailable emotional attachment to people, situations or events. An individual may have a powerful message to share with the world or a beautiful song to sing, yet they dare not step up to the podium or the microphone stand, just in case..! In case of what?

Others may not be able to earn the income they deserve because deep inside they feel they do not deserve any reward. Others may be petrified of enjoying a loving, harmonious relationship just because they had one or two bad experiences somewhere in their past. Consequently, they either avoid approaching their ideal mate or they inadvertently sabotage a wonderful relationship without rhyme or reason. All of these situations hark back to fear-based emotions.

In his lifelong quest to discover more meaning to his life, scientist and engineer, Lester Levenson (1909-1994), decided to take steps to seriously turn his life around. His constant seeking out for truth to life and being unsuccessful left him in a state of dis-ease and depression. His illnesses included regular bouts of jaundice, kidney stones, spleen problems, perforated ulcers, migraine headaches and more. By 1952, he had already experienced two heart attacks. After the second bout, he was told to expect the worse.

Levenson had studied numerous scholars and experts, including Watson ('Behaviourism') and Freud, as well studying philosophies, logic, economics and numerous other major fields of Man. Even with all that knowledge, there were no answers to the questions he had. Consequently, he started with a clean slate by posing simple questions like:

"What am I?"

"What is this world?"

"What is my relationship to it?"

"What is 'Mind'?"

"What is 'Intelligence'?"

"What is 'Happiness'?"

He asked himself what he wanted out of life? The answer for him was happiness. With inspiration from the work of the philosopher and yogi, Paramahansa Yogananda (1893-1952), Levenson developed a system for attaining detachment from all feelings, including positive as well as negative ones. Levenson's *Release Technique* identifies core emotions (energies) similar to those on Dr David Hawkin's *Map of Consciousness* that I discussed earlier in the book. The philosophy behind the Release Technique is that emotions are purely 'energies in motion'.

Whenever attachment to an emotion is created, one is holding onto a feeling that is redundant the moment it has been created internally. For example, when someone is feeling angry with a situation, such as road-rage, that anger consumes a significant proportion of the person's energy. Continuation of that feeling robs the person of vital life force and the joy of living in the present moment. There are only three things that can be done with an emotion:

1. Suppress the emotion
2. Express the emotion
3. Release the emotion

The worse thing to do to an emotion is to *suppress* it. It leads to a real energetic imbalance within the body, such as fight or flight syndrome, which means the stress hormones cortisol and adrenalin are ever-present in the body. Long-term bottling up of such emotions has the effect of creating more free-radicals, leaving the person vulnerable to illnesses and dis-eases such as cancer and heart disease.

Expression of emotions such as anger leaves the person temporarily in a state of self-satisfaction. However, this is then overcome by feelings of guilt, which is a more harmful emotion, which is then suppressed. Hence, it is not surprising that smart people would choose the third option of *letting go of* the emotion. Lester Levenson's Release Technique is still practiced by many hundreds of thousands of people across the planet through his protégé, Larry Crane.

There are numerous other modern methods are available, such as the 'Sedona Method'[150], 'Emotional Freedom Technique' (EFT), etc. Furthermore, many of the ancient spiritual systems also have their own variety of letting go processes, such as those applied by Buddhists, Muslims, yogis, etc. The choice is endless. The key is to find a system that works for you. During one of my interviews with Larry Crane in early 2010, I posed the question of what the difference was between meditating and releasing. He pointed out that if a person was busy in a boardroom meeting and wanted to release stress, it may be a touch challenging. Asking the boss for time out to assume the pretzel position to chant Om's for

---

[150] www.sedona.com

10 minutes may not be the done thing in some cultures! Thus, using a quicker system like the Release Technique will be far more useful in such a situation.

Meditation can be letting go and one has to let go to meditate. Meditation starts where thoughts 'stop'. Thoughts cannot be stopped but the attention moves away from them onto the moment where the thoughts do not have any effect. Whilst in meditation, releasing takes place but it is possible to release without meditating. For example, one could be letting go of frustration they have with a friend or co-worker. During meditation, issues should not be at the forefront of the mind as one is focusing attention on the moment. If a person was letting go of an issue (such as an incident at home with the spouse) they can do that using one of a range of releasing methods. However, a person does not necessarily have to be in a meditative state to release.

Meditation and Prayer

Prayer has a focus on manifesting an output inside the Matrix. Prayer is an ego-centred activity whereby a person's personality is trying to gain an action. Meditation is where the personality ceases to be. The personality is not really doing the meditation when one is in a true meditative state. Even when a person is at the bottom rungs of a meditative state, their personality is not doing the meditation. When one sees a terrible thing happen in the world, it is exactly the same as seeing a wonderful thing happen.

Energetically, they are the same thing. To the enlightened, good things are exactly the same as the bad things. There is no separation. Some may say that one needs to be without ego. Not true. A person cannot live without their ego. Without the personality that makes up the ego, a person would be nothing other than data. They cannot be without ego, but they can be flexible with their ego. When someone does something which is considered horrendous, the person can be flexible enough to recognise the space and the necessity of it.

Otherwise, they would not know what good was unless there was evil. In the duality of the universe, there cannot just be a place of good. Similarly, there cannot be just a place of evil. Just a place of good would be a singularity, i.e. where enlightenment is.

The Science of Kindness and Compassion[151]

There is an incredible amount of evidence that shows that when a person is experiencing a state of compassion, it causes changes in the chemistry of their brain. If a person performs an act of kindness, they release hormones into the bloodstream that have a very powerful affect the heart. Kindness and compassion are now moving into the realms of measurable biochemical changes within the body. There was a study that taught a Tibetan Buddhist meditation practice which is known as the 'loving, kindness, compassion meditation'. This meditation is about helping people to feel a sense of compassion.

They go through a list of people in their mind, starting with their closest loved one and then they extend that onto people that they simply know. Then they extend it to their enemies. Typically they wish each person, happiness, well-being and relief from all of their suffering. This is the compassion aspect of it. When people do this meditation regularly, structural changes in the brain take place. Many of the cells in the brain sprout new connections (neuro-connections) between them. If the brain cell was like a tree, then it would be as if the trees were growing extra branches purely as a result of experiencing this state of compassion.

This translates into two main things. When these structural changes take place (in the front part just above the forehead particularly on the left hand side of the brain), it helps a person feel a greater sense of empathy, a positive emotions, and positive well-being in their life. The average

[151] Taken from *The Consciousness Revolution Show* interview with Dr David Hamilton

person performing this kind of meditation regularly tends to feel better, warmer, happier, more positive, and more optimistic with their life.

The second advantage is that they have a greater capacity to concentrate and to pay attention. That can translate into improvements in many aspects of their life particularly, for example, if they work in a business environment. Having an improved capacity to concentrate and pay better attention is going to produce many rewards for such people. Through regular acts of kindness or regular acts of compassion, the human body produces a hormone in the brain called 'oxytocin'[152], which is also the hormone involved in childbirth.

When a woman is pregnant, oxytocin can help induce labour. It also induces milk production during nursing. If regular acts of kindness or compassion are performed that involve a personal connection with someone for even a second (e.g. through eye contact or a smile), that connection produces oxytocin in the brain. The oxytocin moves to a part of the brain called the 'amygdala'[153], which is responsible for the feelings of fear and anxiety. It can be active at times when a person is mistrustful of other people. The oxytocin turns down the activity level of that part of the brain (amygdala). Consequently, they become more trusting of people.

Oxytocin also helps people become more gentle and generous towards people. They even like people more. The reality is that giving someone something as little as a hug releases a high level of natural oxytocin. Here's the good news: it is free! Oxytocin is not addictive, but the way it makes a person feel can be addictive. It causes other changes in the chemistry of the brain, which may be naturally addictive.

Oxytocin has an incredibly powerful impact on the cardiovascular system, including the heart, veins, arteries and capillaries. Oxytocin is also released from the heart, which is

---

[152] www.en.wikipedia.org/wiki/Oxytocin

[153] www.en.wikipedia.org/wiki/Amygdala

then pumped around the bloodstream. It sticks to the cells that line the arteries ('endothelial cells'). This causes the cells to produce 'nitric oxide'. Nitric oxide dilates (expands) the arteries, veins and capillaries. When this happens, blood pressure comes down. Hence, as oxytocin directly lowers blood pressure, scientists refer to it as a *cardio-protective hormone*.

Scientists are aware that there are important benefits for a person to have rich social networks. The more social connections they have where people offer each other emotional support in times of difficulties, the more oxytocin they tend to have in their bloodstream. Therefore, their hearts are healthier. The social networks are referring to real connections and not how many Facebook friends a person has or how many followers they have on Twitter. These do not count! The secret is to get good at making friends and become softer and gentler towards people. It takes courage to do something like this, but it is a very healthy activity.

There are tactics that can be employed to help dealing with grouchy people who are only happy in their misery. For example, when visiting such a family member, giving a hug every time over time may wear them down to the point that the recipient may even reciprocate the hug. Dealing with such people can be difficult in certain environments such as the workplace. Sometimes, all that can be done is to change one's own attitude and behaviour.

When it comes down to making any change, whether it is in one's personal life or the work environment, the change always starts with oneself. This is done by looking inwards and being brutally honest about one's own behaviour and the way in which one really communicates. If there are any personal behavioural modifications that need to be made, then that is precisely where to start. When a person starts to make changes in their behaviour, which might be an introduction into being gentle, kinder or more patient, honest or more trusting, they may find people begin to change around them.

The heart is the organ of the body that is most affected by kindness. However, it is also the most negatively affected by high amounts of stress and even higher through hostility and aggressiveness. When a person is under a chronic amounts of stress over a long time, they are much more vulnerable to heart disease and heart attacks. The reason for this is that stress produces two phenomena inside the body. First, free radicals get produced as a side effect of excess stress, but they could also be a byproduct of aggression and aggressive tendencies.

Free radicals are also a direct effect of too many fried foods, drinking too much, too often, smoking and other lifestyle abusive behaviours. Second, stress causes inflammation in the body. Inflammation is very important when someone cuts or wounds themselves. It is the body's mechanism for creating protection around a wounded area in order for it to heal properly. For example, when someone breaks a bone, the tissues around it swell up.

Inflammation is also a byproduct of much stress, including aggressive tendencies, poor dietary choices, smoking, etc. If a person is chronically stressed for a period of time, the rise in free radicals causes a rise in inflammation, therefore, directly contributes to heart disease. That is quite simply why chronic stress is bad for the heart. Besides this, constant aggressive tendencies shown on a regular basis have almost the same effect, if not greater, as chronic stress.

These have a more negative effect than having a poor diet or a poor lifestyle. It is abundantly clear that one's inner environment has a strong relationship to one's health and wellbeing. What about the impact of the external environment on personal health? Many people live in less than ideal conditions and in less than optimal environments, e.g. a rough neighbourhood or with family violence or in financially deprived conditions.

If someone lived or still lives in such a hostile environment, it is easy to point the finger at the people and the conditions for the cause of personal suffering. However, being in a hostile environment does not mean one has to be hostile back. Irrespective of how other people are in their attitude and behaviours, the key is that one's own behaviour influences one's health. If a person is in a hostile environment, providing they are not hostile back, then they are not going to suffer the consequences of ill health.

Unfortunately, many people who live in such circumstances tend not to exercise control over their thoughts and feelings. This is one of the reasons why there are so many more busy medical centres and doctor's surgeries in socially deprived urban neighbourhoods. Even scientists and psychologists are recommending what wisdom keepers have been doing for thousands of years. They advocate keeping a list and practising gratitude for things that have happened to them that day.

Dr David Hamilton and Dr John Demartini are advocates of writing a daily list of gratitudes. It certainly helps a person to pay attention to the more pleasurable side of life rather than focusing on the painful experiences. Focusing the mind on different things means the biochemistry of the body begins to respond to where attention is being placed. To be accurate, it is not just about focusing the thoughts. It is also about focusing one's feelings about different things.

Over time, a person will gradually find themselves being more optimistic and feeling emotionally better in a real sense. Some studies of 'gratitude interventions' are producing results comparable to the effects of prozac for people with experiences of mild to moderate depression. For much more information on the studies, check out Dr David Hamilton's books and articles on his website [154].

---

[154] www.drdavidhamilton.com

Consciousness Revisited

Most scientists and metaphysicists struggle to provide a definitive answer to this question. What do people mean by consciousness being 'a sense of awareness'? According to Dr Dean Radin, the mystery is in the...

'...awareness of your own experience after being aware of yourself or self-awareness'

Imagine that all of reality is like the ocean. The ocean water is the medium by which things are created. When the waters of the ocean are observed, waves are seen. If a snapshot was taken, the surf would be seen as a very specific shape that does not appear to be the same as the ocean. It is sticking out of the ocean and has its own structure. On a different time scale (a very fast time scale), the ocean could be seen as a solid object with little mountains on top of it.

Thus, when solid structures around the world are seen, they are being seen through very slow time scales. If things were sped up, mountains would be seen undulating like water and buildings would be rising and falling, etc. A person's sense of the solidness of matter is related to the timescale that they have as a reference point. Consider the ocean as representing the universe. The ocean is the medium from which everything arises. Buoys are placed throughout the ocean to measure the height of each buoy as it moves up and down on the waves.

A tsunami is caused by an earthquake under the ocean. The tsunami is anticipated because suddenly all the buoys, which are normally moving randomly with respect to each other, start moving together. If they all move together at the same time, it is known that the entire ocean has been pushed in some way. They are all moving together in a giant coherent wave. This is what sets off the tsunami warning.

Radin has created an experiment where the ocean referred to here is the ocean of consciousness. It is an ocean or medium in which it is assumed everything exists. Therefore, it is assumed that if millions of minds were simultaneously aware this would cause the equivalent of a tsunami within consciousness. The buoys (our minds) would all be moving at the same time as a reflection of this giant underlying wave of awareness.

These buoys that are being used by IONS are called 'Random Number Generators' (RNG). They are electronic circuits that are doing the equivalent of flipping coins (heads and tails), but the source of the randomness is a quantum event. There are several different forms of RNG's that are being used, but ultimately, they are based on the principle of flipping coins. The experiment was to show whether conscious awareness is related in some way to this deep physical level of reality.

When all minds are focused on a large scale world event, such as the atrocities of 9/11, it creates the equivalent of a giant wave. The giant wave may distort the medium in much the same way that a tsunami distorts the medium of the ocean itself. Such a distortion will be detected by the RNG's as it is taking place at a deep level of reality. So, when a massive event comes along (as was the case of the funeral of Princess Diana), the RNG's record a non-random event. Momentarily, everybody's thoughts, feelings and intentions are focused on the same thing.

Perhaps, they will all start flipping heads for a short while or they may all start flipping tails. A formal analysis can be applied to random sequences coming out of these electronic circuits which are scattered around the world. There are seventy RNG's in different cities around the world. Over a long period of time, data from one of these RNG's in relation to each of the other RNG's, shows that large scale events like 9/11 is the equivalent of a tsunami.

This changes the degree of randomness that is ordinarily expected to be seen in these circuits as they become less random. It is very similar to what would happen when a tsunami distorts the ocean itself and all the buoys suddenly rise up and fall down again at the same time. The experiments carried out with RNG's say that, in moments of high mental coherence, something about the physical world changes. This is from the point of view of an event that occurs somewhere in the world.

Much attention is paid to it and then it is reflected in the RNG's. Some of the events have been large scale meditations cause the same effect, too. There is a suggestion from the experiment that when enough people are meditating at the same time (typically, these are meditations on peace), there is a physical effect on the world at large. Thus, there is the potential for humans to direct the level of evolution that they wish to experience. To create this sea-change, one has to start with a grass-roots effort and slowly build up. Eventually, meditation will no longer be seen as a strange Eastern practice, but a truly powerful ability to transform one's life.

Know Thy Self

The words of the ancient sage, Socrates, ring true to this day. He said:

"Know thyself and you will know the movement of the spheres and the gods and all the universes."

This is a simple statement, but fundamentally it is about getting to understand and know oneself in such a way that there is total unity and balance within. By attaining this level of harmony, one's world outside becomes a reflection of the world inside. That seems easy enough to do. But for most people, that means knowing themselves at an intellectual level. I meet very few people who will say that they do not know themselves. Even if a person did know themselves with 100% accuracy at the intellectual level, it accounts for one out of the five faculties of the mind.

In other words, the maximum they know themselves is 100% of one-fifth (= 20%). Therefore, they do not know 80% of themselves. Knowing oneself includes understanding one's thoughts, emotions, intuition (knowingness), the physical body and the observer[155]. Getting to know one's self involves much more than a few days of contemplation and note-taking. It involves getting an experienced mentor to provide guidance, support and to hold the energy through the transformation period that each person will experience.

At the same time, one needs to allow life force to flow to all the cells of the body by learning to breathe correctly. Most people have forgotten how to breathe. I say 'forgotten' because most people knew how to breathe perfectly when they were a baby. One of the first processes I teach to my students for eliminating stress and creating more inner balance is to breathe more naturally. Allowing oxygen to reach every cell in they body, allows efficient and effective energy flow and intra-cellular communication.

When this happens, the body is in a harmonious state where significant stress reduction can take place. Then, they practice taking daily action to re-member their true power. According to all the great spiritual teachers and scientists I have interviewed, the most powerful form of practice is meditation. The stillness of the mind opens up the doors to the rest of the self. It also creates heightened awareness of the inner and outer environment. Finally, I encourage people to follow the mantra that Richard Wilkins advocates:

"When the student is really ready, they become the teacher"[156].

---

[155] As heard on several interviews on *The Consciousness Revolution Show* with Konstantin Pavlidis

[156] Wilkins, R. *Broadband Consciousness*

Sharing one's knowledge and practice with immediate family, friends, neighbours, co-workers and the community has huge implications on global transformation. However, there is a caveat. Personally, I do not advocate evangelising discoveries to those who do not wish to hear or are not ready to hear. Otherwise, there is a danger of very quickly losing friends who may have been otherwise ready to listen in a few weeks, months or years time. It is much more powerful for a person to teach by being a living example than by merely preaching. This way the student becomes more than a teacher. They become a catalyst for human and planetary transformation. How amazing is that?

Chapter 18: A New Hope

"When there is a consciousness revolution, there is also exponential growth in people's awareness regarding their day-to-day thoughts, feelings, attitudes and behaviours. That is how real difference is made to the world."

Currently, the geopolitical situation across the planet is such that there are ample deceptions, manipulation and control enacted by few individuals over the many. When a culture is in the position of global power, the individuals make their economic and socio-political system the dominant world system. So far, they have been based solely on a competitive model. The goal of such a system is to maximise profit at any expense, including over the needs of the people and the planet. Consequently, this becomes a model based on survival of the fittest, i.e. competition will drive deception.

The *New Universal Order* that has already begun means having transparency in running businesses and organisations. This is becoming more apparent as those organisations behaving in the old ways are being exposed and are fast disappearing. Competition is a self-destructive exercise. Each corporation is trying to thrive at the expense of another company who is also trying to destroy another corporation's profits through greed.

Competition is a zero sum game with no winners. However, this strategy is much more expensive to maintain because, as one competitor is put out of business, another one rises. This applies not only to businesses, but to the human species as a whole. In the long run, it turns out that it is far more efficient to 'feed the enemy'[157] than to eliminate them. There is good news is on the horizon. There are many thousands of people across the world in different positions of authority who understand the New Universal Order. They are waking up and seeing themselves as integral, interconnected collaborators of a much more conscious planet.

The key for individuals new to personal and planetary transformation is to identify what they are naturally attuned to in their desire to make a real difference to the world. Then, all that needs to be done is to begin living that life. Competition has its time and its place. However, complementarity, cooperation and collaboration already play a significant part today. This can be seen from witnessing how many people are ready to give their time, energy and effort in times of natural disaster, such as earthquakes, tsunamis and during famines.

Although it is fascinating to see how people wait till the very last moment to live their collaborative nature, i.e. during crisis. Since the time of Descartes, humans have become increasingly self-centred and, more or less, have chosen to forget they are a part of one unified universe. They have relied far too much on the survival instinct in order to make it through their version of life. Nonetheless, there is now enough individual knowledge, wisdom and experience to be able to construct communities that value the contribution of ALL its members and respects the divine interconnection between all that exists in them and around them.

The Sufis say that God had to manifest Itself to know Itself. According to Dr Elisabet Sahtouris, it is a similar type of process where 'individuation' needs to occur first before the collective can realise that they are part of a universal pool of creation of constant growth and evolution. One is the predecessor for the other in terms of a realisation of its true nature and force.

---

[157] Taken from the author's interview with Dr Elisabet Sahtouris on *The Consciousness Revolution Show*

The master illusionists have used every possible tool and device at their disposal to explain away their Draconian policies that have harmed those in their 'care'. They have also instigated mass killings through all sorts of means beyond the comprehension and the radar of the public. Make no mistake: the master illusionists are not amateurs. They know exactly what they are doing, who they are using, who they are targeting, precisely when, how and exactly why. They have manipulated the concept of democracy beyond a joke. They have jumped on the bandwagon of Malthus and Darwin to justify, divide, destroy and conquer.

The master illusionists have implemented the mass usage of eugenics until one of their own screwed up their plans when he went 'too public' with it prior and during World War II. These illusionists have desecrated the good name of medicine and healing by taking prominent positions in that industry, both in the production of drugs and its regulation. They have 'taken out' any world leader who spoke out or raised the head above the parapet.

In the 21st century, however, things are shifting. There is an awakening process far beyond the wretched imaginations of the master illusionists. They knew this day would come, but just did not figure out it would come so fast, so hard and so intensely. Therefore, they have been trying to and will continue to try to thwart the mass awakening process. In other words, their biggest fear is a consciousness revolution. No arms required. No violence. But no more sitting on the fence either. No more waiting for someone else to do something about it.

The consciousness revolution has already begun. Look around. Entire nations are raising their voices against their dictatorial governments and puppet rulers. They are saying that enough is enough. Recently, Tunisia, Egypt, Algeria and Libya took a stand against their brutal government regime. Over the coming months and years, I would not be surprised in the least to see such actions take place within numerous other nations.

In the developed world, there are countless people educating the masses about health, food supplies, water and many of the topics that have been touched upon in this book. Fascist rule by politicians, serving the interests of corporations, will no longer be tolerated by the public. Employees of such firms will no longer wish to work for these kind of organisations and agencies. When there is a consciousness revolution, there is exponential growth in people's awareness regarding their day-to-day thoughts, feelings, attitudes and behaviours. That is how a real difference is made to the world.

If you have reached this part of the book by now, then you are probably one of those admirable beings who truly will change the fate of this planet. You are a revolutionary. And, the revolution will begin in the emancipation of your mind. Define your purpose. When you are on purpose, you will have a message. Share your message with the world. May peace be with you and peace be around you. May you have the wisdom to shine your brightest light on all that is dark. May you have the courage to bring all that is dark into your light. May the love emanating from your heart reach out to those who are a part of your life and those who have yet to enter your life. And, may your life be blessed with abundance, joy and fulfilment.

Let the new story unfold...

Afterword

While reading this manuscript, my eyes have opened to more than what I have accepted as conventional reality. For me, it is not only the journey of one man, Harun Rabbani, but it is also the journey of us All to what lies beyond the visible. It is a gift that is...

...Beyond Illusions

I stand upon the precipice
Within the Grand Illusions
Veiling my Way...

But there beyond the mist
Lies a golden city of Light
Waiting my Return...

My journey beckons me
To know 'Who I Am' though I am distracted
by words that have gone before...

Somewhere within Time and Space
There comes a 'Silent Whisper'
That says, "Remember"...

And as I walk forward
Parting each veil, I wondered
"Remember What?"

Then in the stillness of that moment

'I Remembered'

I AM the Flower
I AM the River
I AM the Stars
I AM Me
I AM You

We are One - together!

In Beauty,
Ginger Gilmour
Sculptor and artist
www.gingerart.net

Appendix

Appendix I: The Inscription on The Georgia Guide Stones

1. Maintain humanity under 500,000,000 in perpetual balance with nature.
2. Guide reproduction wisely - improving fitness and diversity.
3. Unite humanity with a living new language.
4. Rule passion - faith - tradition - and all things with tempered reason.
5. Protect people and nations with fair laws and just courts.
6. Let all nations rule internally resolving external disputes in a world court.
7. Avoid petty laws and useless officials.
8. Balance personal rights with social duties.
9. Prize truth - beauty - love - seeking harmony with the infinite.
10. Be not a cancer on the earth - Leave room for nature - Leave room for nature.

Appendix II: The Hippocratic Principles

2,500 years ago, Hippocrates, the father of nutrition and medicine, laid out the following 10 rules, which have been largely ignored by the medical profession:

1. The natural way is the only way.
2. Treat the cause of an illness, not the symptom.
3. Look to the spine for illnesses.
4. Throw away your drugs and heal the people with food.
5. Most illnesses can be prevented by eating natural foods.
6. A healthy colon is essential.
7. Do not administer dangerous and harmful drugs.
8. Do no harm to your patients.
9. Do not perform surgery for money.
10. The word protein means 'most important'.

Resources

Recommended Online Resources:

Mark Abadi: www.markabadi.com
Carmen Boulter, PhD: www.pyramidcode.com
Dawson Church, PhD: www.drdawsonchurch.com
Larry Crane: www.releasetechnique.com
Ian R. Crane: www.ianrcrane.co.uk
Jude Currivan: www.judecurrivan.com
David Hamilton, PhD: www.drdavidhamilton.com
Nassim Haramein: www.theresonanceproject.org
Molly Harvey: www.corporatesoulltd.com
Dale Hwoskin: www.sedona.com
David Hyner: www.davidhyner.com
Alex Jones: www.infowars.com
  www.prisonplanet.tv

Konstantin Korotkov: www.new.korotkov.org
Bruce Lipton, PhD: www.brucelipton.com
Deepak Lodhia: www.catalyst-coaching.com
Lynne McTaggart: www.lynnemctaggart.com
Judith Orloff, PhD: www.drjudithorloff.com
Konstantin Pavlidis: www.orassy.com
Dean Radin, PhD: www.deanradin.com
Manjir Samanta-Laughton www.paradigmrevolution.com
Lyndsay Wagner: www.lyndsaywagner.com
William Whitecloud: www.williamwhitecloud.com
Richard Wilkins: www.broadbandconsciousness.com
Rob Williams: www.psych-k.com
The Burzynski Movie: www.burzynskimovie.com
(Cancer)

The Consciousness Revolution Show:	www.exposeillusions.com
Institute of Noetic Science:	www.noetic.org
Natural News:	www.naturalnews.com

The End Game:

www.youtube.com/watch?v=x-CrNlilZho

The Obama Deception:

www.youtube.com/watch?v=eAaQNACwaLw

Zeitgeist Movies:

www.watchzeitgeist.com

The Century of the Self:

www.youtube.com/watch?v=IyPzGUsYyKM

The Ascent of Money:

www.channel4.com/programmes/the-ascent-of-money/4od

Recommended Reading

Begg, David K. H. *Economics*

Boulter, C. *Angels and Archetypes*

Bryson, C. *The Fluoride Deception*

Church, D. *The Genie in your Genes: Epigenetic Medicine and the New Biology of Intention*

Currivan, J. *The 8ᵗʰ Chakra*

Currivan, J. *The 13ᵗʰ Step*

Currivan. J, Laslo, E. *CosMos: A Co-Creator's Guide to the Whole World*

Currivan, J. *HOPE - Healing Our People & Earth*

Dispenza, J. *Evolve your Brain*

Frankl, Viktor E. *Man's Search for Meaning*

Hamilton, D. *How you can Heal your Mind*

Kropotkin, P. *Mutual Aid*

Lipton, B. H. *The Biology of Belief*

Lipton B. H. *Spontaneous Evolution*

Orloff, J. *Emotional Freedom*

Orloff, J. *Second Sight*

Pert, C. *Molecules of Emotion*

Perkins, J. *Confessions of an Economic Hitman*

Sahtouris, E. and Harman W. *Biology Revisioned*

Sahtouris, E. *Earthdance - Living Systems in Evolution*

Samanta-Laughton, M. *Punk Science*

Samanta-Laughton, M. *The Genius Groove*

Schwartz, G. E. *The Afterlife Experiments*

Tellinger, M. *Slave Species of the Gods*

Walton, C. *The Incredible You*

Whitecloud, W. *The Magicians Way*

About the Author

Having spent a decade in the medical devices industry and a lifetime of exposure to religious and spiritual practices, Harun Rabbani turned to investigating the relationship between science and spirituality and its significance to life. His research led to him interviewing and meeting numerous pioneering scientists, spiritual masters, the highest calibre of movement artists and many specialists in the field of consciousness research. Harun is an advocate of human transformation and presents at conferences and seminars in the UK and internationally.

He is a collaborative partner in several key social enterprises, including London's Orassy Kendron, which aim to accelerate Humanity's evolution. His ongoing research into science, education, history, arts and spiritual practices can be heard during his interviews on Radio Nu Rah. Harun continues his Martial Arts, yoga and spiritual practice with experienced wisdom masters. He also invests much of his time sharing experiences and spiritual practice at several international retreats and Life Encounter courses.

www.exposeillusions.com